This is a fully revised and updated version of Hans van den Doel's *Democracy and welfare economics*. It presents the economic theory of political decision-making (otherwise known as new political economy, or public choice), providing students with an accessible and clear introduction to this important subject. The authors identify four different methods of decision-making by which the political process transforms the demands of individual citizens into government policy and public goods and services: negotiation, majority decision, representation, and bureaucratic implementation. These are analysed in turn as independent decision-making models whose effectiveness is examined with reference to economic theory. A final chapter draws conclusions from this analysis, arguing that the size of the public sector is a result of forces that work in different directions at different stages of the political process.

Democracy and welfare economics

Democracy and welfare economics

Second edition

HANS VAN DEN DOEL

formerly Professor of Economics, University of Amersterdam

and

BEN VAN VELTHOVEN

Associate Professor of Economics, Leiden University

Published by the Press Syndicate of the University of Cambridge
The Pitt Building, Trumpington Street, Cambridge CB2 1RP
40 West 20th Street, New York, NY 10011–4211, USA
10 Stamford Road, Oakleigh, Victoria 3166, Australia

First published 1993

Printed in Great Britain at the University Press, Cambridge

A catalogue record for this book is available from the British Library

Library of Congress cataloguing in publication data

Doel, Hans van den.
[Demokratie en welvaartstheorie. English]
Democracy and welfare economics. – 2nd ed/Hans van den Doel and Ben van Velthoven.
p. cm.
Includes bibliographical references and index.
ISBN 0 521 43057 7 (hc). – ISBN 0 521 43637 0 (pb)
1. Welfare economics. 2. Democracy. 3. Bureaucracy.
I. Velthoven, Ben van. II. Title.
HB99.3.D6313 1993
330.15′56 – dc20 92-23167 CIP

ISBN 0521 43057 7 hardback
ISBN 0521 43637 0 paperback

SE

Contents

Preface

The first edition of *Democracy and welfare economics*, written by Hans van den Doel, was published in 1979. Since then, the economic theory of political decision-making has met a steadily growing interest. Many publications, in part theoretical but also – and above all things – of an empirical nature, have seen the light. As a consequence it became more and more desirable, if not necessary, in the course of time to up-date this book. As Hans van den Doel himself was not able to do so on account of ill-health, Ben van Velthoven took charge of the revision which now has led to the appearance of this second edition of *Democracy and welfare economics*.

For this second edition we have critically gone through the whole text. First, of course, recent theoretical insights have been coped with. Then, we have done our best to record the results of empirical research wherever possible. Furthermore we have seized the opportunity to eliminate some obscurities in the original formulation and to clarify the graphical and mathematical derivations, which remain few in number. Finally the sequence of the argument has been altered in a number of places for didactic reasons, while maintaining the quite specific design of the book.

Various persons have contributed to the realisation of this second edition, to whom we want to express our gratitude. Hans Keman, Arthur Schram and Jan Kees Winters kindly read drafts of – chapters of – this book and gave us their comments; Karina Tribels assisted in collecting the relevant literature; Hedy Braun and Karla ter Horst-van Domburg typed large parts of the text; John Haslam of Cambridge University Press provided us with editorial assistance. Our special thanks are to Julie Bivin who took care of the translation of our Dutch writing into proper English.

Finally we want to convey our lasting appreciation to Jan Tinbergen, Piet Hennipman and Truus Grondsma, without whom this book would never have appeared at all. For the rest we refer to the preface in the first edition.

1 Economics and politics

1.1 The size of the public sector

One of the most radical changes which has occurred in the Western economies during the past century has been the rapid growth of the public sector.

Centralisation of power by the government took place through the introduction of statutory control of various aspects of private-sector activities: labour contracts, social security, safety, competition, the environment and town and county planning. Many aspects of decisions taken by private firms regarding production and prices are subject to such legal requirements.

Centralisation of power also took place through the growth of public ownership. In various countries industries like electricity, gas, water, railways, aircraft and air transport (bulk), steel, broadcasting, postal and telecommunication services are wholly or partly in the public sector. Furthermore, considerable parts of the housing stock are publicly owned.

However, the most radical centralisation of economic power did not come about by either statutory measures or public ownership, but by the relative increase in public sector receipts and outlays.

Table 1.1 gives some recent data on ten separate OECD-countries and the total OECD average. In 1989 current expenditure on goods and services of the general governments amounted to 15 to 20 per cent of gross domestic product (GDP), whereas social security transfer payments were mostly between 10 and 20 per cent of GDP. Total government expenditure, which in most countries in 1890 had totalled less than 10 per cent of gross national product, had risen to 35 to 50 per cent of GNP a century later; the total incidence of taxation and social security contributions has grown equally. Figure 1.1 shows the

Table 1.1 *Income and expenditure of government in ten OECD-countries in 1989 (as a percentage of GDP)*

Country	Government final consumption expenditure	Social security transfers	Total outlays[a]	Current receipts[b]
Australia	16.4	8.6[c]	34.3[c]	34.2[c]
Canada	18.7	11.8	44.3	39.6
Denmark	25.1	18.1	58.7	57.4
France	18.3	21.4	49.7	46.5
Germany	18.7	15.6	45.1	44.6
Italy	16.8	17.7	51.7	41.1
Japan	9.3	11.8[c]	32.9[c]	34.3[c]
Sweden	26.0	19.5	60.1	64.1
United Kingdom	19.4	11.9	40.9	39.7
United States	17.9	10.8	36.1	31.8
Total OECD	16.6	13.5	41.2	37.3

Notes:

[a] Total outlays comprises final consumption expenditures, interest on the public debt, subsidies and social security transfers to households, gross capital formation, and purchases of land and intangible assets.

[b] Current receipts consists mainly of direct and indirect taxes, and social security contributions paid by employers and employees.

[c] 1988.

Source: OECD, Historical Statistics 1960–1989, Paris 1991; Tables 6.2, 6.3, 6.5, 6.6.

rise for the US, the UK and Germany. Notwithstanding the fact that the growth of the public sector seems to have been curbed in the past decade, it is apparent that in these countries between one third and one half of national income is spent nowadays, one way or another, via the public sector.

1.2 Economics and political science

The growth of the public sector has posed serious problems for economists and political scientists. We shall begin with economics. Robbins (1935, pp. 1–24) defined *economics* as 'the science which studies human behaviour as a relationship between ends and scarce means which have alternative uses'. This definition gives no

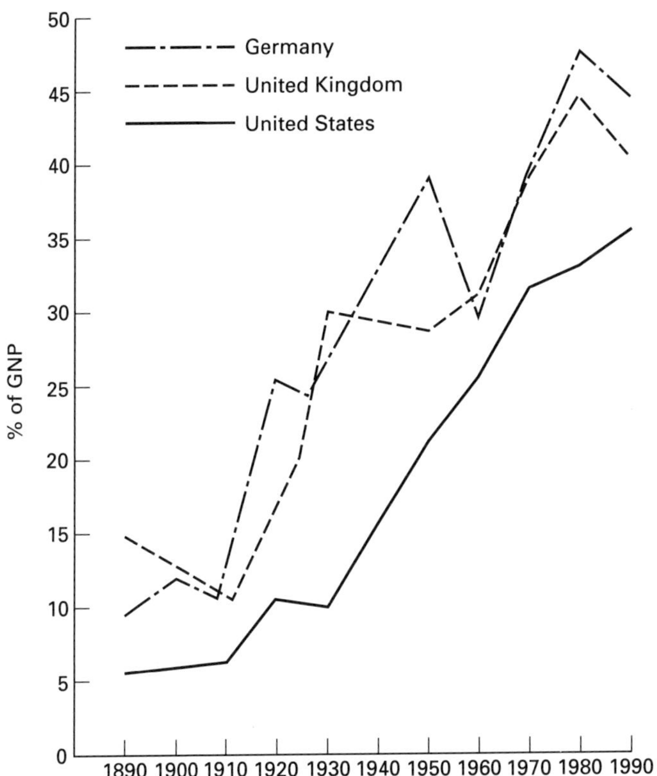

Figure 1.1 Public expenditure as a percentage of GNP[a]
[a] Includes all levels of government
Source: R.A. Musgrave and P.B. Musgrave, Public finance in theory and practice, McGraw-Hill, New York, 4th edition, 1984, figure 7.1; OECD, Historical Statistics 1960–1989, Paris, 1991.

specific economic ends: each end has an economic aspect, provided it involves the use of scarce means, i.e. if the realisation of the end involves foregoing the other desired alternatives. Nor are there any specific economic means: each means is economic provided it is scarce and has alternative uses; a material good is an economic means, but so is the vote which the voter can give to one political party once every four years.

Thus economists (in the tradition of Robbins) view human behaviour from the viewpoint of scarcity. They examine what benefits and costs are involved in certain decisions. When the supply of goods and services is not limitless, people are forced to make a choice: a choice to achieve (to some extent) one end means that the achievement (to some extent) of another end must be foregone. Every choice demands sacrifices consisting of the benefits of the foregone goods and services: 'You can't have your cake and eat it too.'

In theory, economics is an indispensable ancillary science for analysing the choices which must be made within a large public sector. In practice, however, economists ever since Adam Smith have concentrated on the private sector of the economy. The study of the public sector has been left largely to sociologists and, more recently, to political scientists. In so far as economists have included the government in their analysis, they have generally applied the following limitations to themselves. First, they have tended to regard the government, using a monistic concept, as a unitary being, i.e. as an independent individual which maximises its own utility and makes its own cost-benefit analyses. Second, they have usually spoken of the government in normative terms only. Their main subject of discussion has been what the government should do or should refrain from doing. What the government in fact did was important merely because it enabled economists to determine to what extent the norms were met. If, contrary to expectations, the government satisfied the standards, they were pleasantly surprised or saw it as proof of their own powers of persuasion in public discussion. When the standards were unfortunately not met by the government, they took offence, felt despondent or they called for the present politicians to be replaced by better ones. Only Pareto among his contemporaries drew the one correct conclusion when he said that he wanted to study sociology in order to discover why the advice of economists was ignored.

Despite the undoubted value of sociological studies, especially political science or policy sciences, they too have not yet succeeded in providing an adequate insight into the workings of the public sector. Easton (1953, p. 129; 1965a, p. 50) defines the study object of *political science* as: 'those interactions by which values authoritatively are allocated for a society'. Political research seeks to understand that system of interactions in society through which authoritative or binding allocations of values (i.e. goods, services, etc.) are made and implemented. We do not wish to enter into the discussion among political scientists on when an allocation of values is binding. It is important to note, however, that most political scientists assume that it is precisely the institutions of the public sector (pressure groups, political parties, parliament, cabinet, civil servants) that bring about this binding allocation. Thus, not only economics but also political science is an important, even essential, ancillary science for studying the theory of the public sector.

But, in practice, political scientists do not live up to this claim. Political scientists who work from Easton's definition generally neglect the economic aspect of the allocation of values. For the purposes of this book it is important that many political scientists ignore the fact that the institutions of the public sector have costs as well as benefits. Here costs do not (only) mean the costs of salaries and housing of the office and its staff, but are (especially) related to the fact that these institutions do not always decide on an optimum allocation of values (goods and services) which are relatively scarce. The chance that the decisions will be wrong ones as regards the citizens is considerably greater if the process of choosing is wrongly organised. Thus, the binding allocation of values by public sector institutions is not only a sociological but also an economic problem. It is only when political scientists realise the validity of this conclusion that the results of their analyses will be satisfactory.

1.3 Economic theory of political decision-making

The shortcomings in the way in which most economists and political scientists study the public sector can be reduced when economics, sociology and political science are integrated into a new field. A beginning was made with such an integration when, after the Second World War, a new field of economics and political science was developed in the writings of Arrow, Downs, Olson, Buchanan, Tullock, Riker, Niskanen, Frey and others. This new field was given many names (such as mathematical political theory, the economic study of non-market decision-making, public choice), two of which describe it best, namely, *the economic theory of political decision-making* and *new political economy*.[1]

This new field is characterised by a large-scale use of deductive methods of analysis and of mathematical models. A mathematical model is a system of mathematical equations which fit together logically. A combination of deductive theorising and mathematical formulation may provide a number of advantages: the implications of certain assumptions are less easily overlooked; contradictions in logic in the assumptions can be clarified; whoever formulates a theory is forced to list exactly to which phenomena the elements of his theory will apply; complicated structures can sometimes be described more easily; and, last but not least, it becomes easier to test some points of political theories quantitatively. Frey (1970a, p. 21) concludes rightly that such a confrontation with reality can prevent the building of mathematical models from becoming the end rather than the means.

The new field is part of *political science* because it is concerned with positive theories which consider binding decisions made by society about the allocation of values. Special attention is paid to the way in which *government policy* is made. Until now the most important themes of the economic theory of political decision-making have been: supply and demand of public goods within a group, the allocation of values in the process of exchange with different power constellations, the influence on government policy of competition among political parties for votes and the behaviour of bureaucratic organisations.

Finally, the new field is also part of *economics*, both as regards the object of study and the method used. We have already noted that economics, as defined by Robbins, studies the decisions made with respect to relatively scarce goods and services. Thus the economic theory of political decision-making studies the decisions made with respect to relatively scarce public and quasi-public goods. The theory acknowledges the importance of institutions and is especially concerned with how the allocation of scarce means is influenced by the *method of decision-making*.

1.4 Methodological individualism

In respect of method we can speak of a 'structural isomorphism' (i.e. a similarity of form) between the economic theory of political decision-making on the one hand, and micro-economics on the other. This is apparent from the use of the deductive method (discussed above), from the assumption that decisions made by individuals in an economy are intended to maximise the attainment of some objective (section 2.1.1), and from the postulate of *methodological individualism*. The monistic concept of the government as a unitary, independent economic subject is replaced by a pluralistic concept in which the government is seen as a set of individuals (the suppliers) who produce public goods for a set of other individuals (the demanders) who value these public goods on their individual merits.

On the *supply side*, methodological individualism provides a much more thorough insight into decision-making within the government. The government is not seen as a mythical institution raised high above the citizens, but as a set of groups (politicians, civil servants) and individuals (politician a of party x, civil servant b of department y) who may all be pursuing aims which conflict in parts. This view does not permit an *own* responsibility of *the* government (e.g. for the taking of paternalistic decisions), but it does allow for extraordinary positions of power for particular *individuals* who can in consequence make paternalistic decisions on *their* account and experience the political consequences.

On the *demand side*, methodological individualism was introduced to the theory of public finance many years ago by Sax, Mazzola and Wicksell. It has become highly relevant because of the growth of the public sector. When collective decisions are made about what is a large part of everyone's income, many have serious questions about the status of the individual. Some of these questions are, whose aims determine collective decisions? What decisions are made? And how are the costs and benefits of these decisions allocated among the citizens? The increasing size and complexity of the public sector make it wellnigh impossible for voters to know what is important for the benefit of other voters. As early as 1896 Wicksell ((1896)1958, p. 90) concluded that 'each person can ultimately speak only for himself'. The parcel of goods and services provided by the public sector is only at an optimum if social welfare as seen by the individual citizens reaches the highest possible level.

1.5 Welfare economics

In this book we want to present the economic theory of political decision-making in a way that can be characterised as follows:

1. The economic theories of political decision-making are applied to the organisation of democracy and bureaucracy in modern Western economies.
2. The relevant theories are integrated using the concept of a 'political process' which consists of a number of stages succeeding each other logically (namely negotiation, majority decision, representation, and implementation).
3. The decision-making at each stage of this process is evaluated using welfare economics.

Before discussing the concepts of democracy, bureaucracy and political process, we shall give a short exposition of the role welfare economics plays in this book.

Welfare economists concentrate on the joint welfare of the individuals of a group, which is not the group's material wealth but the group's well-being in so far as it depends on economic factors. *Welfare economics* consists of three elements:

1. The formulation of the *conditions* which must be met if the joint welfare of the individuals in a group is to be at an optimum.
2. The study of *how* these conditions can be *realised* by the institutions of this group and by means of policies which will be carried out within the framework of these institutions.
3. The critical assessment of the contribution of *existing* group institutions and the existing group policy to joint welfare.

This definition means that it is precisely welfare economics which has most in common with political science. After all, both political science and welfare economics study the allocation of values for a group, in this case for society. However, welfare economics is not concerned with society's allocation of values alone, but with the resulting social benefits and the social costs. When, in this book, we concentrate on the welfare aspects of a certain allocation, we choose *ipso facto* a one-sided approach. Welfare economics, like economics in general, is a science that deals with only one aspect of reality; it studies the phenomena it observes from only one aspect, namely the aspect of scarcity. Society's allocation of values which are not scarce falls outside its scope.

Pareto, Barone, Lange, Tinbergen and Baumol have concentrated on the welfare economic problem of defining the conditions for realising an optimum social welfare and on the question of how the organisation of an economy (the economic order) affects the social welfare of the totality of individuals. Tinbergen (1959, 1967), especially, makes this problem explicit when he sketches the 'optimum regime'. His question is, what economic order ensures the greatest welfare benefits, i.e. which economic order transforms individual preferences into an allocation of scarce means in such a way that social welfare most closely approaches the optimum? This question will also form one of the mainstays of this book. Whereas Tinbergen concentrates his inquiry on the welfare aspects of the organisation of the economy as a whole, this book will consider the effects of the organisation of the public sector on social welfare.

1.6 Centralisation and concentration

Our interest in the public sector is thus concentrated on its most fundamental element – its organisation. An *economic organisation* has at least three important features:

1. It is directed at, or helps determine, the realisation of a complex of aims external to that of the organisation.
2. It has a structure characterised by the degree of centralisation and concentration of economic power.
3. It has a method of coordinating economic decisions related to this structure.

In the term economic power two elements are combined, namely, economic and power. As noted before, economics studies the behaviour of individuals in so far as it is directed towards the achievement of their ends and involves the use of scarce means which have alternative uses. Following Weber ((1922)1972, p. 28) power can be defined as a specific form of influence, namely, the possibility to influence the behaviour of other individuals in accordance with their own aims. Accordingly the *economic power* of an agency or a person is its influence as far as it can be used in accordance with its ends and is backed by the capacity to apply economic sanctions, i.e. sanctions which are situated in the scarcity of means.[2]

The structure of an economic order is characterised above all by the degree of *centralisation* and *concentration* of economic power. A structure is centralised or concentrated if the power is limited to a relatively small number of agencies or persons. In a deconcentrated or decentralised economy, power is divided equally between the agencies or persons concerned. The difference between deconcentration and decentralisation lies in the direction in which power is consolidated or spread. Concentration and deconcentration are *horizontal* movements, i.e. consolidation or separation of agencies on the same hierarchical level. Centralisation and decentralisation are *vertical* movements, i.e. consolidation of agencies on a higher hierarchical level and the separation of agencies at a lower hierarchical level respectively.

The coordination of the decisions in an organisation is largely a matter of communication. A specific pattern of lines of communication belongs to a certain structure. Bound up with the structural patterns described above there are, in principle, two patterns of communication, namely, one consisting of horizontal and one consisting of vertical relations. Horizontal relations are connections between agencies or persons on the same hierarchical level, vertical relations are relations between agencies and persons of different hierarchical levels. In other words, horizontal relations are based on *equality* of power of the agencies and persons, vertical relations are based on *inequality* of power.

Whether horizontal or vertical relations will dominate thus depends on the structure. A centralised structure means that vertical relations between the agencies and persons will dominate, a deconcentrated structure means the domination of horizontal relations.

1.7 Democracy and bureaucracy

We have already denominated the organisation of the economy as the economic order. Translated into the terminology just given, the *economic order* is, on the one hand, the degree of centralisation and concentration of the economic power of decision-making in an economy and, on the other, the related way in which the decisions are coordinated. It is noteworthy that the theory of the economic order also makes use of typologies which are based on a division into horizontal and vertical forms of coordination. Following German authors such as Eucken (1940), Hayek (1944) and Röpke (1954), two ideal types of main forms of the economic order are distinguished, namely, the 'zentralgeleitete Wirtschaft' (centrally planned economy) and the 'Verkehrswirtschaft' (exchange economy). The *centrally planned economy* is an ideal type of vertical organisation in which the economic actions in an economy are determined by the plan of one agency or individual. An *exchange economy* is a type of horizontal organisation in which all agencies or individuals make separate plans which they coordinate by a process of exchange.

If we consider the German terminologies literally, they have a very wide meaning. A 'zentralgeleitete Wirtschaft' does not only mean the (vertical) forms of organisation in which coordination is by personal commands but also those forms in which orders are given by means of an anonymous manipulation of markets and prices. A 'Verkehrswirtschaft' includes not only the (horizontal) forms of coordination when goods are exchanged in a market for an amount of many per unit, but also coordination by way of negotiations, voting or elections.

This book, however, is not a treatise on the economic order as a whole, but only on one part of it, namely, the economic order within the public sector. A public sector is characterised by the fact that, among other things, there is no exchange of goods for money and also that such an exchange often is impossible (see chapter 2). Nevertheless, in a public sector it is, in principle, possible to have both Eucken's ideal types, albeit in a specific form. The ideal type of the 'zentralgeleitete Wirtschaft' in a public sector has the form of a perfect *bureauc-*

racy. The ideal type of the 'Verkehrswirtschaft' in the public sector has the form of a perfect *democracy*. Within a perfect bureaucracy (economic) actions are determined by the plan of a single individual, the head of the bureaucracy. The other individuals have a subordinate position in the hierarchy. The channels of communication are vertical and coordination is by way of commands (letters, budgets, etc.). Within a perfect democracy, however, all individuals make plans independently and their power is equal. The channels of communication are horizontal and coordination is by way of negotiations, unanimous decisions, simple (or qualified) majorities and/or by delegating decision-making to elected representatives.

With this the concepts of bureaucracy and democracy to be used in this book have been virtually laid down. Bureaucracy is defined as a collection of methods to coordinate (outside the market) the decisions of agencies which, and persons who, are subordinated to each other in the hierarchy. On the other hand, democracy is the collection of methods to coordinate (outside the market) the decisions of agencies and persons who have equal positions.

These concepts of democracy and bureaucracy are ideal types, i.e. abstractions containing only the pure elements from which a concrete political system is constructed. The next section will be devoted to this concrete political system.

1.8 Political system and political process

In principle, a system is a set of elements, which can be limited in number and which are mutually related. The term 'political system' primarily acquired a meaning by Easton's writings (1953, 1965a, 1965b). In complete harmony with his definition of political science (cf. section 1.2) Easton defines a *political system* as 'the set of interactions through which values are authoritatively allocated for a society'. Among the most important aspects of the political system are the political culture (including the conceptions, preferences and aims of the individuals belonging to the system), and the political structure (including the balance of power). The *environment* contains all other systems which together with the political system make up society as a whole.

The special feature of Easton's analysis is that he describes the relations between the political system and its environment in a circular flow model. The political system receives *inputs* from the environment. These inputs are the demands of individuals on government

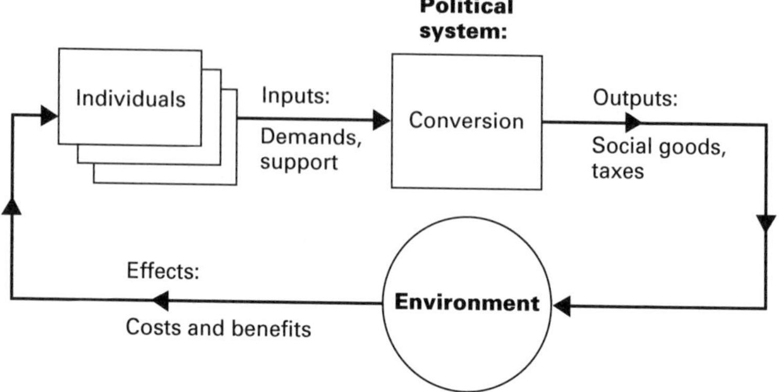

Figure 1.2 Circular flow model of the relations between the political system and its environment

policy and the support they give certain officials. The inputs are *converted* by the political system into *outputs*, i.e. into decisions on policy, such as the production and distribution of public goods and the laying down of rules of taxation. The policy affects the environment (e.g. the types of schools, the structure of cities, the distribution of income) and thus the individuals are affected. These effects, which consist of costs and benefits, in their turn influence the demands and the support of the individuals, and the cycle begins again.

The transformation of inputs into outputs is carried out during the *political process*. In Western economies, this political or conversion process is a complicated process of decision-making which passes through a number of different stages. Each of these stages in its turn might be split up into a number of sub-stages. The process of conversion, in which the aims of individuals are transformed into public goods and services, has at least four stages in each of which a different decision-making method dominates, namely negotiation, majority decision, representation and implementation. The order in which we mention these stages and their respective methods of decision-making is not based on chronology but on logic. For example, we do not exclude the possibility that a majority decision or some kind of negotiation will follow the representation. The logic of the order is that – with the exception of negotiation – none of the stages can exist unless the system has passed through the previous stage at least once. This will be illustrated in chapter 7.

1.9 Further outline of this book

In this book two elements of the flow model will be examined more closely: the process of conversion and the evaluation of its effects. The criteria on which this evaluation is based are considered in chapter 2. The following chapters (3 to 6) will analyse the decision-making methods which are relevant to the four successive stages of the process of conversion as independent decision-making models, namely,

1. *Negotiations democracy*. This stage is examined in chapter 3; it consists of negotiations between the agencies and persons concerned and it aims at reaching a result acceptable to the largest possible majority. An example of such a negotiations democracy is the 'concerted action' of employers, workers and representatives of the government on the division of the national income between wages, profits and expenditure on public goods and services.
2. *Referendum democracy*. This stage is examined in chapter 4; it consists of the decision whether to put the results of the negotiations to the vote, in which case the outcome of the voting is binding. A referendum democracy is not confined to referendums on a single proposal, but it may also be used to vote upon a whole bunch of decisions.
3. *Representative democracy*. This stage is examined in chapter 5; it consists of letting elected representatives conduct the negotiations and take the majority decision. As Schumpeter has pointed out, these elected representatives compete amongst themselves for the support of the voters. Examples of such a representative democracy are the negotiations within, and the decisions by, a parliament and a cabinet.
4. *Implementation bureaucracy*. This stage is examined in chapter 6; it is concerned with whether or not decisions made by parliament and cabinet are implemented by appointed bureaucrats. Examples of such an implementation bureaucracy are the decision-making processes within ministries and within each department of a ministry.

A political process can be compared with a branch of industry specialising in the production of public goods and services. The four stages mentioned are then production stages which link the original producer with the final consumer. In the stages of negotiations democracy and referendum democracy the raw materials can be said to be produced, the intermediate goods are then the product of the representative democracy while the implementation bureaucracy provides the final product for immediate consumption. As is the case in the business world, some stages can be skipped here, e.g. when a pressure group informs the bureaucrats directly about the outcome of their negotiations, thus by-passing the politicians. It is also possible that some stages are integrated, e.g. that the referendum democracy disappears as an independent stage. Yet again, a new and independent stage can split off (differentiation), e.g. if the executives of the political parties take independent positions from their members in parliament.

The comparison of a political process with a set of production stages makes clear that an evaluation of the separate stages is worthwhile only if it then becomes possible to judge how the production process functions as a whole. This is why the elements of the conversion process discussed in this book are reassembled in chapter 7 and are then evaluated in their mutual relationship.

2 Welfare and welfare optimum

2.1 Individual welfare

2.1.1 Aims

In chapter 1 we introduced the theme of this book: the analysis of the political process and the evaluation of its effects. The starting point for our examination will be the postulate of methodological individualism, i.e. our analysis and evaluation will depart from the preferences and behaviour of the individual citizen.

Weber ((1922)1972, p. 12) classified human conduct as traditional, affective, value-rational and purpose-rational. Traditional social conduct is determined by custom. Social conduct is determined affectively, especially emotionally, when it is guided by feelings and emotions which react to external stimuli. Value-rational conduct is determined by the conscious faith in the absolute worth of the conduct as such, independent of any aim. Purpose-rational conduct is, on the contrary, directed at the achievement of an aim. What is true for conduct as a whole is true for decisions in particular. According to Weber a person decides purpose-rationally if he* aims to achieve certain results by his conduct. These results are the purpose of the decision.

Henceforth we fill in the postulate of methodological individualism by assuming that individual *behaviour* is *purpose-rational.* This assumption is part of an honourable tradition in economics, and is also used in other social sciences. The social psychologists, Krech, Crutchfield and Ballachey (1962), for example, observe that 'human action is motivated, or goal-directed'. Simon (1978, p. 5) even states: 'The view of man as rational is not peculiar to economics, but is endemic, and even ubiquitous, throughout the social sciences.'

* It is only for concision that we use the male form rather than both the male and female forms here, and also in other instances throughout the book.

The goals an individual strives for can be economic or non-economic. *Economic goals* are those of which the realisation involves the use of scarce means which have alternative uses. All other goals are non-economic. It is possible to imagine cases in which economic and non-economic aims will conflict; for instance, a consumer's attempt to satisfy his economic needs might have a negative influence on his faith, hope and charity. However, we shall ignore this problem in the rest of this book by assuming that the attainment of economic goals will not influence the achievement of non-economic goals.

There is considerable confusion about the concept of economic goals: in many cases these goals are simply equated with the desire for a high income or for many goods and services. This confusion can be ended by distinguishing between income, wealth, individual welfare (or utility) and social welfare.

Income refers solely to the amount of money a person earns in a specific period. *Wealth*, a wider concept, refers to all the goods and services a person has obtained in this period. Wealth includes not only material goods but also the non-material services, and not only private goods but also public goods. Income and wealth are objective concepts, in contrast to the next two which are purely subjective. *Individual welfare (utility)* is synonymous with the degree to which the needs of the individual are satisfied, in so far as this satisfaction depends on economic factors. Individual welfare is the total of positive and negative utilities. The positive utilities include the pleasure an individual derives from all those goods and services which are in principle capable of satisfying human needs. The negative utilities include the costs of acquiring those goods and services (e.g. the loss of leisure) and the negative external effects which proceed from the actions of others (e.g. the negative effects on the environment). It will be clear from this that welfare is taken as a broad concept, namely the degree of satisfaction of human needs of whatever kind, in so far as it depends on scarce means.

The way in which an individual views his welfare and acts according to this view, can be represented by a set of target variables, an objective function, and a decision rule. *Target variables* are changeable quantities, which the individual i regards as capable of influencing his subjective utility (U^i). One example are the quantities of the m consumption goods and services at his disposal (q_1^i, q_2^i, …,q_m^i). Another example is his work effort (a^i), which on the one hand will affect welfare negatively as the individual has to give up leisure time, but on the other hand may also contribute positively to individual welfare because of the social contacts, the scope to develop one's talents, and the status offered by a job. The *objective function* indicates in which way the target variables influence utility as seen by the individual:

$$U^i = U^i(q_1^i, q_2^i, \ldots, q_m^i; a^i).$$

If the coefficients are known such a function provides an insight into the relative weights given by the individual to each variable. A *decision rule* is the extent to which an individual strives to realise his targets. We assume that each individual will attempt to maximise the level of his objective function.

While, as we have seen, economics and the other social sciences can mostly find each other in the postulate that human action is goal-directed, their roads part when it comes to the assumption that people *maximise* their objective functions (cf. Simon, 1978).

The assumption that individuals maximise their objective functions has been very fruitful for the development of economic theory. For, taking account of the restrictions people have to cope with when pursuing their goals (such as: the outlays on goods and services should not exceed the available budget), it can be derived from the objective functions, through deductive analysis, which behaviour the individuals will predictably exhibit. On the basis of data on actual behaviour, it can next be verified with the help of econometric-statistical methods whether the theoretical predictions have indeed come true. If such might not be the case, this acts as a feed-back to the theory that something is at fault. Perhaps the objective functions have been inaccurately specified, or maybe the relevant restrictions have been inadequately dealt with. And so on.

The apparent fertility for economic theorising of the assumption of individual welfare maximisation is sufficient reason to employ this same premise in our analysis of political decision-making. There is, however, a second reason. In this book we do not only want to analyse, but also to evaluate from the point of view of the individual citizens. This is only possible if it can be assumed that individual citizens do indeed have such a point of view, i.e. strive after a clearly defined goal. If the individuals do not pursue any objective, it would also be impossible to evaluate the various stages of the political process from their objectives.

2.1.2 Consistency

From various sides objections have been raised to the assumption, sketched above, that individuals strive after the maximisation of their objective function. The critique can be summarised in the following three points:

1. The individual objective function does not exist at all, respectively it is not constant and therefore not suited for operational use.
2. Individuals perhaps strive after some goals, but do not do so in a consistent manner.
3. The individual objective function perhaps is consistent, but it is not being maximised.

We shall try to refute these points of critique in this and the next section.

In the first place it is often pointed out that individuals are themselves not aware of the existence of their objective function. But how can such a function then underlie their behaviour? It is further observed that the desires, opinions and aims of people are not constant. On the one hand, people are guided by the desires and opinions of their fellow-beings and by advertising (of commercial and political nature), and they learn from their faults. On the other hand, new products are continually appearing on the market and new issues on the political agenda, which were not taken into consideration until then.

According to Lindblom (1968, pp. 12–28) targets are never given in the political process but continuously changing. Consequently, for him, welfare is a non-operational concept; the exact nature of the objective function only becomes clear when a choice is made between alternative, mutually exclusive policy programmes. Thus, targets and means are related throughout the entire process of choosing and cannot be separated.

Against these arguments the following points can be raised. Even when targets and means cannot be *separated*, it is possible to *differentiate* them for analytical purposes. The fact that a person does not know that he has an objective function does not mean that this function is non-existent. Important is whether the behaviour of the person is directed at the achievement of an aim, and whether it is – either explicitly or implicitly – in agreement with and can be described by such a function. Finally, changes in the objective function over time as such do not need to prohibit the operational use of the concept. Presuming that the objective function at each separate moment exists and can be specified, the function always represents the targets of the individual and their relative weight at that specific moment. And that is what we stand in need of. In section 2.1.4 we shall return to this issue.

The implicit or explicit existence of an objective function is determined not only by the fact that a person aims to achieve certain goals, but also that he does so consistently. First, this means *comparability* of the target variables. A person must be able to compare different, often dissimilar entities, such as a glass of wine and expenditures on NATO, as to their contribution to his individual welfare. Stated differently, the requirement of comparability holds that for each couple of alternatives x and y the individual should be able to say whether he (1) prefers x to y, (2) prefers y to x, or (3) is indifferent between x and y.

Suppose that in a referendum a citizen first votes for stronger defence, and then for lower taxation, as a result from the fact that he has not been able to connect the levels of expenditure on defence and taxation. It must be concluded then that this citizen has been unable to compare the various alternatives in a consistent manner.

The survey article by Thaler (1987) gives a number of illustrations of the fact that people indeed do not always proceed consistently when comparing alternatives. We lift out one example. Tversky and Kahnemann (1981) asked two series of respondents the following questions:

1. Imagine that you have decided to see a play, admission to which is \$10 per ticket. As you enter the theater you discover that you have lost a \$10 bill. Would you still pay \$10 for the ticket to the play?
2. Imagine that you have decided to see a play and paid the admission price of \$10 per ticket. As you enter the theater you discover that you have lost your ticket. The seat was not marked and the ticket cannot be recovered. Would you pay \$10 for another ticket?

Although the individual positions in both cases are completely identical (no ticket and poorer by \$10) 88 per cent of the respondents answered the first question in the affirmative and only 46 per cent the second.

Consistency not only means comparability, it also means *transitivity*. A person must be able to arrange the alternatives transitively, i.e. arrange them in an ordinal sequence. This means that for each triple of alternatives x, y and z the following should hold: if the individual prefers x to y and y to z, then he also prefers x to z.

May (1954) gives an example of intransitive preferences among male mathematical students who were asked about their preferences among brides. The brides were classified as to beauty, intelligence and income. A large minority of the students decided as follows: 1. first, they preferred beautiful, clever but poor brides to beautiful, dumb but rich ones; 2. then, the beautiful, dumb but rich ones were preferred to ugly, clever and rich ones; 3. finally, the ugly, clever and rich ones on their turn were preferred to the beautiful, clever but poor ones. The intransitivity in this example apparently resulted from the fact that the students hesitated on the weight they wanted to give to each of the characteristics.

Koo (cf. Kornai, 1971, p. 136) studied to what extent American households were consistent when they were shopping for food. On the basis of this study, Koo constructed a consistency-index q, which can have a value between 0 and 1 ($0 \leqslant q \leqslant 1$). If a household is 'steadily consistent' in its orderings $q = 1$; if it is 'steadily inconsistent' $q < 0.5$; if it is 'restrictedly inconsistent' $0.5 < q < 1$. The numerical results of Koo's study can be summarised as follows: 1 per cent of the households were 'steadily consistent' in their orderings ($q = 1$); 2 per cent of the households were 'steadily inconsistent ($q < 0.5$); 86 per cent of the households were 'restrictedly consistent' ($0.6 < q < 0.8$).

This conclusion confirms our everyday experience that almost nobody decides totally consistently or totally inconsistently, but that most people are reasonably consistent in their orderings. The hypothesis of rationality is a hypothesis which does not apply at all times. It cannot be used to completely explain the decisions of all people, but the decisions of most can be approximated fairly well. Moreover, it can be assumed that, if we are considering groups of people, the inconsistency of one individual in one direction will be compensated by the inconsistency of another in the opposite direction. Finally, we may suppose that people will learn from their mistakes, and that processes of selection are at work (e.g. through the market or through the evolution of institutions), such that the seriousness of possible inconsistencies will be kept within bounds, if not eliminated.[1]

2.1.3 *Maximisation*

An important part of the framework for the analysis of individual behaviour is the decision rule. It is assumed that the decision-maker decides according to his preference ordering. This means that the decision-maker aims at achieving the highest possible utility, i.e that he tries to maximise his individual welfare. Thus, we regard the individual citizen as a *homo economicus* who, as soon as he knows of possibilities to improve his situation, will no longer be content with the existing situation.

Against the assumption that people will try to maximise the value of their objective function, Simon (1957, pp. 196–206) placed another assumption, namely that people strive only to reach a certain *level of aspiration*. The reasons for this behaviour are situated in the complexity of the economic problems, the limitation of the human brain and the incompleteness of the information, which make it almost impossible for individual persons to determine their optimal way of conduct. The aspiration level can be, for example, an annual salary of $50,000 in combination with a 40-hour working week. A person who has reached this level of aspiration will not try to reach a higher level because all combinations of more than $50,000 and less than 40 hours are equally satisfactory. In the literature such conduct is termed *satisficing*.

The description of decision rules in the form of levels of aspiration has been very popular in the social sciences and was introduced through the work of Cyert and March (1963) into economics (see, e.g. Loasby, 1976 and Etzioni, 1987) and in the economic theory of political decision-making (cf. Frey and Schneider, 1978 and Mosley, 1984). It provides important practical and theoretical advantages. When the rule is not formulated as 'the level of my income must rise as much as is possible' but as 'my income must amount to $50,000 per year', it becomes possible to determine unambiguously whether the goal has been achieved. Furthermore, the concept of the level of aspirations also makes allowance for ignorance and for the complexities of the situation, as noted above.

From the fact that the formulation of decision rules in the form of levels of aspiration has some advantages, it cannot be concluded, however, that individuals do not strive for a maximum utility. The fallacy of such a conclusion can be shown by making a distinction between subjective and objective rationality. A decision rule is *subjectively* rational if a decision-maker attempts to bring his objective function to the highest possible level. A decision is *objectively* rational if the maximum that could be achieved is actually attained. The difference between objective and subjective rationality is due, on the one hand, to incomplete information about possible behavioural alternatives and their implications and, on the other hand, to the impossibility of digesting all information. For example, a chess player acts subjectively, not objectively, rational: he makes his moves without considering all possible strategies, is uncertain about the consequences of each of the alternatives, and is unable to take the effects of each possible move into consideration rapidly.

Because of lack of information and the complexity of the situation, it is often impossible to achieve an objective maximum, and the achievement of an aspiration level of the desired goals will have to be sufficient. Yet, the achievement of this aspiration level does not mean that the decision-maker is really satisfied. As soon as he has more information, his aspiration level will be raised, and he will attempt to increase his utility level. Moreover, the reason that the decision-maker generally is not fully informed lies (among other things) in the fact that the collection and digestion of information takes time and money; if the costs of additional information exceed the benefits, it is quite rational for him to remain incompletely informed. The assumption that a decision-maker will maximise his utility thus means that he will, given his information and the costs of acquiring additional information, prefer the better to the less (taking for granted that he is able to compare the rival alternatives and to arrange them in an ordinal sequence). Riker and Ordeshook (1973, p. 23) conclude: 'unless we ask decisionmakers to play God, maximizing and satisficing are the same thing'.

2.1.4 Measuring individual welfare

Given our assumption that individuals maximise their objective function, it would be very useful to know more about the form and content of these functions. In principle there are two methods of specifying objective functions, to wit: by asking people about their goals (the *interview* method) or by studying their actual choices (the *revealed preference* method). These methods are not equal in value; they both have advantages and disadvantages. The interview method has as its great advantage that people are directly questioned about their goals and the relative weights of the various target variables. A disadvantage is that the results can be less reliable because the respondents have no economic incentive to reveal their true preferences. The latter problem does not arise, or to a less extent, in the case of the revealed preference method, because this method is based on actual choice behaviour. The deduction of the underlying goals from actual choice behaviour is, however, anything but simple. The number of possible goals, the relative weights of these goals, and the restrictions which may have been lying at the basis of the actual choices are so large a priori that it is extremely difficult to determine with any degree of certainty which have been the real underlying goals.

For the measurement of preferences economists distinguish between the *ordinal* and *cardinal* method of measurement. This distinction is related to the measurement scale that is being adopted. In the ordinal approach one makes use of the so-called ordinal measuring scale, in the cardinal approach one employs an interval or a ratio scale.

A measuring scale is *ordinal* if meaning can only be given to the fact that numbers are larger or smaller. An ordinal scale is a means of indicating an order. For example, in an interview three baskets of private and public goods, x, y and z, are put before the respondent who is asked to value the three alternatives by means of a mark between 0 and 10. Suppose the respondent values the three alternatives with 8, 6 and 2, respectively. We can speak of an ordinal scale if we can conclude that the respondent places the highest value on alternative x (valuation mark 8), considers alternative y with valuation mark 6 his second choice and values alternative z with mark 2 least, without it being allowed to give any meaning to the relative differences between the marks. Observe that the same preferential ordering of the three alternatives can also be expressed through the series of marks 10, 5, 0, or 7, 5, 1, or 4, 3, 1, etc. In an ordinal scale the absolute value of the valuation marks is of no importance, only the sequence.

We speak of an *interval* scale if we can attach a meaning to the differences between the numbers such that the operations of adding and subtracting make sense. In the above example, there would be an interval scale if, from the marks given, the conclusion could be drawn that the difference in utility between the alternatives x and y (8 minus 6) is half that between the alternatives y and z (6 minus 2). The ratios between the figures 8, 6 and 2, however, have no meaning. Note that measuring on an interval scale does not lead to a unique result. The information that the utility difference between alternatives x and y is half that between y and z can also be expressed by the series of numbers 7, 5, 1, or 4, 3, 1.

A *ratio* scale is an interval scale in which meaning can be given to the ratios, such that it is meaningful to divide and multiply. A necessary condition here is that the figure ‘zero’ is regarded as ‘nothing’. In the example there is a ratio scale if a mark of 0 means ‘no utility at all’ and if accordingly a value of 8 means four times the utility of a value of 2. Now only the unit of measurement remains arbitrary, i.e. the information on the individual welfare valuation of the three alternatives is preserved if all valuation marks are multiplied or divided by the same (positive) number. The information that alternative x provides a utility that is four times that of alternative z and three times that of alternative y could also have been represented, for example, by the marks 4, 3, 1 instead of 8, 6, 2.

2.1.5 *The measurability of individual welfare*

There are several schools of thought in economics as regards the measurability of individual welfare.

The oldest is derived from the founder of welfare economics, Pigou, who measures utility and social welfare by means of the *measuring rod of money*. According to Pigou the price of a product which someone buys is an expression of what that person is willing to pay for it. Behind that lies the utility the good is offering him. For that reason Pigou considers the price as a measure of utility. Expressing all products in money terms by a multiplication of their price and quantity and summing all these amounts yields a total amount which represents the welfare of the individual. An outcome of zero can be interpreted as no welfare at all. Cf. Pigou ((1920)1946, pp. 11, 31, 57). These basic principles imply that Pigou regards utility as a cardinal quantity which can be measured on a ratio scale.

Paretian welfare theory has criticised this idea that utility can be measured. Important points of critique on Pigou's measure are the following: (1) consumer surplus is neglected, i.e. it is left out of consideration that the consumer often values (intramarginal) units of a product more than what he has to pay for it; (2) incomes can mean quite different things for different persons; an amount of $50, for example, has a quite different value for a beggar than for a multi-millionaire; and (3) the disutility of the employment of production factors is not counted. Pareto thought that utility can be measured on an interval scale only. To use his own words: 'A man can know that the third glass of wine gives him less pleasure than the second; but he can in no way tell what quantity of wine he must drink after the second glass in order to get pleasure equal to that which the second glass of wine provided him' (Pareto, (1906)1971, p. 191).

Up to the present, Pareto's view dominates welfare economics. However, since Von Neumann and Morgenstern (1944) developed an ingenious method to measure individual welfare on an interval scale using interviews, the cardinal concept of utility has regained ground. Their method, which is known in the literature as the *expected utility* method, can be illustrated by a simple example. Suppose an individual can choose between the consumption of a cup of coffee, a glass of milk, a glass of buttermilk and a cup of tea. He prefers these beverages in the given sequence. The cardinal problem is in determining the difference in utility between the various alternatives. Von Neumann and Morgenstern obtain the answer to this question in the following way. For the most and the least preferred alternatives, coffee and tea respectively, arbitrary maximum and minimum valuation marks are chosen, for instance 10 and 0. After that the individual is asked to indicate for each of the other alternatives at which chance p he is indifferent between that alternative and the situation that he gets coffee with chance p and tea with chance $(1-p)$. The valuation mark which belongs to that alternative can then be calculated as $p \times 10 + (1-p) \times 0$. Suppose the individual is indifferent about a choice between a glass of milk (with 100 per cent certainty) and a situation with a 60 per cent chance of getting coffee and 40 per cent of getting tea. Then the valuation mark of milk is $0.6 \times 10 + 0.4 \times 0 = 6$. Assume further that the individual is indifferent between buttermilk and a situation with 20 per cent chance of getting coffee and 80 per cent of getting tea. The valuation mark of buttermilk thus equals 2. In this way we would get a series of marks 10, 6, 2 and 0 for coffee, milk, buttermilk and tea. The distances between the marks give an indication of the intensity with which the one alternative is preferred to the other. Notice that the series of marks only gives an interval scale; with other maximum and minimum numbers chosen at the outset the same preferences could also have been expressed by, e.g., the series 6, 4, 2 and 1. At any rate, it is clear that the chances at which the individual is indifferent provide Von Neumann and Morgenstern with a measure to order 'utilities' cardinally.

The idea that welfare can be measured cardinally by using the interview method has also been taken up by other authors. Van Praag (1968), for example, measures the welfare of households by means of a self-rating interval scale, on which the interviewed persons can indicate their utility level on a scale between 0 and 10. See also Van Praag and Kapteyn (1973), Wansbeek and Kapteyn (1983), Kapteyn (1985). From the answers of the respondents an individual welfare function of income can indeed be derived. One conclusion from this research is interesting enough not to withhold it from the reader, as it refers back to the problem touched on in section 2.1.2, that objective functions may be subject to change over the course of time. The results of Van Praag show that someone with a current income of, say, $20,000 per year who expects his net income to rise by $4,400 will predict an increase in his utility from, say, 5 to 6.5. If this rise does not change the objective function, the individual would value his utility at 6.5 after the rise in income has become a fact. However, the objective function does change. Van Praag found that a rise in income of $4,400 in actuality does not lead to a utility of 6.5 but of 5.5. This means that a part of the increase in income, in the example $2,800, does not lead to a greater utility. As soon as the income has increased, the real rise in utility is disappointing, i.e. it is on average only 35 per cent of the predicted improvement. This is a consequence of *preference drift*: due to habituation effects the objective function shifts with the welfare level which has been reached. Apart from this preference drift there may also be a *reference drift* at work: if for all the people in an individual's reference group incomes rise to the same degree as for the individual himself, the objective function shifts still further, so that the increase in individual welfare as a result of the rise in income will be smaller yet. It is a merit of the work of Van Praag et al. that they have empirically shown that shifts in the objective function may occur but need not detract from an operational use of this function.

Summing up we can state that among economists different views exist as to the measurement of individual welfare. Now the scale on which individual welfare is measured is of little interest, as long as the analysis is confined to individual choice behaviour. In the traditional theory of consumer behaviour economists get on very well with indifference curves, which only require measurement of individual welfare on an ordinal scale. As soon, however, as we want to occupy ourselves with social welfare and with interpersonal welfare comparisons, it is important which measurement scale is being used.

2.2 Social welfare

2.2.1 Interpersonal comparison of utility

As already indicated in chapter 1, welfare economics is concerned not with the utility of a single individual but with the common welfare of all individuals in a group. For the welfare of all individuals combined we use the term *social welfare*. As soon as more than one individual is considered, it becomes difficult to define what is understood by (optimum) welfare. After all, individuals have an endless variety of conflicting interests so that it does not necessarily follow that the goals of all individuals will be realised simultaneously. Particularly for problems of distribution, one individual's preferences may readily conflict with those of others. Welfare economics is thus concerned with how one individual's utility can be compared with that of another individual.

The nature of this problem can be illustrated by an example of a canteen, used by only two persons, a and b. The canteen can provide only one sort of roll, either ham or cheese. Suppose the preferences of both canteen users are such that person a prefers ham to cheese, while the preferences of person b are just the reverse. These canteen users thus have conflicting interests. Which sort of roll should be served? There are in principle two methods of solving this problem. The first method is that of the *interpersonal evaluation of utility*. The canteen owner (or somebody else, like the dietician) then gives a subjective answer to the question whether he or she thinks that ham is of greater value (e.g. healthier) than cheese, or whether he or she takes more interest in a's utility than in b's.

The second method is that of the *interpersonal comparison of utility*. Scientists can try to provide an objective answer to the question which type of roll will ensure the greatest pleasure to the two users of the canteen, taken together, by scientifically weighing the pleasure received by person a from a ham roll and by b from a cheese roll. Welfare economists disagree as to whether it is possible to make interpersonal comparisons of utility. This disagreement is understandable because the question of comparing utility is closely related to the question of measuring utility.

An interpersonal comparison of utility is possible in the example only if the following can be determined:

1. How many ham rolls are needed by a and b respectively to produce the same utility as one cheese roll, i.e. what is the ratio for a and for b of the utility derived from a ham roll to that derived from a cheese roll (measured in the units of utility defined for a and b respectively)?
2. What is the ratio of a's unit of utility to that of b?

To answer the first question a ratio scale is essential; for the second question it is necessary to know 'the terms of trade' between both units of utility. Illustrating the correctness of this proposition is simple.

Suppose the two persons are capable of representing their

Table 2.1 *Valuation numbers representing the pattern of preferences of two canteen users*

	ham roll	cheese roll
person a	3	1
person b	3	6

preferences on a ratio scale; see table 2.1. The table shows that person a values a ham roll three times as highly as a cheese roll, and that b values a cheese roll twice as highly as a ham roll; the valuation numbers have been expressed in the utility units of a and b respectively. Adding the marks of both persons gives $3+3=6$ for ham and $1+6=7$ for cheese. It looks as if the common welfare is best served by cheese rolls. However, the addition of the marks of a and b only makes sense if they are expressed in the same unit. Suppose it was known that the utility units of a are twice as large as those of b; then the valuation numbers of a and b can be converted to a common denominator. The marks of a (3 and 1 in the utility units of a) can for instance be converted into utility units of b to 6 and 2 respectively. Adding again gives $6+3=9$ for ham and $2+6=8$ for cheese, so that now the conclusion can be drawn that person a sets more value on ham over cheese than person b on cheese over ham. It is clear that this interpersonal comparison of utility is only possible because the welfare valuations of the persons involved are available on a ratio scale, and because these individual valuations are expressed in the same measurement unit (respectively, because it is known how these can be converted to a single utility unit).

The use of a ratio scale is thus a necessary but not a sufficient condition for applying interpersonal comparisons of utility. An ordinal scale is at any rate insufficient for an interpersonal comparison of utility. See further Boadway and Bruce (1984).

2.2.2 *The social welfare function*

In section 2.1.1 we argued that individual welfare (utility) can be expressed in terms of target variables, an objective function, and a decision rule. This also applies to collective welfare. The collective objective function, which is better known as the *social welfare function*, expresses the relationship between the welfare of the group and the variables which influence this collective welfare. On the basis of a decision rule it is possible to determine whether the group target has been reached.

There are different schools of thought in welfare economics and each has its own interpretation of the social welfare function; see Boadway and Bruce (1984).

Bergsonian welfare economics (Bergson, 1938; Samuelson, 1947) is the most general approach, as it does not speak out about the question of measuring utility and with that excludes the possibility of interpersonal comparison of utility. Social welfare (W) is deemed to depend on: the quantities (q) of the m goods and services to be consumed by the n individuals; their work effort (a); and any other factors (r, s, and t) which affect the welfare of the members of the community:

$$W = W(q_1^1, \ldots, q_m^1; \ldots; q_1^n, \ldots, q_m^n; a^1, \ldots, a^n; r, s, t).$$

Generality, however, has its price. A welfare function of this kind is empty, until it is specified on the basis of data which can differ from time to time and from place to place.

As to this filling in, the Bergsonian welfare function introduces the possibility of seeing social welfare as (partly) dependent on the degree to which the economic policy targets set by political leaders have been met, irrespective of whether these targets are shared by each citizen separately. For example, the view on social welfare of the Dutch social-democratic party PvdA around 1980 has been formulated by Merkies and Vermaat (1981, p. 112), with the help of responses to a questionnaire, as a welfare function of the Bergsonian type:

$W \quad = -10{,}65\ u - 4{,}46\ p_c - 3{,}46\ LIS - 3{,}99\ WCU + 10{,}18\ CBY$, where:

u = registered unemployment as a percentage of the total labour force;
p_c = the percentage increase in the price index of household consumption;
LIS = the (corrected) share of labour in national income;
WCU = the percentage increase in real labour costs per unit of output in the industry with respect to abroad; and
CBY = the gross burden of taxes and social security premiums as a percentage of net national income (all variables expressed in deviations from their 1977 level).

See also Van Eijk and Sandee (1959), Van Velthoven (1989).

More generally welfare economics does not confine itself to the policy makers, but is precisely interested in the question of how the welfare evaluations of the individual citizens can serve as the basis for statements on social welfare. Starting from the individual welfare of the citizens the Bergsonian welfare function reads:

$$W = W(U^1, U^2, \ldots\ldots, U^n).$$

In this general formulation, the function is, of course, not very suited for operational use.

The social welfare function becomes much more concrete in *Pigovian* welfare economics, which builds on the tradition of utilitarism *à la* Bentham. Social welfare is taken to be the sum of the utilities of each of the n individuals separately:

$$W = U^1 + U^2 + \ldots\ldots + U^n.$$

Pigovian welfare economics originates with the measurability of utility on a ratio scale and with interpersonal comparison of utility on the basis of the assumption that an equal money income gives each individual the same utility. In this conception of social welfare a welfare decrease of one individual can be compensated by the welfare increase of another.

Another concrete specification of the social welfare function has been furnished by Rawls (1971). In his view, social welfare is determined by the position of the person who is worst off in society. Formally:

$$W = \text{minimum}\ \{U^1, U^2, \ldots\ldots, U^n\}.$$

Social welfare increases only if the position of the least favoured improves. The application of this welfare criterion requires an interpersonal comparison of utility as well in order to be able to determine which person is the worst off. The idea, however, that interpersonal comparison of utility might be possible meets with many objections among economists.

Paretian welfare economics, which gained greatly in importance after the Second World War, rejects interpersonal comparisons of utility; utility can only be measured on an ordinal scale. Moreover, collective welfare is seen as exclusively dependent on the individual welfare evaluations of the subjects involved; interpersonal evaluation of utility is out of order. Paretian welfare economics does not have a fully specified social welfare function on offer. But it does dispose of a decision rule which makes it possible to avoid judging the distribution of utility and to draw conclusions which are valid for all distributions of utility.

2.2.3 *The Pareto criterion*

To avoid conclusions about the desired distribution of utility, Pareto formulated a criterion for social welfare about which a consensus among the members of a group is not a priori excluded. The Pareto criterion states that social welfare can be said to have increased when one or more members of the group concerned have become better off and no one is worse off. In such a case a *Pareto improvement* is said to occur.

The criterion is not only a standard for detecting an improvement in social welfare but also for determining how long such increases can continue. According to the criterion, social welfare is at an optimum as soon as it is no longer possible to increase the level of utility of one or more individuals without reducing the utility of one or more other individuals. Thus, social welfare is said to have reached its *Pareto optimum* if no (further) Pareto improvement can be realised.

It should be noted that the Pareto optimum which would be reached eventually through such Pareto improvements, strongly depends on the initial distribution of resources. Stated differently, with another initial distribution can go another Pareto optimum. The Pareto optimum thus need not be unique. See also Bohm (1987, pp. 2–6).

A number of objections, both theoretical and practical, have been raised against the Pareto criterion; see e.g. Rowley and Peacock (1975). Hennipman (1977, pp. 117–51) has refuted the most important theoretical objections and has shown that they are often based on the misunderstanding that the criterion of Pareto contains a value judgment. Many critics wrongly interpret the Pareto criterion as a norm ('it is a good thing to make one man better off if nobody else is made worse off') or, more strongly even, as a commandment ('no one should be made worse off'). Pareto ((1906)1971, pp. 1–3) himself never tired of denying that he wanted to give recipes for achieving the highest possible degree of happiness, benefit or well-being instead of an ethically neutral criterion for judging economic efficiency.

Value judgments about increases in social welfare cannot be made without knowing which social groups benefit from the increase. If, for example, only those individuals with relatively high incomes were to profit from an increase in social welfare, the effect would be to widen income differences and this might result in the increase being rejected even though the Pareto criterion has been fulfilled. The application of the conclusion based on the Pareto criterion must therefore always be weighed against the value judgment underlying a certain distribution criterion.

Another important point of critique is that the Pareto criterion does not pay (sufficient) attention to the benefit people derive from freedom as well as to the intrinsic value of rights; cf. Nozick (1974), Rowley and Peacock (1975). Paretian welfare economics will indeed consider rights and liberties from the point of view of whether they contribute to social welfare and not as unassailable entities. Authors like Rowley and Peacock (1975, p. 83), on the other hand, advocate a liberalist view in which the maintenance and extension of negative liberties – defined as the absence of coercion by certain individuals on others – is given precedence. They suggest that the application of the Pareto criterion and of a liberalist set of values can lead to different results; the first approach will, for instance, more easily lead to a positive judgment on regulation than the second. In practice, the contrasts seem rather less serious than the differences in the theoretical premises might lead us to suspect. In the first place, Paretian welfare economics is compatible with the existence of rules, obligations, established rights, etc. The value of such institutions, however, is not to be found in their concurrence with one or other preconceived ethical ideal, but in the fact that such institutions may be necessary for the optimisation of social welfare in a world of scarcity. See chapter 3 for an application of this line of thought to the explanation of the existence of a government; see also Buchanan (1987). Second, different rights and liberties may come into conflict with each other, so that it will yet be necessary to balance the pros and cons and government intervention (e.g. regulation) may become inevitable. The proclamation of absolute rights and liberties does not give any hold as to the grounds for striking this balance; Paretian welfare economics, on the other hand, provides us with a clear criterion.

The practical objections to the Pareto criterion concern the problem that changes in social welfare which comply with the criterion do not often occur. Nearly every improvement in utility for some individuals is associated with a fall in utility for others. For those cases the Pareto criterion does not give a decisive answer as to increase or decrease of social welfare. In other words, the Pareto criterion does not yield a complete ordering.

To meet this objection, the later literature, building on suggestions by Kaldor (1939) and Hicks (1939), has formulated the *compensation principle* which is also known as the *neo-Paretian* criterion. The neo-

Paretians examine whether the individuals that are better off as a result of economic change (the gainers) can compensate those that are worse off (the losers). If a certain change results in an increase in welfare for the gainers which is so large that, after the losers have been fully compensated for their welfare loss, there is still a net increase in welfare left, this change is, on the basis of the Pareto criterion, a *potential* social welfare improvement. In order to determine unambiguously whether there is such a potential improvement in social welfare Scitovsky (1941) suggests that two compensation tests be performed. In the first test gainers are asked whether they are prepared to compensate the losers for the loss they will incur as a result of the change. In the second test the losers are asked whether they are prepared to compensate the gainers if the change does not take place. Should the first test have a positive result and the second a negative, then it cannot be said that social welfare *will be* increased by the change, but we can say that it is *possible*, on the basis of the Pareto criterion, that the change would increase social welfare.

The compensation principle does not require that the compensation really takes place. One reason for this is that actually computing the compensation payments and carrying them into effect probably will turn out to be a difficult and costly operation. As a second reason it is put forward that the actual execution of the compensation payments is only important for the distribution of welfare, an issue which the Pareto criterion just seeks to avoid; compensation should be the subject of a separate decision with regard to the distribution of welfare.

2.3 Optimum welfare

2.3.1 The two fundamental theorems of welfare economics

Paretian welfare economics has developed two fundamental theorems with respect to the functioning of a pure exchange economy which is characterised by perfect competition on all markets; see, for instance, Stiglitz (1988, pp. 63–4), Boadway and Bruce (1984, p. 64). The first theorem says that – under certain conditions – a market economy leads to a Pareto-optimal (Pareto-efficient) allocation of the scarce means of society. The second theorem states that – again under certain conditions – every Pareto optimum can be attained by a market economy, provided it starts from the appropriate distribution of resources.

These two fundamental theorems seem to give expression to the idea that any government could safely leave the whole process of the allocation of resources and the production of goods and services to the market, i.e. to the private sector of the economy. As far as there is a role for the government in the economy, it is restricted to the redistribution of the ownership of resources and, with that, of the entitlements to income; thus the government can bring about that Pareto optimum which yields the most desirable distribution of welfare over the individuals.

However, things are not so simple. The two theorems only hold, as was already indicated, under certain conditions. If in practice those conditions are not fulfilled, it is said that *market failures* occur. Many markets are not characterised by perfect competition; for quite a number of goods and services no market exists at all; producers and consumers are not completely informed as to all alternatives and prices; and the price and market system does not always yield a stable equilibrium on all markets. These examples of market failure, which may hamper the realisation of a Pareto-optimal allocation, can be as many reasons for government intervention.

2.3.2 External effects

Our aim is to throw light on the coordinating methods of democracy and bureaucracy in the public sector of an economy. In chapter 1 we sketched the growth of the public sector. The types of activities usually performed within the public sector are generally described in the welfare economic literature as: activities to provide public goods, to take action in case of decreasing costs and external effects, and to bring about income transfers. In order to be able to view briefly all these activities from a welfare theoretical point of view, we shall concentrate at first on a category which largely combines the above elements – external effects.

External effects can be defined as positive or negative influences which lie outside the market and which affect the conditions of production or the level of satisfaction in other households. Well-known examples of external effects are the way in which some industries harm others by polluting the air and water, the obstruction of the view by a building, and the traffic congestion and the danger on the roads resulting from motorised vehicles. One can also think of the benefits the whole community experiences from good education, proper housing and a suitable system of social security, which preclude the citizens from being confronted with slums and beggars.

When the conditions of production in other firms are affected, the term used is external effects *in production*; when the level of satisfaction in other households is affected, the term used is external effects *in consumption*.

According to Buchanan and Stubblebine (1962) external effects in consumption are present if, for example:

$$U^a = U^a(q_1{}^a, q_2{}^a, \ldots, q_m{}^a, q_j{}^b).$$

This means that the utility of an individual a depends not only on his own consumption pattern, but also on the consumption of another individual b. Here it is just one specific good j that is at stake, but there may be more. This cross-dependency operates outside the market and can both be positive and negative by nature. When a's utility is positively affected by b's consumption there is a *positive* external effect (external economy); when a's utility is negatively affected by b's consumption the external effect is called *negative* (external diseconomy).

If individual b, for example, builds a sea-wall for his own use, this will inevitably protect individual a as well. This means that a's utility is then positively influenced by b's consumption. If, on the other hand, b plays his transistor radio too loudly, a will experience negative external effects.

External effects are of great interest for a welfare theoretical analysis, because they can lead to inefficiencies, i.e. to non-Pareto-optimal outcomes. The reason for this is that individual b, when deciding about his consumption of good j, will take due account of his own costs and benefits, but not of the positive and/or negative external effects of his decision for person a (and possibly others) when these effects do not affect him in any – financial or other – way.

In the case of a positive external effect for a, the total social benefits of the consumption of good j by person b are higher than the private benefits b is taking account of. Person b will therefore be inclined to consume a quantity of the good which is too small from a social welfare point of view. A Pareto improvement is easily contrived. That is, if individual a would pay a (small) contribution to b to induce him to increase his consumption of good j (a little), both a and b, but in any case one of them, could be better off.

The opposite holds in case of a negative external effect. The total social costs of the consumption of good j by individual b would be higher than his private costs. Person b will therefore be inclined to consume too much of the good from a social welfare point of view. If person a would pay a (suitable) compensation to b at a reduction of his consumption of the good, both a and b, but at any rate one of them, could be better off. As an alternative one could have b pay a fine as a compensation for the nuisance and damage he is causing others. Then, b is forced to take account of the negative external effects, and thus of the total social costs, of his consumption; he will no longer be inclined to consume too much of the good. Similar reasonings apply to external effects in production.

While it is clear that the presence of external effects can lead to non-Pareto-optimal outcomes, nothing is as yet implied as to the necessity and the form of government intervention. If, for example, only a few persons are involved in the occurrence of a certain external effect, they could start negotiations with one another to accomplish Pareto improvements. For that process to become successful it is a necessary prerequisite that the property rights are clearly defined and that the observance of these rights can be commanded. Coase (1960) has even argued that – under certain conditions – any arrangement with respect to the liability for the damage of a negative external effect, irrespective of whether liability would rest on the person causing the damage or on the victim, would lead to a Pareto-optimal outcome (see Cooter and Ulen (1988)).

Things become different in the case of larger groups and if we are dealing with indivisibilities and non-exclusion in consumption, i.e. with public goods. We shall discuss the latter in the next section.

It is further worth mentioning that Hochman and Rodgers (1969) – starting from the theory of external effects – have argued that the issue of income redistribution can also be addressed by the Pareto criterion. This standpoint diverges from our earlier conclusion in section 2.2.3 that the application of the Pareto criterion and the question of how to judge the distribution of welfare could be separated. Now, Hochman and Rodgers assume that the individual welfare of people with higher incomes is dependent on and positively related to the incomes of the persons with a less favoured position in society. Under that assumption, redistribution of income from high to low income groups could indeed increase the utility level of both, i.e. lead to a Pareto improvement. From that assumption one could also explain the phenomenon of voluntary contributions to all kinds of charity funds.

2.3.3 *Public goods*

In the literature we can find various attempts to define the characteristics of pure and impure public goods (see, for instance, Cornes and Sandler (1986)). We would like to summarise the common element in these analyses as follows.

Public goods are goods which, once they have been provided for one individual, can be provided for others without extra cost. This special characteristic means that one person's consumption is no rival to the consumption of another person. If one individual consumes a private good, for example an apple, then that apple cannot be eaten by anyone else. Consumption by one makes consumption by another impossible. However, if one person drives across a bridge, this in no way precludes others from driving across this bridge. Marginal production costs are, of course, incurred in the growth in the number of bridges built. But, within certain limits, no marginal consumption costs are incurred by a growth in the number of people using a particular bridge. A bridge is a consumer good which is technically indivisible. As the number of users increases, the once and for all production costs can be divided among more and more consumers, so that the average costs per consumer are continually decreasing.

Public goods, as defined above, can be classified on the basis of two criteria.

Exclusion by producers

The most important criterion is the answer to the question whether the producer of a public good is able to exclude individual consumers from consuming it.

In the case of some public goods, it is technically *impossible* to prevent other consumers from benefitting. Such goods are inevitably at the disposal of others as well. Well-known examples of such public goods are: lighthouses, national defence, sea-walls and the ironing-out of the business cycle.

In the case of other public goods, it is technically possible to prevent other consumers from benefitting. This can be done by denying entry to some consumers or by charging an entrance fee, for instance a toll. When a bridge has been built it *can* be made available to others without extra costs, but it is *not necessary* to do so. Examples of this type of public goods are: roads, railways, harbours, recreation areas, fire departments and civil rights.

Even though it is technically possible to split the second category of public goods into units which can be sold in the market, the implementation of this possibility can lead to much wastage. Once a single person is provided with such a good, it can also be made available to others at no extra cost. For as long as the use of such a good is not greater than the available capacity permits, it is better for all consumers to buy the public good together and to apportion the costs among one another, than to let each individual separately buy the good in the market. Collective acquisition of the good and splitting it into units which then are sold in the market for a price pro rata of consumption, may also be economically undesirable. A price per unit can put an unnecessary break on the use of the good, while the cashing of these prices entails additional costs.

However, in the case of the first category of public goods, it is technically impossible to split them into saleable units even if this would be desirable from an economic point of view. In respect of goods such as national defence and sea-walls, a quid pro quo transaction (an exchange for a sum of money per unit) is ruled out in that the use of these goods cannot be made dependent on the payment of an entrance fee.

Notice that the category of public goods for which the element of 'joint consumption' is combined with the impossibility of exclusion represents a clear case of positive external effects.

Exclusion by the consumer

Public goods can thus be classified according to whether or not producers are able to exclude certain consumers from consuming them. Another classification is whether or not a consumer himself can choose to consume the good. A consumer can decide independently whether he will drive along a certain road or enter a certain harbour. However, he cannot decide independently whether he will be defended by a dike or an army corps, and whether or not he wishes to profit from an incomes policy or from the ironing-out of the business cycle. Once a dike is built or a business cycle ironed out, an individual consumer can in no way decide to remain unaffected.

In table 2.2 public goods have been classified according to all criteria used so far. The horizontal division shows whether some consumers can be excluded from consumption by the producer of the public good. The vertical division is on the basis of whether an individual

Table 2.2 *A typology of pure and impure public goods*

	Person is able to choose amount of consumption		Person is unable to choose amount of consumption	
	Utility increased by consumption	Utility decreased by consumption	Utility increased by consumption	Utility decreased by consumption
Persons can be excluded from consumption	Recreation area Roads Cable television	Polluted beaches	Fire departments Civil liberties	Infectious diseases The military draft
Persons cannot be excluded from consumption	Lighthouses Socialised medicine Knowledge	Excess sunshine Airport noise	Public order National defence Pollution control Flood control	Air pollution Floods

Source: Riker and Ordeshook (1973), p. 261.

consumer himself can choose to consume or not. Public goods with a positive and a negative effect on utility are shown separately.

Samuelson (1954, 1955) calls the goods shown in the bottom right-hand corner *pure public goods*. These goods satisfy two conditions simultaneously – consumers cannot be excluded nor can they exclude themselves. All other public goods are impure, as in one form or another they all have private as well as public elements. Either the producer can limit the provision to certain individuals, or the individuals can limit their own consumption, or both.

The distinction between pure private goods and pure public goods has been elegantly expressed in mathematical terms by Samuelson (1954):

1. The total consumption of a pure private good, for example butter, can be divided between two persons so that one consumes less butter as the other consumes more. If Q_i represents the total consumption of butter and q_i^a and q_i^b the quantities consumed by a and b respectively, then $Q_i = q_i^a + q_i^b$, i.e. total consumption equals the sum of the separate amounts consumed.
2. The total consumption of a pure public good, for example tanks, cannot be divided between two persons. Tanks are provided equally for everyone; they are consumed in their totality by everyone. If Q_k is the total consumption of tanks, and q_k^a and q_k^b are the tanks consumed by a and b, then, by definition, $Q_k = q_k^a = q_k^b$.

2.3.4 *The individual welfare optimum*

In section 2.3.3 we stated that it would be economically undesirable to split a public good into saleable units (e.g. through the levying of toll) even if this were technically possible. That conclusion was somewhat premature because whether something is economically desirable can only be judged on the basis of an explicit criterion for optimum social welfare. To that end we introduced in section 2.2.3 the Pareto criterion.

Seen from the viewpoint of a single individual, it is relatively easy to define his welfare optimum. For the sake of clarity we shall confine the analysis to pure private and pure public goods. General starting point for the argument is that for the single individual the positive difference between the total benefits and the total costs of goods and services should be as large as possible. That holds for (pure) private as well as for (pure) public goods. On the basis of Gossen's first law – the law of diminishing marginal utility – it can be taken for granted that after the first unit of a specific good has been consumed, each successive unit will give less satisfaction, i.e. will provide fewer benefits than the previous one. On the other hand the costs to an individual of foregoing other expenditures of his income do not weigh less heavily for each successive unit. However, as long as the benefits of the marginal unit – i.e. the least useful unit – exceed its costs, the individual's total positive balance will increase. It is only when the costs of the marginal unit exceed its benefits that the total positive balance will decrease. A necessary condition for achieving optimum individual welfare is, therefore, that for the individual marginal benefits equal marginal costs.

As to public goods this implies, according to founders of public finance such as Sax and Wicksell (Musgrave and Peacock, 1958, pp. 177–89, 72–118), that the cost of the last pound spent by the individual on contributions or taxes then just equals the benefit he receives from the last quantity of the public good he consumes that was financed by this pound.

Following Marshall the total benefits, less total costs, for an individual can be analysed using the concept of *consumer surplus*. The benefit is expressed by the highest price an individual would, if necessary, be prepared to pay for a specific quantity of a certain good. The costs consist of the price the individual actually pays. An individual's consumer surplus then is the maximum amount of money he would, if necessary, be prepared to pay for a specific quantity of a good, less the amount of money he actually pays. Translated into this terminology a person only then has reached his individual welfare optimum if his consumer surplus is at its maximum.

The consumer surplus is illustrated by means of figure 2.1. This figure is based on the continually repeated question, what is the maximum amount an individual will, if necessary, be prepared to pay for the first unit of a certain good (butter, tanks), for the second unit, for the third unit, etc? These amounts, which represent the marginal benefits, are shown in the figure by the height of the successive columns. For the sake of simplicity we assume that the marginal costs of the good in question are constant for the individual concerned. For each additional packet of butter the same price (p) has to be paid; for every extra tank the tax to be paid will be increased by the same amount (p).

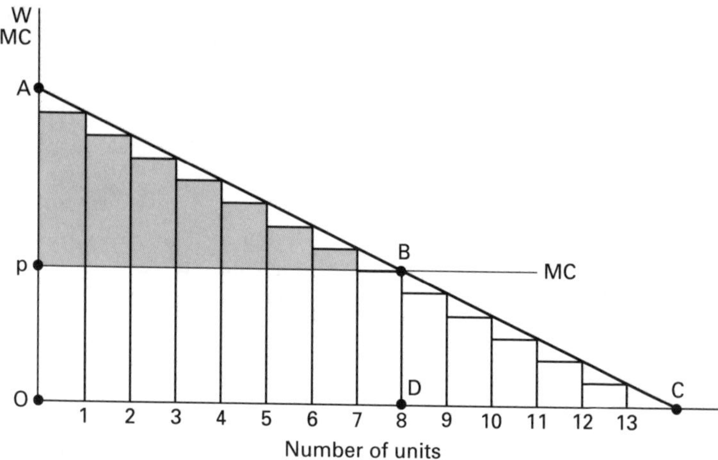

Figure 2.1 The consumer surplus of a good for a single individual
W = marginal benefits
MC = marginal costs

If an individual wishes to achieve his optimum utility then, among other things, it is essential that his marginal benefits equal his marginal costs, which is here the case at 8 units. The maximum amount the individual would be prepared to pay for 8 units is the sum of the columns 1 to 8, approximately the area covered by the quadrilateral ABDO. The total amount he actually pays is shown by the oblong pBDO. His consumer surplus, which is at a maximum when he buys 8 units, is therefore the shaded part of the triangle ABp.

It is known that the individual demand curve for a good gives the relation between the price of the good and the quantity the individual is prepared to buy at that price in a given period. In that sense the line ABC in figure 2.1 represents the demand of the individual for a good (butter, tanks). At price or tax amount p per unit the individual is prepared to buy 8 units of the good. In an analogous fashion one can read out at other prices or tax amounts per unit what number of units of the good the individual is willing to buy.[2]

2.3.5 *The demand for a public good*

In figure 2.1 the line ABC represents the demand by one individual. Let us now turn to the demand of a group of people. It is

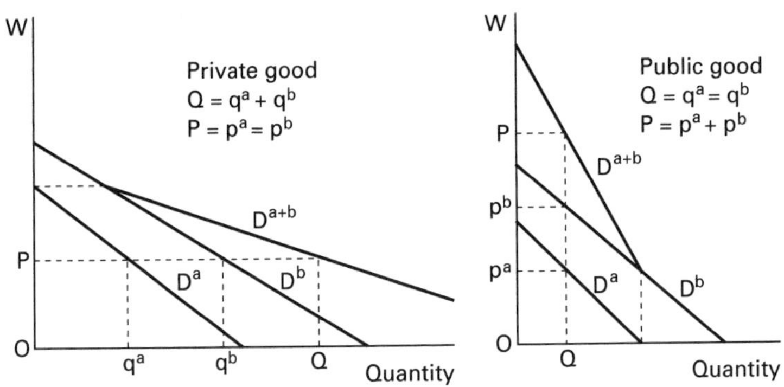

Figure 2.2 The addition of individual demand curves to total demand
W = marginal benefits
Q = (joint) quantity
P = (joint) price
q^a, q^b = quantity person a, b
p^a, p^b = price person a, b

known that the total demand for a pure *private* consumption good, expressed as a quantity, is equal to the total of the amounts demanded by the individuals separately. This is shown on the left-hand side of figure 2.2. In this figure the curves D^a and D^b represent the individual demands for butter by persons a and b, respectively. For both consumers the (market) price P is the same, so that $p^a = p^b = P$. Individual a is interested in buying q^a packets of butter at this price, individual b in q^b packets. The total amount demanded at this price is equal to the sum of the individual quantities, i.e. $Q = q^a + q^b$. An analogous reasoning holds at other values of the (market) price. The total demand for butter (D^{a+b}) can thus be obtained by *adding* the individual demand curves *horizontally*.

In section 2.3.3 we explained that the total demand for a pure *public* good differs from the total demand for a pure private good. In the example, a and b do not need to own their own tank to defend themselves; they can both use the same tank for that. The quantity Q of a pure public good is consumed in its totality by a as well as by b: $q^a = q^b = Q$. Adding the number of tanks demanded by a and b horizontally would therefore be misleading, as it would imply double counting. It is significant only to add the preparedness of a and b respectively to pay a certain price (tax amount) for the same tank. If a is prepared to contribute an amount p^a per tank and b an amount p^b, then the total preparedness to pay is given by: $P = p^a + p^b$. This conclusion is graphically represented on the right-hand side of figure 2.2. The total demand for tanks is obtained by determining for each tank – 1, 2, 3, . . . , n – the total preparedness to pay as the sum of the contributions which a and b together are prepared to make. The total demand for tanks is thus not obtained by a horizontal but by a *vertical addition* of the individual demand curves.

2.3.6 *The social welfare optimum*

The Pareto criterion helped Samuelson (1954) to make general statements on the optimum social welfare of a large number of individuals, when this social welfare also depends on public goods. We shall limit ourselves to the case of two individuals and a single pure private and a single pure public good.

Let us first consider the (social welfare) optimum for two individuals and one *private good* – butter. As the marginal cost of butter equals P, it becomes possible to see from the left-hand side of figure 2.3 that the individuals a and b reach their individual welfare optimum when they consume q^a and q^b packets of butter, in both cases at price P per packet. At these points the marginal benefits for both a and b are equal to the marginal costs, so that for each individual the consumer surplus is at a maximum, that is, equal to the shaded areas of the triangles A″C″P (for a) and A′C′P (for b).

Suppose that there is an omniscient and benevolent dictator (e.g. the philosopher-king in Plato's *Politeia*) who decides on the level of output of the good and its distribution between a and b. Assume furthermore that the philosopher-king decides that the total quantity of butter produced will amount to Q_{opt} at a price P per packet. This point represents a potential optimum (in neo-Paretian terminology), because the total consumer surplus is at a maximum, namely, equal to the area covered by the square A′BCP.[3] This point also represents a real optimum in Paretian terms provided total consumption is divided among a and b so that a consumes quantity q^a and b quantity q^b. After all, such a division means that everyone's individual position is at an optimum and the king cannot improve the position of either individual without worsening the position of the other.

By analogy we can also derive the (social welfare) optimum for two individuals and a *public good*. If the marginal costs of tanks equal P, it is possible to read from the right-hand side of figure 2.3 that, when there is no group action, person a will be at an optimum when he does

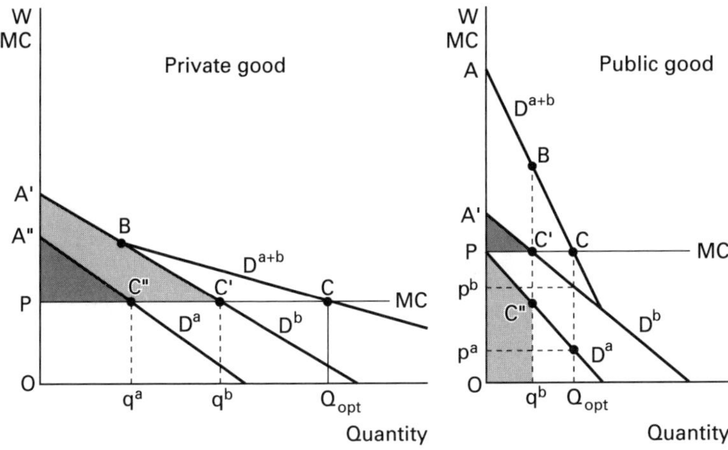

Figure 2.3 The social welfare optimum for a pure private and a pure public good

W = marginal benefits
MC = marginal costs
P = price
q^a, q^b = quantity person a, b
p^a, p^b = price person a, b
Q_{opt} = social welfare optimum

not buy a single tank and b's individual optimum will be reached at q^b tanks. At these quantities the respective individual marginal benefits of a and b equal their individual marginal costs. Thus q^b tanks are bought in total. However, because tanks are a pure public good, both a and b will profit from the purchase. The consumer surplus of a then equals the shaded quadrilateral $PC''q^bO$ (since he pays nothing for the tanks) and that of b will equal the shaded area of the triangle $A'C'P$. The total consumer surplus equals the area $ABC'P$, that is, equals the total benefit (the area ABq^bO) minus total costs (the area $PC'q^bO$).[4]

Suppose once again that a philosopher-king decides on the level of output and the distribution of the public good. Assume also that the king decides that Q_{opt} tanks are produced at price P per tank. This point represents a potential optimum because the total consumer surplus is at a maximum, namely, equals the whole area of the triangle ACP. The action of the philosopher-king has thus increased the total consumer surplus by the triangle BCC'. The potential optimum can be transformed into a real Pareto optimum by dividing the total costs between a and b such that a contributes p^a per tank and b p^b. Such a division provides each person with an individual optimum position and the king can improve the position of the one only by worsening that of the other. Thus, the social welfare optimum for a public good has the following characteristics:

1. The individuals contribute so that for each individual the marginal benefits equal that individual's marginal costs.
2. The total contribution of the individuals combined equals the total costs of the public good.
3. The sum of the marginal benefits of the individuals equals the marginal costs of the public good.

In summary, we conclude that the social welfare optimum for private goods differs in at least two respects from that for public goods. In an optimum situation (pure) private goods are consumed in different quantities by different consumers at the same price, but (pure) public goods are consumed in the same quantity by different consumers at different prices. The optimum for private goods means that *for each consumer separately* the marginal benefits equal the marginal costs of the good. However, the optimum for public goods means that their marginal benefits, which represent the *sum* of the marginal benefits of all consumers, equal the marginal costs of the good.

In order to reach a Pareto optimum for private goods it in principle suffices if each individual separately weighs his (marginal) benefits and costs. The market mechanism thus is capable – under certain conditions – of producing the optimum quantity of private goods. Those conditions notably are that individuals should be well-informed and strive after maximisation of their utility, and external effects should be absent. Thus we have come back to the first fundamental theorem of welfare economics; see section 2.3.1.

The market mechanism is, on the other hand, not capable of producing the optimum quantity of public goods. In the market every individual acts for himself, so that no or insufficient care is taken to sum the (marginal) benefits of all consumers before these are weighed against (marginal) benefits.

In so far as welfare depends on public goods, the social welfare optimum can only be obtained by an institution capable of adding the marginal benefits of individuals. In the following chapters a number of such institutions will be examined, namely, negotiations democracy, referendum democracy, representative democracy and bureaucracy. All these institutions are logical stages in the political process, i.e. the process of conversion of individual needs into public goods.

3 Negotiation

3.1 Freedom of exit and non-commitment

In chapter 2, we considered the conditions for a social welfare optimum. We formulated this welfare optimum from the point of view of a philosopher-king who stands outside the economic and political process and who wants the best for his subjects. We stated that with regard to private goods and services, one can, in principle, rely on the market mechanism for realising an optimum. With regard to public goods, we have not yet answered whether an optimum is attainable in social reality, and if so, under which circumstances. This topic will be discussed in chapters 3 to 6.

In this chapter on *negotiations democracy*, we shall consider whether groups in which the members negotiate with each other on the basis of freedom of exit and non-commitment, are able to establish the particular policy that is optimal for the joint welfare of the citizens in that group. It is important to reflect on groups because every collective action takes place by or on behalf of a group, and a system of purely individual transactions in a free market has not – in general – been suitable for the delivery of public goods. *Freedom of exit* (voluntarism) means that the members are free to leave the group. *Non-commitment* means that group decisions are not binding for the individual group members. Examples of groups which are more or less organised on the basis of freedom of exit and non-commitment are interest groups, trade unions, military alliances (e.g. NATO in peace time) and international organisations (the United Nations).

Studying negotiations democracy is important for two reasons. First, the negotiations democracy is an independent decision-making model which occurs fairly frequently. Second, group negotiations are an important element of any democratic political system. Analysis of negotiations, therefore, is necessary to understand the functioning of the entire system.

This chapter is divided into six sections. After some introductory remarks in section 3.2 about the important difference between self-interest and group-interest (between individual and collective rationality), we investigate the circumstances under which a group of individuals with a common goal will act to achieve that goal. Subsequently, the question arises of whether a group is able to function in such a manner that a result is realised which is optimal for the group. In section 3.4, we give a preliminary answer to this question using the exchange model of Lindahl and others; we deal with the question more extensively in section 3.5 where we apply game theory concepts. In section 3.6, we examine the practical results of a negotiations democracy by using a number of examples and relating these results to the theory.

3.2 Self-interest and class-interest

The starting point of any economic reflection on groups is the assumption that the members of the group make subjective, rational decisions. As explained in section 2.1, this assumption means that the individual members of the group:

- strive to achieve their own goal;
- understand this goal as welfare, and that they view welfare as dependent on group decisions with regard to certain goods and services;
- are able to compare the various alternatives and to order them into a set sequence;
- will prefer a higher welfare to a lower.

In his book *The logic of collective action*, Olson (1965) provided the first consistently formulated and systematically elaborated economic theory of groups. In this book, he defines a *group* as a number of individuals with a common goal, i.e. a number of subjects striving for *the same individual goal.*

This conception can be found in the work of the classical economists. Marx, especially, based his definition of *class* not on irrational social ties of its members but on economic factors. He distinguished between a *Klasse an sich* and a *Klasse fur sich.* A *Klasse an sich* is determined by production relations. Those who own the means of production belong to the 'capitalist class', the bourgeoisie, while the non-owners make up the 'proletariat'. According to the Marxist view, at a certain moment the members of a class become aware of their position. The owners will strive to expropriate the surplus value formed during the process of production, while the exploited proletarians will begin to resist. It is at this point that the classes *an sich* ('as such') become classes *für sich* ('for themselves'); both classes are then characterised by their position in the production process.

Marx held great contempt for those socialists who believed that human behaviour is based on an inborn altruism for neighbourly love. Together with Engels he wrote in *The Manifesto of the Communist League*:

> 'The bourgeoisie, wherever it has got the upper hand, has put an end to all feudal, patriarchal, idyllic relations. It has pitilessly torn asunder the motley feudal ties that bound man to his 'natural superiors', and has left remaining no other nexus between man and man than naked self-interest, callous 'cash payment'. It has drowned the most heavenly ecstasies of religious fervor, of chivalrous enthusiasm, of philistine sentimentalism, in the icy water of egotistical calculation' (Marx and Engels, (1848)1962, p. 54).

Marx regarded ideology as a cloak for self-interest. He ridiculed the Church of England in his remark that it would pardon an attack on 38 of its 39 Articles of Religion more readily than it would an attack on 1/39 of its income.

The emphasis Marx laid on self-interest and purposiveness made him a target for criticism. The sociologist Mills argues that in Marx's view, class action will always come about if the members of a class are rationally aware of: (1) the interests of their own class; (2) the interests of other classes; (3) the fact that the interests of other classes are illegitimate; and (4) the possibilities of using certain means for collective action (1951, pp. 325–8). He concludes: 'This idea is just as rationalist as liberalism in its psychological assumptions', for it is based on 'a calculus of advantage'. Yes, this idea is 'utilitarian, and more closely related to Bentham than Hegel'. The error of this view has long been proved, according to Mills, by the existence of widespread political apathy. 'Indifference', he concludes, 'is the major sign of the . . . collapse of socialist hopes.'

Olson (1965, pp. 105–10) defends Marx against Mills' attack; he agrees with the notion that every class action is based on a calculus of costs and benefits. However, Marx made one fundamental error in logic, according to Olson. In Marx's view, when a proletarian pursues his individual interest in a rational manner, this then means that he will further the interest of his class. Through an invisible hand, harmony will automatically come about between individual and collective rationality. Wicksell, however, gave Olson the idea that this implicit assumption is incorrect. When it is assumed that an individual will serve his own interest, it does not necessarily follow that he serves the interests of his class. This is apparent in Marx's own example of the exploiting class – the entrepreneurs. All entrepreneurs strive for the same goal, namely maximising profits. Decisions by individual entrepreneurs aimed at realising this goal will, in a situation of perfect competition, as is well known from economic theory, result in the group making no profit at all in the long run. The individual pursuit of profit will inevitably lead to an accumulation of decisions to expand the production of profit-making products, and this will result in a drop of the market price until the profits disappear. In this case, individual rationality is in conflict with collective rationality. What is true for entrepreneurs might also be true for the proletariat. It is logically inconsistent to accept the notion of conflicts between the individual and collective optimum in the case of the entrepreneurs but to deny this possibility, a priori, in the case of the proletariat.

3.3 The participation decision

3.3.1 The large group

The residents of a district, the inhabitants of a municipality, the citizens of a country, or the workers in a branch of industry can all be viewed as members of a group. Since the members of a group partially share the same interests, they can attempt to achieve a result which is optimal for the whole group through cooperation on a voluntary and non-committed basis. Olson (1965) then poses the question, if and under which circumstances can it be expected that individuals will participate in processes of collective action and decision-making?

In Olson's opinion individual decisions on whether or not to participate are based, as pointed out before, on a subjective, rational assessment of costs and benefits. An individual citizen in a *large group* will reason that the effect of his contribution to the realisation of the common goal is negligibly small. If, indeed, there is no appeareance of the common goal being realised, it is highly unlikely that the contribution of one extra individual will make a difference. The individual, therefore, is tempted to regard the (marginal) benefits of participation as equal to nil.

The following are included in the costs of participation:

the time needed for the actual participation in collective action;
the financial burden related to participation in common activities (such as travel expenses, contribution);
the information costs which include the costs (in time and money) resulting from collecting the information necessary to participate (for example knowledge about various points of view and knowledge about opportunities to influence).

These costs are clearly recognisable for the individual and are in total greater than nil.

A subjective, rational assessment of costs and benefits will then inescapably lead to the conclusion that it is better for the individual to abstain from participation. As soon as the citizen assumes that others will realise the desired policy anyway, it is only to his advantage to abstain from participating which will save time and money. In this case, one could speak of *positive apathy*. *Negative apathy* is also possible. When others do not cooperate to achieve a desired policy, or when it is expected that others will not be successful, it does not make sense for the individual citizen to go into action alone or to participate in the action of others. Time and money that could possibly be invested can be regarded as lost beforehand. In short, from whatever assumption a citizen starts, he does not participate according to this theory.

According to Olson, Marx thus assumed wrongly that rational behaviour of the members of the proletariat will lead to mass participation. Large numbers of individual proletarians will sponge on the urge to act by the doers – in so far as these exist – because they view the collective optimum as subordinate to their individual optimum.

It follows from Olson's model that participation will be very small when the policy is optimal. In this situation, many citizens will be of the opinion that things will go well even without their contribution. In the case of positive apathy previously described, there is no inconsistency between mass non-participation and realisation of the collective welfare optimum. However, based on Olson's model, it can also be predicted that participation will be small if the policy is far removed from the optimum. Then many citizens are of the opinion that their individual political contribution will not matter anyway. It is clear that this case of negative apathy does not contribute at all to realising a group welfare that is optimal in terms of the Pareto criterion.

3.3.2 A positive participation decision

According to Olson's theory, the participation decision in large groups will in principle turn out negatively. This raises the question under which circumstances a participation decision will be positive. According to the theory, the individual will decide to participate when the expected benefits exceed the costs. Several factors can contribute to this.

First, the *outcome of the group action* could be of great value to the individual. In that case it will serve the individual to his advantage when he acts, irrespective of what others do. Others can then profit without undertaking anything; they are the so-called 'free riders'. Think, for instance, of a landowner who builds an anti-flood dike from which other people in the region profit as well.

Second, participation in group activities does not only need to serve a collective interest. Participation can also result in all sorts of private benefits. In this case, Olson speaks of *selective incentives*. These private benefits can be of both a material and non-material nature. Examples of the first category are the right to individual legal aid that is part of the membership of a trade union and the use of tourist services as part of the membership of a national tourist association. Of a non-material nature are power, prestige and the social contacts that individuals can derive from, for instance, functioning actively within a political party or participating in a demonstration against nuclear weapons. These private benefits can be more or less accidental by nature, but selective incentives can also be consciously designed to persuade an individual to participate and become a member of an organisation. Selective incentives can be shaped in the form of a reward for participation; they can also take the form of punishment or a fine in case of non-participation. The closed-shop system of the trade unions in Britain and the US and picketing at strikes are examples of the latter situation.

In recent literature (Mueller, 1986), one finds the idea that learning processes occur when individuals are frequently rewarded – for instance in education – for a cooperative attitude and punished for non-cooperative behaviour. By means of these learning processes, reputation effects and social norms develop which will subsequently lead a life of their own and stimulate cooperative behaviour in the future. Elster (1989, p. 105) defines a *social norm* as 'the propensity to feel shame and to anticipate sanctions by others at the thought of behaving in a certain, forbidden way'. Furthering this idea in his model of the individual participation decision, Naylor (1990) adds a factor to the cost-benefit assessment which describes 'the valuation by the individual of the reputation effects that derive from acting according to the social norm'. This factor has a positive influence on the decision to participate in collective action, and especially to remain participative.

Third, it needs to be understood that the *costs* to the individual as a result of information, organisation and implementation are not equal for every type of collective action. Signing a petition of a district committee involves completely different costs than financing a weather satellite for tornado warning. We must add to this that the costs for collective action in the future will decline noticeably as a result of the speedy development of information technology.

The aforementioned factors come together in the *small group*. There is a much more direct relation between the contributions of individual members and the success of collective actions in a small group than in a large group. The input of each individual has immediate, noticeable consequences for the collective result. Furthermore, social control is larger in a small group so that cooperation is more quickly rewarded in the sphere of social contacts (a pat on the shoulder by friends and colleagues, prestige) while non-cooperation will be punished (disapproval, rejection). Finally, costs for organisation, information, and decision-making carried by the actives will be considerably lower in a small group than in a large. It will be clear that all these factors, separate or in combination, will contribute to higher individual benefits when participating in group activity and/or to lower costs. Under such circumstances, the individual will be more quickly inclined to make a positive participation decision.

3.3.3 Implications and practice

Olson's theory describes the circumstances under which individual group members will and will not participate in activities that are important for realising common goals. Accordingly, as more group members decide positively about participation, the chances for the realisation of collective action and the creation of a common organisation naturally increase. Let us review some interesting implications of this theory.

1. It is not to be expected that all groups with a common interest will work on their common interests in equal measure. Small groups with very specific interests will more easily and more quickly

organise and establish collective action than large groups with diffuse interests. The (very) small group of electronics producers in the EC, thus, is better able to lobby in favour of protectionist measures than the large and diffuse group of consumers can resist the price increases that result from it.

2. When types of collective action will result in higher costs for participants at some point, they will occur less often. From this point of view, it can be expected that petitions will acquire more support than demonstrations, that more people will join a labour union than will strike, and that more people will vote than will join a political party.
3. Because organising for collective action is problematic and involves costs, it is to be expected that it will take some time before it gets off to a good start. On the other hand, organisations that have developed selective incentives often survive, even when the collective goal for which they were once created is no longer sought. Existing organisations are sooner inclined to establish a new field of activity than to abolish themselves. The consequence is that as societies have had longer periods of political stability, greater numbers of organisations for collective action will exist (Olson, 1982, p. 41).

A considerable amount of empirical research material is available that supports these and other aspects of the economic theory of participation.

The unequal degree of organisation of various social groups can be illustrated with a number of examples regarding the Netherlands. Between 90 and 100 per cent of Dutch enterprises, both in terms of their absolute number and their size, are organised in employers' associations, to which we should add that many enterprises are a member of various associations. On the other hand, only 29 per cent of employees are affiliated to a trade union, and the consumers' union has only about 5 per cent of the population of 18 years and older. A significant private organisation for those entitled to social security transfers and government subsidies does not exist at all. These differences in degree of organisation appear to be explained by the size of the groups involved, the nature of their common interests (specific or diffused), and the above-mentioned time factor.

The importance of cost, in time and money, to the degree and manner of participation is emphasised by the fact that in 1987 46 per cent of the electorate participated in a petition versus only 19 per cent in a demonstration and 12 per cent in an action group. A similar trend is found in the more specific political sphere. While the voter turnout for national elections is around 80 per cent, the membership of political parties is made up of less than 4 per cent of the electorate, and of those members only a minority actively participates within the party. Comparable data for Britain can be found in Parry et al. (1992).

We can add to this that the politically active are not representative of the Dutch population: males, the highly educated, and higher-income individuals are more politically active than females, the lower-educated and lower-income individuals. These differences in participation can be explained in a large part by differences in education. This concurs with Olson's theory when it can be assumed that the costs for an individual to acquire the necessary information for political participation decrease the higher the education he possesses. Apart from this, it has been established that differences in opinion between the politically active and the politically inactive are small.

The hypothesis that the number of organised interest groups in the country increases the longer the period of stability is maintained is confirmed by research of Murrell (1984), who investigated 24 OECD countries (see also Mueller and Murrell, 1986).

Finally, we should mention the research by Opp (1986) on the anti-nuclear movement in West Germany. It is clear that selective incentives of a non-material, social nature play an important role in the decision to participate.

3.4 Voluntary exchange

3.4.1 The Lindahl equilibrium

In the previous section, we investigated if and under what circumstances groups of individuals with a common goal will act to further the realisation of that goal. The next question then is whether those groups are able to achieve such a policy that the result is optimal for the group.

Lindahl ((1919)1958), Johansen (1965, pp. 123–53) and Buchanan (1968, pp. 11–48) have studied the conditions under which a voluntary and non-committed basis for a collective optimum can be realised by means of *negotiation* and *exchange*. The negotiation model they describe has four characteristics. First, the negotiators possess a more or less equal position of power. Second, all citizens simultaneously negotiate the nature and size of collective provisions, and everyone's share in the costs. It is evident that the low share in the costs per unit for the one will result in a high share for the other. Third, the demand curve for each individual shows a declining trend. This means that the quantity of a collective provision demanded by an individual will be larger when his share in costs per unit is lower. Fourth, during the negotiation process, each negotiator will behave in accordance with the Pareto criterion which means that he is prepared to accept an improvement in the position of others if he himself will not suffer for it.

Such a negotiation model seldom occurs in reality. Nevertheless, a discussion of this abstract notion aided by the method of the declining abstraction is necessary in order to acquire insight into collective decision-making as it actually occurs.

In the model by Lindahl et al., the negotiation process between every pair of individuals a and b is roughly as follows. When at the start individual a pays a low share in the cost per unit, then he desires many units, meaning a high collective provision level. Individual b in that situation pays a much higher share per unit and therefore wishes fewer units, hence a lower provision level. Individual a will then offer b a smaller share in the costs per unit in order to persuade b to accept a higher provision level. When, on the other hand, b, at the start of the negotiation process, pays a relatively low share in the costs per unit, the roles are reversed. No matter how extreme the frames of reference for a or b are, somewhere there is middle ground (a certain collective provision level and shares in the costs per unit for both) in which both a and b can find one another and in which each individual position has reached equilibrium between costs and benefits. Once a and b have found common ground, then they together will negotiate with c and find consensus in the same manner. This repeats itself until an individual equilibrium between costs and benefits is established for every citizen.

The negotiations between a and b, hence, will lead to an exchange between them. By using traditional demand and supply curves, Buchanan (1968, pp. 22–32) was able to make the development of this exchange graphically plausible. In figure 3.1, D^a and D^b represent the demand curves of a and b, previously shown on the right-hand side of figure 2.2, for, for instance, canons. For the sake of simplicity, the marginal costs of the good have been assumed constant and equal to P. If a and b would act completely independent from one another, a will refrain from buying while b will purchase q^b canons. If we assume

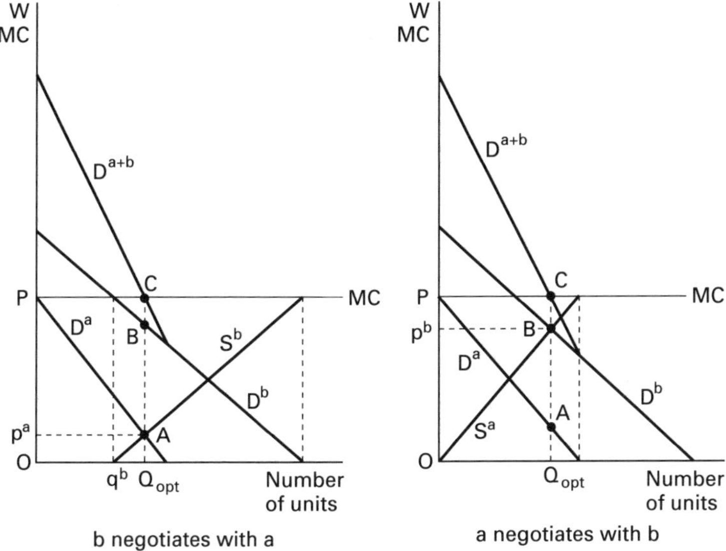

Figure 3.1 Demand and supply of a public good
W = marginal benefits
MC = marginal costs
P = price
Q = quantity
opt = optimal
q^a, q^b = quantity individual a, b
p^a, p^b = price individual a, b

that we are dealing with a (pure) public good, then both consume q^b units, but a consumes this quantity without having to pay any price. Now there is a possibility that an exchange between a and b is realised that is profitable for both. Buchanan shows this possibility by raising the question, what price must b receive from a in order for him to be willing to purchase even more canons? And vice versa – what price would a be willing to pay in order to persuade b to indeed buy more canons? When both questions result in the same answer, then it is profitable for both to trade more canons for a higher share in the costs for a.

Buchanan bases his answer to the first question, namely how much b wants to receive, on the fact that b too will appreciate more canons than q^b positively, as is clear from the demand curve D^b. In order to buy additional canons, b wants to assure that at *minimum* the difference between his marginal benefits of these canons and the marginal costs is paid for by others. It is therefore possible to draw a supply curve S^b (see the left-hand side of figure 3.1) that indicates at which level of contribution of a individual b is prepared to buy more canons above the initial amount q^b.[1]

Buchanan bases his answer to the second question, namely how much individual a is willing to pay for extra canons, on the marginal benefits that a derives from these canons. The marginal benefit at any arbitrary number of canons is depicted graphically by a's demand curve. The *maximum* costs per canon that a wants to accept for his account in case of purchase beyond q^b, is thus depicted by that part of demand curve D^a that is on the right of point q^b.

From point q^b up to the intersection of S^b and D^a the (maximum) amount that a is willing to pay for an extra amount of canons exceeds the (minimum) contribution that b wishes for the purchase of these canons. This, therefore, opens opportunities for a mutually advantageous exchange. Beyond the intersection S^b and D^a, the maximum amount that a wishes to pay for additional canons is smaller than the contribution that b wants to receive at minimum; in this case an exchange is no longer possible. Assuming that both parties will utilise all possibilities for mutually advantageous exchange, they will meet at the intersection of S^b and D^a. At that point, b exchanges his willingness to purchase Q_{opt} instead of q^b canons against the willingness of a to pay a contribution p^a for each additional canon instead of paying nil. Both will profit from this exchange because between q^b and Q_{opt}, the marginal valuation of a for extra canons (D^a) exceeds his contribution in the costs (p^a). Likewise, the marginal valuation of b for extra canons (D^b) exceeds his contribution in the costs ($p^b = P - p^a$).[2]

In the above we assumed that b takes the initiative and purchases the canons, while a contributes to the costs. Naturally, the roles of a and b can be reversed. Individual a is himself not prepared to buy any canon at price P. As is apparent from demand curve D^a, a appreciates canons positively, but his marginal benefits are smaller than the marginal costs. The picture changes when individual b would contribute in the costs. In order to decide on the purchase of canons, a will at *minimum* want to see the difference met between his marginal benefits and the marginal costs. The curve S^a on the right-hand side of figure 3.1 indicates at which contribution of b, individual a is prepared to purchase canons. D^b, on the other hand, indicates the *maximum* contribution that b is prepared to pay for each canon.

When a and b completely utilise the opportunities for mutually advantageous exchange, they will meet at the intersection of S^a and D^b. This intersection corresponds with Q_{opt} canons, the same quantity as above. Individual a will purchase a total of Q_{opt} canons, while individual b will contribute p^b for each canon. For both the exchange is advantageous. Indeed, until Q_{opt} the marginal valuation of b for extra canons (D^b) exceeds his contribution in the costs (p^b). Likewise, the marginal valuation of a for extra canons will exceed his contribution in the costs ($p^a = P - p^b$).[3]

We notice that the final result of the negotiation process will be that Q_{opt} canons are purchased, independently of who has taken the initiative. This outcome is known in the literature as the *Lindahl equilibrium* (see also Roberts, 1974).[4]

Referring to section 2.3.6 and figure 2.3, we further notice that the final result meets the conditions of a Pareto optimum in the case of a public good, because it can be read from figure 3.1 that Q_{opt} corresponds with the intersection of D^{a+b} and MC. In other words, the sum of the marginal benefits of a and b equals the marginal costs as a whole; furthermore, every individual pays such a contribution that each individual's marginal benefits are equal to each individual's marginal sacrifice. This conclusion holds general validity; the outcome of the negotiation model of Lindahl c.s. is Pareto optimal.

There is an old saying: 'where two are trading, one will be wailing'. This proverb is thus not applicable to voluntary exchange ('without coercion and deceit'). Assuming that parties participating in an exchange process possess a more or less equal amount of negotiation power, Lindahl, Johansen and Buchanan proved that through exchange the result for both a and b can improve. Phenomena in politics such as wheeling and dealing, exchange, compromise and coalitions are thus a priori not inconsistent with the pursuit of higher social welfare. Quite the contrary, it is through exchange that a higher welfare level is reached than would have been possible otherwise. There are cases in which policy satisfaction for the one does not inhibit policy satisfaction for the other.

3.4.2 *Evaluation*

The model discussed in the previous section is based on a large number of assumptions. Of these, the first two are the most important. The assumption that a and b possess an equal amount of negotiation power means that we are dealing with *democratic* negotiation processes. In many negotiation processes, however, the power balance is not equal. The assumption that all group members negotiate simultaneously about the nature of the collective provision and about each other's share in costs is even less realistic. This assumption will hold, at most, for *small* groups. In large groups, most group members will make decisions in isolation from one another. A well-known example is provided by price theory. In an oligopolistic situation (few suppliers), each individual producer will have to consider the reaction of competitors when setting a price. In a situation of perfect competition (many suppliers), the individual company will accept the price behaviour of its rivals and adapt to that. In the first case, the company assumes that the height of its own price will influence the price set by others, while in the second case the company will assume that its own behaviour does not influence the market price that is valid for all.

Representatives of interest groups in a negotiations democracy who negotiate with each other and with the government, themselves form a small group. The interest groups, however, are not monolithical but consist of large numbers of members who all pursue their own goals. As long as the negotiation process is characterised by freedom of exit and non-commitment, these members do not feel bound to the outcome of the negotiation. The fringe members, in particular, will decide independently whether they will accept the policy of the group representatives, and these representatives will take this into consideration. In fact, large numbers of persons are thus involved, directly or indirectly, in the decision-making process. But it is because of this that Lindahl's assumption that all persons simultaneously negotiate with each other is not realistic. In the large groups of a negotiations democracy, every subject will assume that his individual contribution to the negotiation process will not affect the outcome.

The consequences of this will be dealt with in the sequel of this chapter with a discussion of game theory.

3.5 Game theoretical approach

3.5.1 The Prisoners' Dilemma Game

A *game* is a mathematical simulation of the interaction of the behaviour between various individuals, in which a logical connection is made between the goals of the subjects, their actions and the results they achieve. The subjects whose behaviour is analysed are called

Table 3.1 *Outcome matrix Prisoners' Dilemma Game*

		prisoner b	
		silence	confession
prisoner a	silence	(-1;-1)	(-30;0)
	confession	(0;-30)	(-15;-15)

players. The way in which a player will act in a particular situation is called a *strategy*. And the result of a strategy is described as an *outcome*. This outcome will be evaluated on the basis of the utility experienced by each of the players.

Depending on the number of individuals who participate in the game, we can distinguish among two-person and n-person games. Moreover, the plays are divided into zero-sum games and variable-sum games (mostly positive-sum games). When the interests of two players are completely opposite, we speak of a *zero-sum game* in which the profit of one results in an equal loss of the other. *Positive-sum games* are games in which the players have partially common interests. The Lindahl exchange process, described in the last section, was an example of a positive-sum game because more welfare for the one did not inhibit the acquisition of more welfare by the other.[5]

The consequences of the situation in which the individuals in a large group have a negligible influence on the outcome of the decision-making process can best be clarified with a two-person, positive-sum game known as the *Prisoners' Dilemma Game* (see, among others, Luce and Raiffa, 1957; Hardin, 1982; Axelrod, 1984). This name is derived from a game situation developed by Flood and Dresher around 1950 and elaborated upon mathematically by Tucker shortly thereafter (Hardin, 1982, p. 24).

In the game situation, two prisoners together have committed a serious crime. If both prisoners remain silent, the proof of their crime cannot be provided; in that case they will be sentenced for a relatively unimportant offence like forbidden possession of arms and be imprisoned for one year. When one of them confesses and provides proof of the other's guilt, then he will be released immediately, and the other will face a sentence of 30 years in prison. When both confess and thus provide proof of each other's mutual guilt, both will receive a sentence of 15 years.

Table 3.1 shows an *outcome matrix* in which the various alternatives are expressed in terms of number of years in prison. The first

Table 3.2 *Utility matrix Prisoners' Dilemma Game*

		prisoner b	
		silence	confession
prisoner a	silence	(3;3)	(1;4)
	confession	(4;1)	(2;2)

number of each alternative in the outcome matrix refers to the sentence of prisoner a and the second number to that of prisoner b.

Based on this outcome matrix, a *utility matrix* (pay-off matrix) is constructed in table 3.2. A utility matrix shows the effects of the various alternatives on the individual welfare of the players. When we assume that welfare effects can only be measured at an ordinal level, and that the players will prefer a lower sentence to a higher, then the four possible alternatives can be categorised in the sequence 1, 2, 3, 4 in which 1 is the least preferred and 4 is the most preferred alternative. In the utility matrix, the first number of each alternative indicates the individual welfare of a and the second number that of b.

The utility matrix shows that the two prisoners have a common interest in remaining silent so that they can expect only a short prison sentence. They then both achieve the next to best priority (3;3), which is also Pareto-optimal because it is impossible to increase the welfare level of one of the prisoners without decreasing that of the other.[6]

However, each prisoner has an individual interest in confessing so that he:

1. will not serve a one-year sentence when the other is silent, but will be released immediately;
2. will not serve a 30-year sentence when the other confesses, but only 15 years.

When both prisoners are isolated from one another so that they cannot influence the decision of the other and cannot make binding and enforcible agreements, it can be predicted that both will confess and provide proof of each other's guilt. Dror wittily concludes (1968, p. 152): 'As a result, both rational prisoners will spend fifteen years in prison thinking about the limitations of pure rationality.' The Prisoners' Dilemma, however, does not prove that 'extra-rational decision-making processes are demonstrably better than pure rationality', as Dror supposes, but only that individual rationality does not lead to collective rationality in the case where individuals cannot influence the other's decision.

The problem elucidated by the Prisoners' Dilemma can be formulated differently. Both prisoners have a common interest in agreeing upon a *cooperative* strategy. That is the strategy in table 3.2 that results in a Pareto-optimal outcome (3;3). This cooperative strategy does not correspond, however, with an equilibrium in the game. Indeed, the non-cooperative strategy is *dominant* because each player will choose it, irrespective of the strategy of his opponent. When the strategy of his opponent is cooperative, then he chooses the non-cooperative strategy to realise the highest possible utility level 4 instead of the alternative with utility level 3. When the strategy of his opponent is non-cooperative, then he too chooses a non-cooperative strategy to realise utility level 2 instead of 1. The result is that both, despite their mutual interest, will choose a non-cooperative strategy that results in utility level 2. When the players cannot influence each other's decision, then the result (2;2) is thus the *equilibrium* of the game, but the result is not optimal in terms of the Pareto criterion.

3.5.2 The Prisoners' Dilemma Game applied to public goods

In earlier parts of this chapter, we noted that pursuit of common goals by large groups of people can and will cause problems. This is important for understanding the functioning of the negotiations democracy, since large groups – users of collective provisions, taxpayers – are usually involved. In a large group, the individual does not enjoy a personal relationship with other individuals. Most individuals will assume that their individual contribution to collective action and to collective decision-making processes will have a negligible influence on the future.

Game theory, and especially the Prisoners' Dilemma Game, is an often used instrument for analysing the functioning of a negotiations democracy. By means of a simple game we shall now illustrate the provision of public goods in a negotiations democracy on the basis of freedom of exit and non-commitment. In this illustration, we examine the provision of a typically Dutch public good, namely a sea-wall.[7]

In the example, two persons will at first take part in the negotiation game. One person is a representative of the employees who face the

Table 3.3 *Construction of a sea-wall. Outcome matrix (net benefits in billion guilders) and utility matrix*

		Outcome matrix		Utility matrix	
		employees		employees	
		positive decision	negative decision	positive decision	negative decision
employers	positive decision	(0.5;0.5)	(-0.5;1.5)	(3;3)	(1;4)
	negative decision	(1.5;-0.5)	(0;0)	(4;1)	(2;2)

decision of whether they want to contribute a part of their wages in order to provide the wall. The other person represents the employers who are considering whether they will relinquish part of the profit on behalf of the wall. We assume that both representatives have full authority on behalf of their supporters.

Both groups (employers and employees) will benefit equally from the sea-wall; for both groups these benefits will amount to 1.5 billion guilders. Total benefits thus amount to 3 billion guilders. The total cost of constructing the wall amounts to 2 billion guilders. When these costs are divided equally between employers and employees, each group will have to contribute 1 billion guilders.

If both the employers and employees decide to contribute to the sea-wall, the total benefits will amount to 3 billion guilders and the total costs to 2 billion, which amounts to a net benefit of 1 billion, or 0.5 billion per group (see table 3.3, top left). If one of the groups would contribute and the other not, then the cost of the wall will be carried entirely by the contributing group, which will suffer a net loss of 0.5 billion; the other group, which does not contribute, would profit from the wall without sharing in the costs and would therefore make a net profit of 1.5 billion (see table 3.3, top right and bottom left). When neither of the groups contributes, the wall will not be built and both costs and benefits will be nil (table 3.3, bottom right).[8]

It is important to note that three outcomes are optimal in terms of the Pareto criterion. In table 3.3, these are top left, top right and bottom left. In none of the three cases is it possible to enlarge the benefits of one group without decreasing the benefits of the other group. In all three cases, the sea defence is realised and the sum of the net benefits is 1 billion guilders. The difference between the three alternatives has merely to do with the distribution of the costs and hence of the net benefits over both groups. The bottom right outcome in the table is not optimal. Yet this non-optimal alternative is the outcome of the game.

The employees can base their decision on whether or not to contribute on two assumptions:

1. the employers decide positively about their financial cooperation in the project;
2. the employers decide not to contribute.

If the employers decide positively, then it is in the interest of the employees to decide negatively. After all, their net benefits will then rise from 0.5 billion (top left) to 1.5 (top right). If the employers decide negatively, then the employees will do so as well. Their net benefits will rise from −0.5 billion (bottom left) to 0 (bottom right). In all cases the employees will therefore decide negatively. In this example, the employees are willing to take advantage of the readiness of the employers to make sacrifices, but they are not prepared to accept the employers taking advantage of them.

Mutatis mutandis, the employers will make the same calculation; they too decide negatively in all cases. The employers themselves are prepared to be 'free riders' in the employees' train, but at the same time refuse to offer a lift to the employees in their limousine.

Employees and employers thus decide not to contribute, so that the wall is not built. The common interest requires that one of the three Paretian optima will be reached, but in fact none is. As a consequence of their non-cooperative attitude, both employers and employees will be worse off than if they had cooperated. Here, there is no invisible hand which brings the self-interest of one category of citizens in harmony with the self-interest of the other category.

The example discussed above is unrealistic in at least one respect. It concerns negotiations between only two persons, namely a representative from the employees and one from the employers, who both held *carte blanche* from their supporters. Both individuals are oligopolists and they will take into account the fact that their behaviour will influence the behaviour of the other. Each negotiator will realise that a unilateral refusal to participate in the costs of the sea-wall will not mean that the other will then bear all the costs, but that the other will also refuse and that the wall will not be constructed at all. Under such circumstances, it is probable that they will cooperate.

In reality, however, large numbers of persons are involved in collective decision-making processes. The individual citizen (an employee, an employer, a store owner, a non-active) will then assume that his individual decision on whether or not to contribute does not influence the collective provision level. It is then that the Prisoners' Dilemma Game becomes important provided that the game is not played between two individuals but between one individual on one side and all other individuals on the other. In the case of public goods, an individual citizen in a negotiations democracy always has two options:

1. the citizen assumes that the public good will be paid for by others, even when he himself does not contribute to the costs;
2. he assumes that others will not cooperate to establish the provision of the good, even when he himself contributes.

The first assumption has already been dealt with by Wicksell ((1896)1958, p. 87) in his theory about parasitical behaviour with regard to public goods. As soon as a citizen assumes that the others will provide the public good, then it is to his advantage to limit his own contribution to a minimum. He is then the free rider a on the left-hand side of figure 3.1 who, as long as the exchange has not taken place, will profit from the benefits of the quantity q^b provided by b, without sharing in the costs.

The consequences of the second assumption have been examined, induced by Olson's work. When others do not contribute to the realisation of a public good, it depends on the demand curve whether it is worthwhile for a citizen to provide the good alone. Most of the demand curves of individual citizens are low in comparison to the marginal costs of a public good. If they are as low as demand curve D^a or lower, then citizens will achieve their individual optimum only by doing nothing.

3.5.3 Democratic acceptance of coercion

In the Prisoners' Dilemma Game, no collective provision is realised despite the fact that it is in the interest of all participants to achieve it. The Prisoners' Dilemma is caused by a specific utility matrix (pay-off matrix). In the examples, the Prisoners' Dilemma is created because under all circumstances the individuals will prefer a light rather than a severe prison sentence, and a low rather than a high contribution in costs. It is to be expected that the way out of the Prisoners' Dilemma is sought by changing the utility matrix. This can be achieved by attaching *sanctions* to certain outcomes so that cooperative strategies become more attractive and non-cooperative strategies are discouraged or even precluded.

The sanctions can be positive or negative. Positive sanctions consist of offering an individual reward to those who cooperate in achieving a socially desirable outcome, so that cooperative behaviour becomes the dominant strategy. To stimulate participation, political parties, trade unions and student organisations can, for instance, decide to offer individual services in the form of ombudsman activities for their constituents, legal aid, or study advice (the selective incentives in section 3.2.3).

In reality, negative sanctions are more common because they are easier to apply. In general, negative sanctions mean that those who do not join in a cooperative strategy will be punished individually. This punishment can be administered by people outside the group but also by people inside. In the example of the two prisoners, it is possible that 'whistle-blowing' on a partner will be met by third persons with ostracism from the criminal underworld, but it is also possible that the two are able to communicate with one another and arrange that the one who speaks will face punishment from the other (in- or outside prison).

If the members of a group punish themselves in the case of non-cooperation (i.e. non-participation or non-contribution), Kafoglis (1962, p. 47) speaks of 'a voluntary acceptance of coercion', which we would like to describe as a *democratic acceptance of coercion*. The members of the group themselves then make provisions to escape their Prisoners' Dilemma through democratic means (for instance via majority decisions). Olson (1965, p. 86) mentions the paradox which has frequently been observed in American manufacturing industry: over 90 per cent will not attend meetings or participate in union affairs, yet over 90 per cent advocate mandatory union membership.

Before Olson, Wicksell ((1896)1958, pp. 89–97) already drew attention to a notable example of a democratic acceptance of coercion, namely the acceptance of compulsory taxation by and to the citizens of a state. This sheds light on an often occurring paradox that citizens evade paying taxes as much as possible, yet vote for higher taxes for everyone including themselves. Their self-interest demands that they contribute as little as possible, but their collective interest requires that everyone, without exception, is taxed up to a certain amount so that collective provisions can be realised.

3.5.4 *Social welfare without coercion?*

The necessity to accept coercion resulting from the Prisoners' Dilemma has troubled many social scientists. On the one hand, various authors doubt the reality value and relevance of the Prisoners' Dilemma Game for processes of collective decision-making. On the other hand, ways to escape the dilemma without coercion have been examined. In this and in the next sections, we will present the suggestions and objections – deconcentration, an altruistic morality, alternative outcome matrices and the Prisoners' Dilemma Supergame.

Several sociologists have pointed out that cooperative action can be stimulated through *deconcentration* of decision-making in small groups. This is advocated, for instance, by Schumacher (1973) in his booklet *Small is beautiful.* From an economic point of view as well there are many advantages in deconcentration. The first is mentioned by Taylor (1976, p. 132), who notes: 'the more numerous the players, the more likely it is that the problem of the provision of public goods will take the form of a Prisoners' Dilemma'. In small groups individuals will behave as oligopolists and feel *themselves* responsible for the influence of their own behaviour on the result achieved by the group, including themselves. The second advantage of deconcentration is that an existing Prisoners' Dilemma can be removed without coercion because those who do not join in a cooperative strategy can be held responsible by *others* and be, for instance, discredited. Such immaterial sanctions are only effective when the individuals are sensitive to it and when the sanctions are selective, that is to say targeted only at individuals who choose an unwanted strategy. Such discriminatory selectivity can only be realised in small groups (Van den Doel, 1977, pp. 223–6). A third advantage of deconcentration is that people acquire the opportunity to *choose* to which group they want to belong. In this respect, Tiebout (1956) points out that through social and geographic mobility, groups of people and communities can be formed with more homogeneous preferences where, in principle, the provision and finance of public goods could be better tuned into the preferences of the individual members.

The responsibility which individuals in a small group feel for the occurrences *within* the group does not extend to what happens *outside* the group. This is the other side of the argument in favour of deconcentration. De-amalgamation of municipalities can, for instance, stimulate free rider behaviour. Citizens in smaller neighbouring towns will then – if possible – make use of the collective provisions in the large central town, but want to avoid paying their share. Other examples are easy to find. A firm that has introduced self-management by the workers will, just like a capitalist firm, make use of the possibilities to foul the environment and to pass part of the production costs on to its neighbours. People are quick to act when the medication they are taking appears to have nasty side effects, but they hardly move themselves when the same products are being exported to the Third World.

Indeed, it can be recommended not to enlarge the decision-making unit beyond what is necessary to internalise the external (for instance, spatial) effects of collective provisions. A further reduction of scale will again call forth further parasitical behaviour by one group towards another.

3.5.5 *Altruistic morality*

This might be the reason why Sen (1974) and Hirsch (1976, pp. 237ff.) consider it possible to escape from the Prisoners' Dilemma through cooperative behaviour as a consequence of an altruistic morality. Sen has designed two variations on the Prisoners' Dilemma Game (PD), namely the Assurance Game (AG) and the Other Regarding Game (OR). The preferences based on self-interest, which Sen calls PD-preferences, remain unchanged. Individuals, however, do not act according to these PD-preferences, but to another utility matrix which is determined by a 'moral code of behaviour' (Sen, 1974, p. 62).

The *Assurance Game* results when individuals cooperate as long as others will do so as well and only end the cooperation when others behave non-cooperatively. Then individuals act according not to PD- but to AG-preferences as can be illustrated by the example of the prisoners: 'I consider one year in prison less objectionable than betrayal of my partner provided that he thinks the same way; if my mate is prepared to let me down, I'll repay him accordingly.' It appears from the utility matrix in table 3.4 that there are two equilibria in the Assurance Game. When one of the players acts cooperatively, then a Pareto-optimal equilibrium is realised. As soon as one of the players ceases to cooperate, then an outcome is achieved that does not meet the Pareto criterion.

The *Other Regarding Game* is even more altruistic. It assumes that

Table 3.4 *Utility matrices based on PD-, AG- and OR-preferences*

Prisoners' Dilemma (PD)		Assurance Game (AG)		Other Regarding Game (OR)	
(3;3)	(1;4)	(4;4)	(1;3)	(4;4)	(3;2)
(4;1)	(2;2)	(3;1)	(2;2)	(2;3)	(1;1)

individuals are always cooperative, even when others refuse to be so. In this case, individuals act on the basis of OR-preferences, for example: 'Betraying my partner is worse than spending 30 years in prison.' The utility matrix in table 3.4 shows how in this case a Pareto-optimal outcome is always assured.

The weakness of Sen's analysis is that he does not indicate how to ensure that people will live up to the moral code. He suggests the possibility that 'society may evolve traditions by which preferences of the OR-type are praised most, AG-preferences next, and PD-preferences least of all' (1974, p. 61). If, however, one of the moralists decides to return to egotism, the cooperative balance will be disturbed. Yet, Sen's models are useful because they clearly reveal the role which morality could perhaps play.

3.5.6 Alternative outcome matrices

In his variations, Sen accepts that underlying preferences have a PD nature. Taylor and Ward (1982) go one step further by claiming that PD-preferences are not at all to be counted on. They believe that two alternative game situations, namely the Assurance Game and the Game of Chicken, usually offer a better description of decision-making processes with regard to collective provisions.

The utility matrix in the *Assurance Game* takes the form as seen in table 3.4. In the view of Taylor and Ward, this form is not a consequence of an altruistic morale, but comes about because the outcome matrix has a different content. More specifically, if one party is cooperative, the (marginal) benefits for the other party to be cooperative will exceed the (marginal) costs.

Let us return to the example of the sea defence and take some inspiration from the building of the Oosterschelde dam in the Netherlands. Say it takes 1 billion guilders to construct a closed dam, in which case the benefits for both parties, employers and employees,

Table 3.5 *Construction of a sea-wall as Assurance Game*

		Outcome matrix		Utility matrix	
		employees		employees	
		decide positive	decide negative	decide positive	decide negative
employers	decide positive	(1;1)	(-0.25;0.75)	(4;4)	(1;3)
	decide negative	(0.75;-0.25)	(0;0)	(3;1)	(2;2)

amount to 0.75 billion guilders. It takes 2 billion guilders to construct a half-open dam, which offers more in terms of environmental protection and fishery interests, so that the benefits for both parties amount to 2 billion. We further assume that both parties involved will or can put up a maximum of 1 billion. Table 3.5 presents the matching outcome matrix (net benefits in billion guilders) and the utility matrix.

The Assurance Game has two equilibria, namely (4;4) and (2;2). Since the first of these equilibria provides a more satisfactory result, it can be assumed that both parties will prefer cooperative behaviour. The collective provision thus comes about in a Pareto-optimal form without any problems.

The second alternative by Taylor and Ward is the *Game of Chicken*. The process of collective decision-making will take the shape of a Game of Chicken when, for both parties, the individual benefits of the collective provision will exceed the total costs, even when the other party does not cooperate. Let us again take the sea-wall as an example. We again assume that the total costs will amount to 2 billion guilders. The benefits, however, are now 2.5 billion for both parties, thus 5 billion in total. Table 3.6 presents the resulting outcome and utility matrices.

The Game of Chicken results in three Pareto-optimal outcomes, namely (4;2), (3;3) and (2;4). Of these (4;2) and (2;4) are the equilibria in the game. Although this means that the Game of Chicken does not have a cooperative solution (3;3), it is not a problem from the point of view of social welfare because the sea-wall is realised, either through the employees carrying the costs, or the employers.

The alternatives by Taylor and Ward express that a process of collective decision-making on the basis of freedom of exit and

Table 3.6 *Construction of a sea-wall as Game of Chicken*

		Outcome matrix		Utility matrix	
		employees		employees	
		decide positive	decide negative	decide positive	decide negative
employers	decide positive	(1.5;1.5)	(0.5;2.5)	(3;3)	(2;4)
	decide negative	(2.5;0.5)	(0;0)	(4;2)	(1;1)

non-commitment does not necessarily result in a Prisoners' Dilemma Game and that public goods can be provided. This finding is, of course, not entirely new in view of our earlier discussion of the Lindahl equilibrium (section 3.3.1). More specifically, the cooperative equilibrium of the Assurance Game in table 3.5 is, in fact, a Lindahl equilibrium. The important question remains to assess what the *reality value* is of Taylor and Ward's alternatives.

In analogy to our evaluation of the negotiation model of Lindahl c.s. (section 3.3.2), we can assume that the Assurance Game will occur especially in the case of small numbers of negotiators. The Assurance Game is characterised by a direct and positive relation between one's own contribution and the collective result. In larger groups, this relation is lost. Thus, the average citizen will not acknowledge a direct and positive relation between his own tax payments and the size of, for instance, the national defence.

Within larger groups, however, smaller subgroups can often be distinguished. When some individuals communicate with one another, it is conceivable that they will act when they set so much value on a collective provision that their individual benefits will exceed the sacrifice even if they bear the costs (almost) alone. The difference between the views of Marx and Olson thus becomes clear in yet another aspect. If the large group or class is based on homogeneous preferences, then no public goods will be provided despite the group interest because there is no one whose preference for a particular good is so strong that he will provide it on his own. Only when the group is of a mixed composition, then subgroups possibly can engage in collective action and achieve certain provisions. These collective provisions, however, will be fewer in number and lesser in quality than is optimal for the group as a whole. Moreover, those who profit strongly by the action or provision will be forced through the parasitical behaviour of others to bear a relatively large share of the costs.

With regard to the Game of Chicken in table 3.6, we would like to remark that it does not offer a true way out of the Prisoners' Dilemma either. First, it assumes that for each player in the negotiation process, the individual benefits will exceed the total costs. That will only occur in specific cases. Either it is about small provisions that can be realised at relatively low costs, or the participants in the negotiation process represent large groups with considerable financial backing (employers and employees, for instance, or nation-states in international discourse). Assuming freedom of exit and non-commitment within these large groups, the Prisoners' Dilemma again becomes relevant.

Second, it is not certain that a solution is achieved in the Game of Chicken. When it is certain that the first party will not cooperate, it is in the interest of the second party to pay for the provision entirely, but of course the second party still would prefer the first party to bear the costs. Every party, thus, has an interest to stay inactive as long as possible in order to force the other to carry the burden. The weakest party will pay the bill. If, however, no one bends then it cannot be predicted whether the provision desired by everyone will be realised. In this case as well, all parties could well be interested in democratic acceptance of coercion in which the costs are shared and it becomes certain that the provision is realised.

3.5.7 *The Repeated Prisoners' Dilemma Game*

Our examination of the Prisoners' Dilemma Game so far has focussed on the game as it is played only once. In itself, the decision-making regarding the construction of a sea-wall is, indeed, a one-time event; it will or will not be built. In many instances, however, there is more going on. The parties that negotiate now about a sea-wall might meet again tomorrow about employment policy, and the day after tomorrow about another matter. Furthermore, a large number of collective provisions do not concern a one-time, but periodically returning expenditure. The police and defence budgets, for instance, are set annually. For all these cases, the Prisoners' Dilemma Game does not offer an adequate description because it does not take into account the future consequences of the strategic choices of today. To underscore this shortcoming, the Prisoners' Dilemma has been elaborated in literature into a, finitely or infinitely, Repeated Prisoners' Dilemma Game; see Taylor (1976), Axelrod (1984).

In a *repeated game*, the original game situation occurs several times, and each player has knowledge of the strategies chosen by other players in previous games. Analysing a Prisoners' Dilemma Supergame is not easy since the number of possible strategies is enlarged. Naturally, a player can decide to always follow a cooperative strategy or always follow a non-cooperative strategy, but he can also choose some intermediate strategy in which his attitude in the course of time can vary depending upon the strategies of his opponent. An example of this is the strategy of complete retaliation in which the player is cooperative at first, but breaks the cooperation completely as soon as the other player behaves non-cooperatively, even if only once. Another example is the *Tit-for-Tat-strategy* which means that a player is cooperative the first time the game is played, and in the next rounds copies the strategy (cooperative/non-cooperative) that was taken by the other party in the previous round. And so, many variations are conceivable.

Let us assume that, at first, the number of times that the game is played is known and *finite*, and that the players know from one another that they are rational and aware of the pay-off matrices. What, then, can we predict about the outcome of the repeated game? In order to find out, we use the method of backwards induction. Consider the last time that the game will be played. Because there are no future rounds, the players face a normal, single PD-game, and both will opt for a non-cooperative strategy. Now look at the second-to-last game. Since the optimal strategy in the last round is known, and independent of what happens in the second-to-last game, the players in this second-to-last game will not have to take possible consequences for the future into account. But if one does not have to think of the future, the second-to-last game, too, is a normal, single PD-game, and both players will opt for a non-cooperative attitude. Thus, reasoning backwards to the first round, we come to the conclusion that the players in all rounds will be non-cooperative. Rational behaviour and complete information for all players leads to the same prediction for a finitely repeated PD-game as in the case of a single PD-game.

The situation becomes entirely different when the game is repeated an *infinite* number of times, referred to in the literature as a *supergame*. In this case, naturally, the backwards induction argument is not applicable. Now it is interesting that there is no longer one best (dominant) strategy independent of the strategy chosen by the other player. If the opponent always opts for a non-cooperative strategy, then there is nothing else for the other player than also always to choose a non-cooperative strategy. If the opponent is continuously cooperative, then it is interesting for the other player to become a free rider by always choosing to be non-cooperative. If, however, the opponent chooses for some intermediate strategy such as complete retaliation, then a non-cooperative strategy is not always the best answer. The player ending the cooperation may profit in the present as a result of his parasitical behaviour (utility level 4 instead of 3), but will also suffer a loss in the future as a result. Since the opponent will follow his bad example, the player will in subsequent games not realise utility level 3 but 2. Everything now depends on how his individual welfare profit in the present relates to his welfare loss in the future. In this, the time preference of the player is important. The *time preference* expresses how a player values the present (present amounts) to the future (future amounts). The higher the time preference, the more a player will value present welfare profits over future losses; he will then be sooner inclined to break with the established cooperation. If, however, his time preference is low, it is in his own interest to maintain cooperation.

Of course, this case of an infinitely repeated Prisoners' Dilemma Game is of limited relevance, as the participants in actual decision-making processes generally have only finite lives. Fortunately, Kreps et al. (1982) have shown us yet another way out of the predicament of non-cooperation in a PD-context. Their analysis allows for *incomplete information* in a finitely repeated Prisoners' Dilemma Game, which precludes the straightforward application of the backwards induction argument as well. This incomplete information might pertain to both players attributing a (small) chance to the possibility that the pay-off matrix is not of the PD-variety after all so that non-cooperation need not be the dominant strategy. Incomplete information may also pertain to the one player not being entirely certain that his opponent is perfectly rational and attributing a (small) chance to the possibility that the opponent plays, for instance, Tit-for-Tat. Kreps c.s. point out that in both cases cooperation may ensue in all but the last few rounds of the game.

Axelrod (1984) has carried out a series of computer experiments with the Repeated Prisoners' Dilemma Game in which he made a large number of possible strategies play against one another. The

Tit-for-Tat strategy came out as the winner in these experiments. On average, this strategy offered the best result and the highest welfare level. Axelrod (1984, p. 54) attributes this success to the fact that Tit-for-Tat is:

nice, because it never starts itself with non-cooperative behaviour. That prevents unnecessary problems.

retaliatory (provocable), because every non-cooperative move of the opposite party is immediately met with a non-cooperative countermove. That discourages free rider behaviour by the opponent.

forgiving, because Tit-for-Tat is prepared to return to cooperative behaviour after a non-cooperative move. Thus cooperation can be restored after disturbance.

clear. The opposite party can easily understand the strategy, which enhances sustainable cooperation.

The computer results suggest that, once one or more subgroups of individuals exist within a group, who are willing to cooperate, this cooperative behaviour can become dominant in the whole group through a process of evolution. Because a nice, cooperative stragegy like Tit-for-Tat appears to be successful, it is to be expected that persons and institutions taking a non-cooperative strategy, and being less successful because of it, will in due course change to a more cooperative strategy or end up in the margin of the group and become insignificant. By way of illustration, Axelrod (1984, pp. 73–87) describes how a system of live-and-let-live could develop between soldiers of opposing parties during the trench war of 1914–1918 in France.

To sum up, the findings above suggest that persons in a Prisoners' Dilemma will prefer cooperation to non-cooperation under certain circumstances. These conditions are that the persons involved realise that they will meet more often and that their preferences are sufficiently targeted toward the future, and/or that information is incomplete.[9]

3.5.8 *The end of 'laissez faire'*

In section 3.1 we argued that a negotiations democracy consists of two elements: freedom of exit and non-commitment. Freedom of exit is the freedom of the individual to leave the group (by, for instance, ending the discussion). Non-commitment is the freedom of the individual to unilaterally refrain from contributing to the costs. Thus, in a negotiations democracy none of the individuals has the power to force others to participate in group deliberations or to accept the outcome of the negotiations.

In previous sections, it has become clear that small groups have reasonable chances of achieving a result that meets the Pareto criterion. In a small group, the individuals feel responsible for the common result and can be held accountable by others. Related to this is that in a small group the outcome matrix will more quickly take the form of an Assurance Game, while, furthermore, the chances for cultivating an altruistic morality will be better. Finally, it is very likely that the members in a small group will meet one another in future negotiations and anticipate on that.

For large groups, there is little or no hope of achieving a Pareto-optimal result. Such an optimum can only be achieved when the individuals can be forced to contribute to the costs of the public goods. When the members of a group understand the correctness of this conclusion and decide themselves that those who do not participate or contribute will be met with certain negative sanctions, then we have a case of *democratic acceptance of coercion* (see section 3.5.3). Such an acceptance, however, means that the basis of a negotiations democracy disappears. Democratic acceptance of coercion may not mean the end of negotiations, but it is the end of the voluntary nature of it. It is the end of *laissez faire, laissez passer*, because it has become clear that in a voluntary process of exchange in large groups there is no invisible hand that will harmonise the self-interest of the one with that of another.

Based on this line of reasoning, we can defend the proposition that the *existence of a government* in all modern economies can be explained by the individuals' pursuit of optimal welfare. Members of a large group need an instrument with which they can punish each other in case they do not live up to duties flowing from agreements made within the group. The instrument that is regarded as most suitable is instituting a government which holds a monopoly on the use of physical violence and can therefore force individuals to comply with group decisions. In this context one can think of a national or local government, but the function of a group's government can also be served by the board of a society, association or club.

Taylor (1976) made clear that this explanation for the existence and functioning of government has already been provided by political theorists such as Hobbes and Hume in the seventeenth and eighteenth centuries. Indeed, it can even be found in the works of the Chinese philosopher Han Fei Tzu in the fourth and third centuries BC. According to Taylor, Hobbes looked upon individual preferences as a mixture of egotism and malice while Hume regarded preferences as a mixture of egotism and benevolence in which egotism dominates. The result is the same. Using quotations, Taylor shows that both in fact described a Prisoners' Dilemma in which the individuals get caught, that both came to the conclusion that coercion is necessary in the interests of all individuals, and that both deduced the existence of government from this. While Hobbes was limited to a static version of the Prisoners' Dilemma, Hume had an eye for the time factor and for the negative influence of a high time preference. Where Hobbes explained the functioning of government mainly from the necessary provision of the public good 'peace and security', Hume more broadly formulated the welfare effects of government: 'bridges are built; harbours open'd; ramparts rais'd; canals form'd; fleets equipp'd; and armies disciplin'd; every where, by the care of government' (Taylor, 1976, p. 126).

In relation to this explanation for the existence of government, Buchanan (1975) speaks of a *constitutional contract*, without necessarily thinking of historical reality. It is sufficient for him to understand the existence and functioning of government as if all citizens voluntarily and unanimously agree. If so, then government fulfills a function, and its existence is legitimised. If not, it remains to be seen whether there are possibilities for constitutional reform that lead to a Pareto-improvement and can therefore acquire everyone's approval (see further Brennan and Buchanan, 1985). Heckathorn and Maser (1987) show that this theory can well be used to understand historical reality such as the creation of the US constitution in 1787.

We also want to mention a recent study by Ostrom (1990) about common pool resources such as fishing grounds and communal pastures, which, according to the logic of this chapter, will be subject to overexploitation when not properly governed. Ostrom describes a series of concrete cases in which groups of individual users effectively managed to organise themselves in a situation of voluntarism and non-commitment, and succeeded in preventing misuse and degeneration of the resource. The successful examples that she mentions include communal tenure of high mountain meadows and forests in Swiss and Japanese villages, irrigation systems in Spain, and water extractions from groundwater basins in California. It appears to be imperative that the group is able to build up a feasible (affordable and credible) system of (mutual) monitoring and enforcement through a process of incremental changes in which, with each step, the transformation costs are not too high and the net benefits are positive. When all users are involved in detecting and punishing misuse, each invididual can assume he will be punished if he does not comply. At the same time, however, the certainty is created that he cannot be exploited for long by others who do not comply. Thus, democratic acceptance of coercion within the group provides the basis for cooperative behaviour.

3.6 Negotiations democracy in practice

3.6.1 International cooperation

Instituting a government that wields sufficient instruments of force will end the voluntary and non-committal nature of a negotiations democracy. Yet, in practice, a negotiations democracy occurs fairly often. Examples of groups that are more or less organised on the basis of freedom of exit and non-commitment are action groups, trade unions, military alliances (NATO), and international organisations (UN). Through some examples in this and the next section, we shall show the results of negotiations democracy in practice, and test these results against the theory. This section deals with international negotiations democracy, the next section will present an example drawn from the Dutch national negotiations democracy.

Olson and Zeckhauser (1966) have applied the theory of negotiations democracy to *military and political alliances*, especially NATO. They regard NATO as a collection of member states who have formed a group based on freedom of exit and non-commitment in order to provide a public good. The common goal is the build-up of a credible defence apparatus that will deter potential aggressors. The defence goods that belong to this apparatus are placed into two categories by Olson and Zeckhauser – armed forces and infrastructural works.

With regard to armed forces, the decisions of the alliance are the result of negotiations in which every country bears the costs of its own army in the end. Because a large country has a larger territory and a longer border, it will have to spend more on defence than a small country in order to realise equal protection against foreign aggression. In addition, a large country will have more inhabitants and therefore a higher national income than a small country and can thus permit higher expenditures for defence. Finally, a large and rich country probably runs a higher risk of being attacked and therefore benefits more from a strong defence than a small, poor country would. For reasons such as these, the demand for defence provisions will be higher in large countries than in smaller countries. From the theory it can then be predicted that, when coercion is lacking, the large countries will contribute an unreasonably large share to the armies of the alliance, while smaller countries will be tempted to hide under the umbrella provided by the large countries and will thus behave as free riders. Olson and Zeckhauser (1966) test this hypothesis with reality. Indeed, it appears that large countries contribute considerably more to the NATO forces given the size of their national income than one would expect. Frey (1984) confirms this hypothesis on the basis of more recent data not only for NATO but also for the Warsaw Pact. See also Kennedy (1983).

Various authors have argued that the Olson-Zeckhauser hypothesis has lost expression in the course of time. Murdoch and Sandler (1984) suggest that the change to a strategy of flexible response from the early seventies onward, gradually altered the nature of the good that the alliance provided. Through military specialisation within the alliance, a certain complementarity would have come about between the efforts of the different allies, thus reducing the incentive to free ride. In addition to this, Oneal and Elrod (1989) point out that a number of participants (Portugal in its colonial wars in Africa until 1975; and, more recently, Greece and Turkey in their animosity over Cyprus) have derived clear private benefits from their military expenditures.

Olson and Zeckhauser separately deal with the costs for NATO infrastructure (bases, depots, pipelines). They indicate that these costs are shared according to percentages worked out in a negotiated agreement. Every ally pays a percentage of the costs of every extension of infrastructural works of NATO. Here, the possibility of parasitical behaviour is not large, according to the theory. Added to this is the fact that small countries economically profit most, and therefore have an individual interest in, these infrastructural provisions. Indeed, it appears from the facts that smaller countries carry more costs of the infrastructure than should be expected in view of their national income.

Concluding this discussion of NATO, we would like to refer to a recent study by Oneal (1990). Based on a thorough analysis of the defence-burdens of fifteen NATO allies for the years 1950–84, he concludes that when the intensity of the Cold War, the exceptional importance of private interests to Greece, Turkey and Portugal, and the growing interdependence in Europe are taken into account, 'the relation between GDP and defence burden hypothesized by Olson and Zeckhauser (1966) still holds generally' (p. 429). 'The theory of collective action continues to provide valuable insights into the structure of the alliance' (p. 445).

One can attempt to draw comparable conclusions for political alliances. Parasitical behaviour, for instance, can be seen in the United Nations; the richest countries, having probably the largest interest in maintaining existing international relations, pay by far the largest contribution. The United States carries a third of the UN budget; the five permanent members of the Security Council (US, Soviet Union, Great Britain, France and China) together carry two thirds of the total budget; 90 per cent of the contribution is paid by 20 per cent of the members (Kennedy, 1979).

Various authors have analysed *international aid policy*. Provision of development aid by rich countries to poor countries is a public good for those rich countries in so far as it contributes to the stabilisation of world peace and the satisfaction of the collective conscience. If we assume that providing development aid is a public good, and that the large countries have the most interest in maintaining world peace, then we can again assume that small countries will parasite on the larger. Olson and Zeckhauser (1966) indeed find empirical support, though modest, for this hypothesis.

But there is more. Development aid can be provided multilaterally (through international organisations) or bilaterally (through mutual agreement between a rich and a poor country). In the latter case, there are selective advantages for the rich country to give aid. These can be of both a political-strategic as well as an economic nature. In the economic field, for instance, development aid might stimulate the exports of the donor country, might help in dumping surplus stocks of agricultural products, might improve the investment climate in the recipient country, and might enlarge the production of raw materials that the donor country specifically needs (Frey, 1984, p. 87). From the fact that multilateral aid is considerably less than bilateral aid (about $\frac{3}{4}$ of the official development aid is bilateral by nature, and only $\frac{1}{4}$ is transmitted through multinational institutions; cf. Todaro, 1989,

p. 482), we see the importance of selective advantages confirmed. We can add to this that research by, among others, McKinlay (1978) and Maizels and Nissanke (1984) proves that in the allocation of bilateral aid to LDCs, strategic, political and trade interest factors with regard to donor countries are significant, and recipient need variables are not.

Dudley (1979) and Mosley (1985) point out that development aid expenditures by a donor country are not only positively correlated with the size of its own national income, but also with the expenditures of other donor countries. This could indicate that development aid is not at all an international public good. Donor countries apparently find obnoxious other countries providing aid as well; they enlarge their aid when others do so in order to maintain their influence in the international arena. This race for aid is advantageous for the developing countries, who receive more aid than they would have if the donor countries operated in isolation or if aid was regarded as an international public good.

The findings above can thus be interpreted that, as long as there is no authoritative world government, the specific self-interests of the donor countries will be dominant.

A last example of the functioning of the international negotiations democracy is provided by the attempts of the *International Whaling Committee* since 1947 to protect the whale against extinction and maintain a commercially viable whaling industry. Taylor and Ward (1982) suggest that this international negotiation is a Game of Chicken. If all whaling countries continue with unlimited pursuing of whales, then the whale population will most certainly cease to exist. Further commercial exploitation of the whaling industry is then impossible. When, on the other hand, a limited number of countries continues to catch whales, then the whale population can be maintained at safe levels, and the involved countries can continue the commercial exploitation of their whaling industry. It is thus a common interest to limit the number of whaling countries. The question then becomes, which countries will remain in the industry. Every country who wants to belong to that group has an interest in being as non-cooperative as possible in order to encourage other countries to stop sooner. Taylor and Ward established that Japan and the Soviet Union have been very tenacious in maintaining a non-cooperative strategy, thus succeeding in being among the last whaling nations.

3.6.2 Wage-restraint and full employment

The national negotiations democracy is discussed by Van den Doel, De Galan and Tinbergen (1976) using The Netherlands as an example. It concerns the fight against unemployment which rapidly increased in the seventies and subsequently remained high and persistent. The authors purposively do not express an opinion as to the causes of unemployment. Regardless of the cause, the fight against unemployment is necessary to stimulate extra investments in the private as well as the public sector of the national economy. Since employees have indicated that they wish to maintain income transfers in the sphere of the social security system, room for extra investments must come out of wage restraint. But, in an economy in which wage negotiations are based on voluntarism and non-commitment, such wage-restraint will, according to the authors, not result to a sufficient degree. The reason for the failure of wage-restraint is that the central federations of trade unions and the central federations of employers' associations have no binding authority to overcome antagonist interests. Thus, the individual employees and employers and the separate unions and associations are caught in a large-scale Prisoners' Dilemma.

Suppose, for reasons of logic, that all employees and employers agree that it is worthwhile to pursue an active and effective employment policy. But they do not agree about the distribution of income; each individual will strive unabatedly to improve his income position in relation to others. When the goals in the field of employment and income distribution are combined, it appears that every employee and employer has ordered the alternatives as follows:

1. His lowest priority is the creation of employment of which he alone bears the burden while others take advantage of him; his relative income position is worsened, but since the offer of an individual does not amount to much, employment is not re-established.
2. The second priority is that no employment needs to be created, so that no one needs to pay, including himself; his relative income position remains unchanged, but employment is not restored.
3. The next to last highest priority is the creation of employment at everyone's expense, including his own; his relative income position remains unchanged and employment is restored.
4. Creating employment at the expense of others is the highest priority; his relative income position is improved and employment is re-established.

An individual employee or employer (and a specific trade union or a specific employers' association) is uncertain about the decisions of others. As long as he is not able to bind other employees and employers (and the other unions and associations) to his decision, he will fear alternative 1 when he decides to sacrifice for employment, because if the others do not follow his move his own income position gets worse without the intended result of increasing employment. As long as the other employees and employers are not able to bind him with their decisions (and attack him with sanctions), he will be tempted to opt for the highest priority which is the fight against unemployment at the expense of others so that his relative income position improves. Because of the non-binding nature of the decision-making process he is caught in a dilemma – he wants to create employment, but refrains from it because of his desire not to pay and for fear that others will do the same. Since all individual employees and employers reason this way, no one sacrifices. Thus employees and employers (and their unions and associations) who can only engage in more or less non-committing negotiations, will neither realise the highest possible alternative, nor alternative 3, but alternative 2. The goals in the field of unemployment are therefore not achieved.

In the opinion of Van den Doel, De Galan and Tinbergen, there are at least two possibilities to escape from this Prisoners' Dilemma. The common element between them consists of equipping the involved persons and groups with the authority to impose sanctions against those who pursue full employment but try to evade the necessary sacrifices.

The first method is the imposition of sanctions by the government. It is the method of a *central income policy*. Representatives in parliament will, after ample deliberation with the organisations of employees and employers, make the final decision about wages and other incomes and instruct the cabinet to see to it that everyone, or almost everyone, will share in the cost of an effective employment policy. In terms of the Prisoners' Dilemma, this method means that government excludes the parasitical alternatives 1 and 4 and puts the choice between alternatives 2 and 3 in the hands of the majority.

The authors point out that the majority will only accept such coercion (democratically) when three conditions have been met:

1. public goods and goals to be achieved through collective means carry relatively large weight in the individual objective functions of the people involved;

2. the people involved believe that government (cabinet and parliament) is able to achieve these goals;
3. the people involved do not look upon government as an instrument of a 'hostile' group, but as their own instrument by means of which costs and benefits can be distributed equally.

There is a second method to escape the Prisoners' Dilemma. In this method it is not the government but the trade-union movement which is equipped with the authority to make binding agreements about wages, prices and collective provisions. This method can be summarised in three rules for behaviour. First, the government confronts the unions by formulating certain policy alternatives in which a certain size and composition of the public sector is combined with a certain wage-increase or wage-restraint. Second, the trade-union movement organises a referendum among its members about these alternatives. Third, both the government and the unions will make known beforehand that they consider the outcome of the referendum binding for the decision about the size of the public sector and the height of the wage level. This method is a step in the direction of a *corporate state*.

The choice between the first and second method cannot be based on the Pareto criterion but depends on, among other things, the relative power that people are willing to give to members of the unions and all other citizens.

How does this view on wage formation in the Netherlands relate to practice? It is clear that wage-restraint evolved only with great difficulty since the development of high unemployment in the mid-seventies. In the first instance, only a few were convinced of the structural nature of the unemployment. The readiness to sacrifice for employment was lacking; people with low incomes were of the opinion that other income groups should pitch in as well, etc. In the seventies and the early eighties, government was forced to intervene several times in wage formation.

As high unemployment persevered, union circles were slowly preparing to use part of the wage-space for the fight against unemployment. As time went by, the offers became larger, and when in 1980 unemployment again rose to unprecedented levels, even a willingness to accept real wage declines developed – although not without pouting. In the course of the eighties, a process of substantial wage-restraint occurred despite the fact that since the formation of the Lubbers cabinet in 1982 the government refrained from intervention in wage formation. The consequence of the wage restraint was that output in the private sector and the competitive position *vis-à-vis* other countries improved, private investment and exports expanded, as did employment in companies.

Wage-restraint on a voluntary basis does, therefore, appear to be possible. This indicates that wage negotiations are not a simple Prisoners' Dilemma Game. When unemployment appears to be structural, it is more correct to regard annual wage negotiations as a Repeated Prisoners' Dilemma Game. And, indeed, in our theoretical exposé in section 3.5.7, we saw that a Repeated Prisoners' Dilemma Game can, under certain conditions, lead to cooperative behaviour.

4 Majority decision

4.1 Majority versus unanimity

4.1.1 Referendum democracy

In this chapter we discuss the referendum democracy, a decision-making model in which the group members make *binding* collective decisions without the intervention of representatives.

As an independent model such a direct democracy seldom occurs. On a national level some countries have a mandatory and decisive referendum but only with regard to changes in the constitution (like Denmark, Ireland, Austria, Spain and Australia). Liechtenstein works with a combination of voters' initiatives and plebiscites. At the initiative of at least 600 members of the electorate, proposals can be submitted to parliament; if the parliament rejects the proposal, then it is submitted to a decisive plebiscite. Although a parliamentary democracy, Switzerland comes closest to being a direct democracy. Next to a mandatory and decisive referendum with regard to changes in the constitution, the country also has a voters' initiative. If at least 50,000 voters choose to do so, laws and decisions of a general nature that passed through parliament can be submitted to a decisive citizens' vote. The population can also submit a request to change the constitution. This takes at least 100,000 of the electorate. After a parliamentary debate, a decisive referendum is held. Between 1951 and 1983 42 voters' initiatives came up in Switzerland and 116 referendums were held.[1]

Although a referendum democracy hardly occurs as an independent model, a discussion is necessary because even in its abstract form, a referendum democracy has three elements which return in other decision-making models. The first element is that the group has a *government* that can monitor and enforce group decisions so that freedom of exit and non-commitment – the central characteristics of a negotiations democracy – are eliminated. The second element is that this group government can not only enforce the implementation of unanimous decisions, but also can guarantee that *majority decisions* are lived up to by the minority. The third element is that both the majority and the minority can be composed of individuals with *different* objective functions.

The structure of this chapter is as follows. In section 4.1 we compare the binding majority decision with the unanimity rule. Section 4.2 addresses the matter of whether majority decisions can be consistent. Section 4.3 analyses some of the effects of majority decisions on social welfare.

4.1.2 The unanimity rule of Wicksell

In order to prevent an individual from being exploited by others, Wicksell ((1896)1958, pp. 87–97) formulated his famous *unanimity rule* which states that all decisions about public goods and the concomitant division of costs must be unanimous. Thus, the unanimity rule appears to create the institutional guarantee for making political decisions that meet the Pareto criterion. Conversely, unanimity could be the proof that the Pareto criterion is met. When unanimity is lacking at first, and political decision-making cannot take place, the winners can try to compensate the losers so that the losers can yet agree to the change proposed by the winners, and unanimity is reached after all. This function of the Wicksellian rule can be put on a level with that of perfect competition in the market economy. The unanimity rule is sometimes referred to as the economic policy optimum theorem (Hennipman, 1977, p. 237), in order to express that the rule can be viewed as the political counterpart of the economic optimum theorems of Paretian welfare theory (see section 2.3.1).

The unanimity rule of Wicksell and the Pareto criterion may be in line with one another in a utopian society, but the situation is more complex in a non-utopian society. In a non-utopian society, unanimity does not have to be regarded as a confirmation of the existence of a Pareto optimum. Nor is a lack of unanimity proof of a Pareto optimum not being reached. In a fundamental essay, Hennipman (1977, 231–53) analyses the different factors involved.

First, Hennipman points to the fact that in reality it is not true that all individuals will always prefer a Paretian optimum to a non-optimal situation, not even when the losers are completely compensated. Pareto improvements can mean, for example, that welfare has increased unequally. The Pareto criterion does not include a judgment on matters of distribution; it is sufficient to state whether or not a Pareto improvement occurs. It is conceivable, however, that the subjects whose welfare relatively declines will vote against the measure out of *jealousy*, even if their welfare increases in an absolute sense.

Moreover, it was pointed out in section 2.2.3 that the Pareto optimum cannot be given an unconditional normative validity. Subjects will always test a Pareto improvement against their ultimate *ethical norms*, for instance in respect of the income distribution. They can prefer a non-optimal situation with an equal distribution to a Paretian optimum with an unequal distribution.[2]

But even when the welfare improvement meets both the Pareto criterion as well as the ethical norms of the subjects, unanimity is not assured. It is possible that the individuals are *insufficiently informed* about the benefits and costs related to a particular project, and thus reject the project without good reason.

Furthermore, in a situation where decisions can only be made unanimously, each individual is in a powerful negotiation position. By threatening to veto each group decision he can, when he plays his cards right, make the others carry a disproportionate share of the costs (Buchanan, 1968, pp. 92–7).[3] The outcome of this type of multilateral negotiations resulting from *strategic behaviour* is indeterminate. It is not certain that a Pareto optimum will finally be achieved; a stalemate can occur because no proposal meets unanimity. At best an optimum is achieved with serious delay and greatly increased costs of decision-making.

4.1.3 Simple or qualified majority?

Thus, unanimity in political decision-making only has meaning as an ideal like, for instance, the ideal of perfect competition. It is totally useless as a practical norm. Wicksell recognised this when he diluted the condition of unanimity 'for practical reasons' to a qualified majority of, for example, 75 per cent or 90 per cent which he called 'relative unanimity'. The question arises as to whether it would not have been more practical to lower this percentage further to, say, 51 per cent. The higher the percentage, the more the Scylla threatens

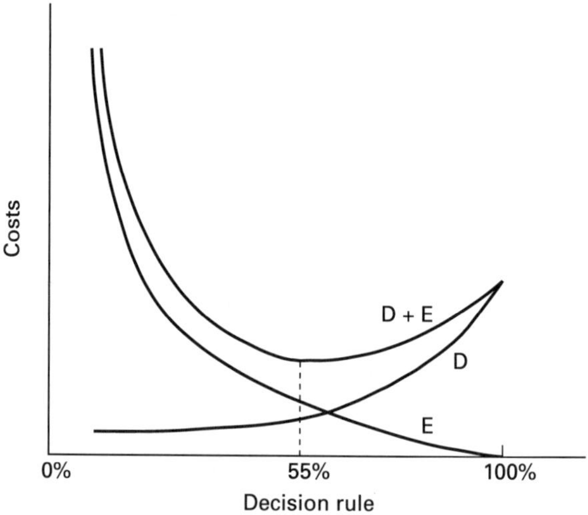

Figure 4.1 The choice of the decision rule by an individual

that small groups will exploit their power and transform the negotiation process to a Polish Diet or an Indonesian Musjawarah. The lower the percentage, the closer one comes to the Charybdis where the majority will appropriate all the benefits of the public goods and will charge the minority with the payment of the costs.

In *The calculus of consent* Buchanan and Tullock (1962, pp. 63–84) indicated how both dangers can best be avoided. The graph in figure 4.1 shows their solution. The horizontal axis gives the decision rule, i.e. the percentage of group members whose approval is required for a specific group decision to be made. The vertical axis represents the expectations that each individual cherishes with regard to the costs he carries in that decision rule. These costs have been subdivided by Buchanan and Tullock into two categories, namely external costs and decision-making costs.

External costs (curve E) arise because some individuals cash in the benefits of collective decisions but shift the costs to other individuals. External costs thus arise because the group forces an individual to contribute to collective action that is not wanted by the individual (at that price). From the point of view of the individual in question, external costs are the result of wrong decisions. They are equal to the reduction of individual welfare as a result of those wrong decisions.

The higher the percentage required for a group decision, the lower the chance of wrong decisions being made, so that curve E will show a declining trend.

Decision-making costs (curve D) are the individual investment of time and energy in the process of negotiation, expressed in money. The closer the requirement of unanimity comes to being met, the higher the decision-making costs will be because, among other reasons, strategic behaviour of individuals becomes more profitable. Curve D thus has a rising trend.

According to Buchanan and Tullock, an individual will choose the decision rule which minimises the sum of both cost categories. In the example of figure 4.1, that is the case with a group decision which requires 55 per cent of the vote.

Although the position of curves D and E is hard to identify empirically, we can draw a number of logical conclusions from the model of Buchanan and Tullock. It is clear that the simple majority rule – in which half-plus-one of the votes is decisive – is as arbitrary as any other decision rule. There is no reason to prefer 51 per cent to 55 unless it can be shown that the total cost curve always is at a minimum at 51 per cent.

The optimum decision rule varies with the nature of the collective decision. When it concerns constitutional decisions, i.e. decisions on decision rules (revisions of the constitution), the external costs will be relatively high so that the minimum of the total cost curve moves to the right. In this case, individuals desire relative unanimity and accept the higher decision-making costs it involves. After all, a faulty constitution has continuing consequences and the effects are unpredictable: today's dictator is often tomorrow's victim of his own rules. If, however, the decisions are allocative, i.e. decisions on collective actions based on given decision rules, then the external costs will be substantially lower, so that the minimum of the total cost curve moves to the left. Most individuals will prefer a decision rule that involves small decision-making costs, for instance a simple majority. In this case costs and benefits have a once-only nature and their size is, to some extent, predictable.

Buchanan and Tullock thus present a paradoxical situation in which it is optimal for the individual welfare of the citizens to discard the possibility of achieving a Pareto optimum. The decision-making costs for reaching a Paretian optimum are, after all, prohibitive.

4.1.4 *The iron law of oligarchy*

Buchanan and Tullock's model sheds light on the functioning of *das eherne Gesetz der Oligarchie* (the iron law of oligarchy) formulated by the sociologist Michels (1911). He sketches an inevitable process of evolution for each democracy, and calls it oligarchisation. A small, independent and complacent group of political leaders, riding on the waves of a democratic movement, will always succeed in imposing its will on the masses. Michels' interpretation of this process was *sociological*; he did not describe the direct but the *representative democracy* and his crown-witness was the social-democracy. His explanatory model rests on two pillars: the necessity of organisation and the growing independence of leadership in politics. Van Doorn (1969, pp. 17–18) simplified Michels' theory into a quasi-syllogism:

democracy means influence of the masses;
influence of the masses implies organisation; the masses unite and show their fist;
organisation necessitates leadership; the fist must strike accurately;
leadership implies the subordination of the masses;
subordination of the masses to a group of leaders is termed oligarchy.

Thus, democracy leads to oligarchy, not through fatal coincidence or malicious intent, but because of an imminent law.

It is possible to reach the same conclusion when it concerns a *direct democracy* by using an *economic* line of reasoning. The economic analogy of Michels' law rests, for the sake of simplicity, on only one assumption: the desire of all individuals to avoid high costs of decision-making. The essence of this economic approach can also be simplified into a quasi-syllogism:

in the eyes of its protagonists direct democracy only makes sense in the case of mass participation;
mass participation results in high decision-making costs for each participating individual (section 4.1.3);
these decision-making costs are so high that all individuals accept decision rules by which the decisions are taken by a minority;
this minority is always composed of the same group of people, namely those individuals who strive for political power and/or who value public goods so highly that their individual benefits exceed the costs even when they pay nearly all the costs of participation themselves (section 3.3.2);

decision-making by a permanent minority is termed oligarchy. Thus, mass participation in a direct democracy results in oligarchy, not because the leaders seize power, but because of the voluntary abdication of the masses.

4.2 Majority decision and collective consistency

4.2.1 Collective intransitivity

In chapter 2 we started from the assumption that all individuals in a group decide consistently, which means that they can compare the policy alternatives with each other (the requirement of comparability) and that they can arrange them in a fixed order (the requirement of transitivity). But the eighteenth century philosopher De Condorcet, the nineteenth century mathematician Dodgson (better known as Lewis Carroll), the twentieth century welfare economist Arrow (1951) and the econometrician Black (1958) have shown that the mere fact that the individuals in a group pursue a consistent goal does not necessarily mean that the group also has a consistent goal. This can be clarified by an example (which, by the way, is not derived from direct but from representative democracy).

Assume that a parliament is divided into three political groups: right, centre-left, and radical-left, and that none of these groups holds an absolute majority. Assume also that the right and centre-left prefer a moderate socialist for prime minister to a radical socialist, that centre-left and radical-left opt for a radical socialist prime minister instead of a conservative one, and finally that right and radical-left prefer an outright conservative to a moderate socialist. The collective preference ordering is then intransitive even though the individual preferences of right, centre-left and radical-left are consistent. This type of collective intransitivity can lead to a situation such as was characteristic of the Fourth Republic in France (1946–59): continual cabinet crises, rapid succession of governments, each party has a turn to provide a prime minister, and the individual citizen loses faith in democracy as the method to coordinate decisions.

4.2.2 Arrow's Impossibility Theorem

The example in the previous section indicates that majority decisions do not always have to lead to a consistent collective preference ordering. Arrow (1951) formulated a general proposition on this matter, known as Arrow's Impossibility Theorem.

Arrow distinguishes a number of conditions to be met before one can speak of a reasonable, fair procedure of transposing individual preferences into a collective preference ordering. Based on Sen (1970, pp. 35–46), we can present these conditions as follows:

1. The individual freedom of choice must not be restricted. Each member of the group is allowed to hold any conceivable individual preference ordering (*condition of unrestricted domain*).
2. The procedure is such that there is a Paretian connection between the preferences of the individual group members and those of the group as a whole: when all members of a group prefer alternative x to alternative y, then the group as a whole will also prefer x to y (*Pareto principle*).
3. The collective order of two alternatives can only be dependent on the preferences individuals hold with regard to these two alternatives; in other words, the order of two alternatives x and y is not influenced by the introduction or cancelling of a third alternative z, as long as the individual orderings of x and y do not change (*independence of irrelevant alternatives*).
4. There is no dictatorship within the group: the outcome of the vote is determined by more than one individual (*non-dictatorship*).

Each of these minimum conditions for a voting procedure looks quite reasonable by itself. Together, however, their impact is disastrous. *Arrow's Impossibility Theorem*, the mathematical formulation and proof of which are outside the scope of this text, has the following purport: under conditions 1 through 4, there is no method to sum the individual preference orderings into a consistent collective preference ordering. Stated differently, the only possibility of reaching a consistent collective preference ordering under conditions 1, 2 and 3 is by appointing a dictator. Again, in other words, if the voting procedure meets a reasonable set of conditions, the outcomes can be paradoxical. We shall illustrate the meaning of the theorem by discussing some voting procedures.

Let us first assume that the group members decide on a *unanimity* basis. The unanimity rule satisfies the four reasonable conditions mentioned above: alternatives are not excluded a priori; as long as the group members agree, that is also the group decision; at each decision the individuals will always present their best alternative; and there is no dictator. Arrow's theorem predicts problems at a collective level in this situation, and indeed, there are – the unanimity rule does not lead in all cases to a complete ordering at the collective level. In other

Table 4.1 *Preference orderings of three individuals a, b, and c*

individual a	x>y>z
individual b	y>z>x
individual c	x>y>z

words, the collective preference ordering does not (always) meet the demand of comparability.

Let us take the example in table 4.1. A group consists of three individuals a, b and c. At a particular decision the group can choose among three alternatives x, y and z. Each of the group members has a consistent individual preference ordering with regard to the three alternatives. In table 4.1 the symbol '>' is used to indicated that one alternative is preferred to another. Thus, individual a prefers x to y and y to z (and, because of the transitivity of his preferences, also x to z). When the group members now attempt to transfer their individual preference orderings into a collective one, they will soon agree that y is collectively preferred to z. They cannot, however, agree on placing x in relation to y and z. In this example it is therefore not possible to achieve a *complete* collective preference ordering through unanimity.

Let us now examine the *majority decision*. This voting procedure too satisfies the conditions of Arrow, as can easily be seen. In many instances there will be no problems at the group level. Take for instance the individual preference orderings from table 4.1. Bringing y to a vote against z will result in a 3-0 win for y. Then bringing x to a vote against y will result in a 2-1 win for x, and a vote of x against z will result in a 2-1 win for x. At the group level this yields the following consistent preference ordering: x>y>z.

Arrow's theorem, however, teaches us that forming a consistent collective preference ordering does not always occur without problems. Take, for instance, the individual preference orderings of table 4.2. In a majority decision, alternative x wins with 2-1 from y and y with 2-1 from z; but z in turn wins with 2-1 from x and x again with 2-1 from y etc. The collective preference ordering then is: x>y>z>x>y . . ., etc. In this case the collective preferences are *not transitive*; they show a *cyclical* pattern. Table 4.2 gives us an example of the so-called *paradox of voting* (also known as the Arrow-paradox or the Condorcet-paradox). Despite consistent individual preference

Table 4.2 *Individual preference orderings*

individual a	x>y>z
individual b	y>z>x
individual c	z>x>y

orderings, the majority decision in some cases leads to collective inconsistency.

Thus far we have illustrated the theorem of Arrow with the well-known unanimity rule and majority vote. Arrow's theorem also concerns other voting procedures. As an example we take a look at the voting method designed in 1781 by the French mathematician De Borda and later elaborated by Black (1958, pp. 59–66). Assuming that four alternatives are under debate, the *Borda-method* presents two options. The first version (the Borda-count) holds that each individual ranks the alternatives in his preferred order and gives the highest-valued alternative four points; the next to highest alternative is given three points, etc. The alternative which receives the highest total number of points will then be chosen by the group. In this case, each voter has $4+3+2+1=10$ points to distribute. The second version of the Borda-method (cumulative voting) holds that every individual can distribute the ten points as he sees fit. He is allowed, for instance, to give all ten points to one alternative. The first version implicitly assumes that an individual orders the alternatives according to an interval-scale in which the welfare difference between each subsequent alternative is always the same. Using the second version, it is assumed that an individual is capable of ordering his preferences according to a ratio-scale: when an alternative does not receive any points, we must conclude that it does not provide any welfare for the individual.

Each voting method is based on a certain interpersonal utility evaluation. Both the pairwise votes that Arrow proposes as well as the Borda-method are based on the value judgment that the welfare of each individual is equally important. After all, Arrow and De Borda allocate the same number of votes to each individual. But where Arrow prefers a system of 'one person, one vote', De Borda prefers a system of, for example, 'one person, ten votes'.

The Borda-method has encountered several objections in the literature. Important is that this voting method abandons the third condition of Arrow, to wit that the outcome of a vote between two

Table 4.3 *Application of the Borda-method*

	two alternatives	three alternatives
individual a	x>y	x>y>z
individual b	y>x	y>z>x
individual c	x>y	x>y>z
	Borda-count	Borda-count
alternative x	2+1+2=5	3+1+3=7
alternative y	1+2+1=4	2+3+2=7
alternative z	—	1+2+1=4

alternatives may only depend on the preferences of the individuals with regard to these two alternatives. It is possible that the introduction of a third alternative will influence the decision fundamentally. We can illustrate this by applying the first version of the Borda-method to the example of table 4.1. When the individuals a, b and c can only choose among the alternatives x and y, then, based on the Borda-count, they will collectively prefer x to y; see table 4.3. Adding the third alternative z has important consequences, however, for the collective ordering of x and y, and this occurs despite the fact that alternative z is valued lower than y by all individuals and thus has no chance of being chosen. Although for each individual the mutual ordering of x and y is unchanged, the group as a whole becomes indifferent between x and y.

Although the Borda-method represents certain advantages – especially by offering better possibilities to express the intensity of preferences – the *sensitivity* of the method to the introduction (or exclusion) of irrelevant alternatives does not make the method an appealing alternative to the majority decision.

The last voting procedure that we would like to mention is *approval voting*. This method has been put forward by the work of Brams and Fishburn (1983). Under approval voting a voter can vote for (approve of) as many alternatives as he wishes, but for each approved alternative he can cast only one vote. Thus, when there are three alternatives, the voter has three options: he can cast an approval vote for his most valued alternative, he can vote approval for the top two alternatives, or he can vote for all three. The alternative which receives the highest total number of (approval) votes wins.

The advantage of this method is its greater flexibility for the voter.

He can support more than one alternative and make a distinction between those alternatives that he regards acceptable and those that he does not. This method concurs with the notion of satisficing as discussed in section 2.1.3. While the voter is given the opportunity to present more information about his preferences than only his top-alternative in an ordinal scale, he is not forced to assess each alternative in detail as is required with the first and second version of the Borda-method.

This method also has certain disadvantages, of which the *indeterminacy* of the outcome must be mentioned specifically. This can be illustrated by an example from Saari and Van Newenhizen (1988). Assume that there are three alternatives x, y, and z and 15 voters. Six of them hold the preference ordering x>y>z, 5 hold the order y>z>x, and 4 the order z>y>x. When all voters only vote for their first preference, x will get 6 votes, y will have 5 votes, and z gets 4; x wins. If only the last group of voters casts approval votes for the best two alternatives, then x will get 6, y will get 9, and z will get 4 votes; now y wins. When all groups cast approval votes for their top two alternatives, then x will get 6, y will get 9, and z will get 15 votes; z wins in this case. To sum up, with given individual preference orderings the outcome of the vote depends on the number of alternatives that the different voters decide to support. Since the voting procedure itself leaves all options open, this procedure does not result in a determinate collective preference ordering. This conclusion is in line with Arrow's Impossibility Theorem which tells us that no voting procedure is ideal.

4.2.3 *Manipulation, agenda control and strategic voting behaviour*

No voting procedure is ideal. One of the most important problems is that voting procedures can be vulnerable to strategic behaviour and manipulation. In the Borda-method, for instance, as we have just seen, it is possible that the outcome of the vote is *manipulated* through the introduction of a policy alternative that, in itself, stands no chance. In the absence of z, alternative y would have been outvoted; with z present, alternative y and x end up *ex aequo*. Individual b thus has great interest in bringing alternative z into the discussion, even if it is not his first choice.

In principle, the majority decision is just as vulnerable to manipulation. Take the example of the voting paradox in table 4.2. Without further decision rules, a pattern of cyclical majorities can occur in which the group is not able to make a definite choice between alternatives x, y and z. In order to break through such a stalemate, additional rules are often made. The chairman could be given the decisive vote, or it could be forbidden that a certain proposal is brought to the vote more than once. When a is the chairman of the group, he could see to it that z is the proposal to be voted on, after which y will first be brought to the vote as an amendment, and then x. In the first voting round z will be outvoted in favour of y, and in the second round y will be outvoted in favour of x. The final choice of the group is then x, not accidentally the highest priority of chairman a. If b (respectively c) would be the chairman, however, the agenda would probably look quite different, in order that the final choice would be y (respectively z).

We can conclude that it is of great importance for the ultimate decision who *controls the agenda*. That person (or group) determines whether an issue will appear on the political agenda, which alternatives will be considered, and in which sequence these alternatives will be voted on. See also Shepsle and Weingast (1981), Ordeshook and Schwartz (1987).

Strategic voting behaviour represents a second type of manipulation. So far we have assumed that group members will vote according to their true preferences. Under certain conditions, however, it might be profitable for an individual to deviate from that at the vote. Let us take again the example of table 4.2 and use the voting sequence imposed by chairman a above. When a and c vote according to their true preferences, it might be worthwhile for b to vote strategically. When b votes according to his true preferences, the final outcome will be x, his lowest priority. On the other hand, when b would give his support in the first voting round (y against z) to z instead of y, the second round would be between z and x, and the final choice of the group would be alternative z, b's second priority.

A necessary prerequisite for successful strategic voting behaviour is that the individual is completely informed of the preferences of the other group members and on their voting behaviour (will the others also vote strategically, and if so, how?). This condition will seldom or never be met. De Bruin (1991, p. 212) therefore concludes that manipulation of the outcome of the vote through insincere voting may be possible in theory, but seems precluded in practice.[4]

4.2.4 *The probability of the voting paradox*

With the majority decision there is a chance that a voting paradox occurs (section 4.2.2, table 4.2). The collective preference

Table 4.4 *The voting paradox: probability that the majority decision does not yield a winning alternative (in percentages).*

		number of alternatives				
		3	4	5	10	15
	3	5.6	11.1	16.0	32.4	41.8
	5	6.9	13.9	20.0		
	7	7.5	15.0	21.5		
	9	7.8	15.6	22.4		
	11	8.0	16.0	22.9		
number of individuals	13	8.1	16.2	23.2		
	15	8.2	16.4	23.5		
	17	8.3	16.5	23.7		
	19	8.3	16.6	23.9		
	21	8.4	16.7	24.0		
	23	8.4	16.8	24.1		
	25	8.4	16.9	24.2		
	∞	8.8	17.5	25.1	48.9	60.9

Sources: Garman and Kamien (1968), Niemi and Weisberg (1968), DeMeyer and Plott (1970), Gehrlein and Fishburn (1976). See also Berg and Bjurulf (1983).

ordering is intransitive then. A pattern of cyclical majorities comes into existence without a definite decision being made, or a decision is being made through manipulation (4.2.3) or chance (by flipping a coin for instance). Whichever way, the situation is rather unsatisfactory. It is therefore understandable that the voting paradox has generated quite some reaction.

Several authors have tried to assess the *probability* that a voting paradox will really occur. If this probability is (almost) nil, the voting paradox can be regarded as a theoretically interesting problem which does not merit further attention from a practical point of view. Table 4.4 provides more information on this probability for different numbers of alternatives and different numbers of group members.

Table 4.4 suggests that there is a reasonable chance of a voting paradox to occur, and that the probability increases rapidly with the number of alternatives being considered. We need to keep in mind, however, that in calculating the probabilities it has been assumed that all possible individual preference orderings of alternatives are equally likely. In the case of three alternatives x, y and z this means that the six possible rankings, $x>y>z$, $x>z>y$, $y>x>z$, $y>z>x$, $z>x>y$ and $z>y>x$, are all equally likely to represent the preference ordering of an individual.

In general, there will be some sort of *consensus* in a group and in a society about the relevant norms, values and goals. This consensus will find expression in a certain degree of uniformity of preferences of the group members. Several studies have shown that the probability of a voting paradox diminishes to the degree that the *social homogeneity* increases. 'There is an inverse relationship between similarity of opinion and paradox likelihood' (Berg, 1985, pp. 378–9).

This conclusion is supported by the empirical research of Jamison (1975). In 1972, this author requested a group of students to submit their individual preference orderings with respect to the Democratic candidates for the presidency of the United States. As expected, there was a certain agreement among the respondents as to the ranking of the candidates. As a result the probabilities of a voting paradox turned out to be considerably lower than those presented in table 4.4; the probabilities calculated on the basis of these data varied from 1 to 3 per cent with three alternatives and from 4 to 12 per cent with five alternatives. Remarkably, the degree of agreement was not so large that the chances were reduced to nil. In other words, we must remain aware of the possibility of the occurrence of a voting paradox.

4.2.5 *The voting paradox: an empirical example*

Even though the literature reflects a virtually unanimous opinion that the voting paradox must occur reasonably often, it has been complained that examples of its occurrence in practice can hardly be found. This complaint, however, is not justified. Empirical examples of the clear role of the paradox in the United States Congress can be found in: Riker (1958, 1965), Farquharson (1969, pp. 52–3) and Blydenburgh (1971). Van den Doel (1973, 1975) describes two instances in the Second Chamber of Dutch Parliament.

As an illustration, we shall summarise the first case in Blydenburgh (1971). This case concerns decision-making in the US House of Representatives on the Revenue Act of 1932. This act was designed to raise over a billion dollars in revenue to offset the costs of attempts by the Hoover administration to counter the Great Depression. The bill's major tax device was a 2.5 per cent manufacturers' sales tax on all companies doing more than $20,000 business annually. In the

Table 4.5 *Patterns of preference orderings over the sales (S), excise (E) and income (I) tax alternatives*

group	members	preference ordering
a	162	I>E>S
b	38	E>S>I
c	16	S>E>I
d	69	S>E>I
e	71	S>E,I
f	30	against all taxes

course of the deliberations, two major alternatives came to the fore. One amendment suggested an excise tax heavily taxing only certain industries, the other proposed an income tax alternative.

Of the 396 Congressmen who actually participated in the voting, 10 abstained on one or more of the votes. For the 386 members who completed their vote, Blydenburgh tried to reconstruct the preference orderings over the sales (S), excise (E) and income (I) tax alternatives, by making use of the outcomes of the various voting rounds, supplemented with information from remarks on the floor of the House and from press statements. Acknowledging the risk involved in this method of reconstructing preference orderings, the results are given in table 4.5.

The groups a, b, c and d have a complete ordering over the three alternatives. For group e, the most preferred alternative clearly is the sales tax; the ordering of the excise and income tax alternatives could not be determined. One interpretation, which we shall follow here, is that group e is indifferent between E and I. Group f, finally, opposes all tax alternatives, which can be interpreted as not having any preferences among the alternatives.

Leaving indifferences out of account it can easily be inferred from the data in table 4.5 that alternative E is preferred to S by 200 versus 156 members of the House, while S is preferred to I by 194 versus 162. However, I in its turn is strictly preferred to E by 178 versus 107 members. Apparently, the collective ordering of the tax alternatives is subject to a cyclical majority problem – E>S>I>E.

Due to the prevailing voting procedures of the House, which led to successive roll calls for the three alternatives, cycling did not show up in practice. The excise tax was voted on last, and became the major revenue source of the 1932 Revenue Act.

Blydenburgh notes that the excise tax would undoubtedly have been defeated had it been voted on first. Had the sales tax been introduced last, that would have been the alternative to be finally adopted. Whether the income tax would have passed if it had been introduced last, is not entirely certain; that would have depended on the actual voting behaviour of group e in that case.

4.2.6 *Single-peakedness of preferences*

Black (1958, pp. 14–25) tried to formulate the conditions which need to be met if collective transitivity is to be ensured. The gist of his conclusion is that the collective preference ordering will always be transitive if all individual preference orderings have a single-peaked shape graphically. In order to understand what Black means with this, we shall briefly explain his method of graphic representation of individual preference orderings.

In figure 4.2, the horizontal axis represents three policy alternatives x, y and z, and the vertical axis shows the valuations of these alternatives by individuals a, b and c on an ordinal scale. The distance between the valuations 1, 2 and 3 is meaningless; only the sequence in which the points are drawn counts. The left-hand side of the figure corresponds with the data from table 4.1. Individuals a and c rank their preferences as $x > y > z$. This preference ordering is single-peaked; from the highest preferred alternative x the valuation line monotonously declines to the right. The preference ordering of b ($y > z > x$) is also single-peaked.

In Black's view, it is necessary that one positioning of alternatives can be found in which none of the curves is multi-peaked. More precisely his proposition says: when a collection of *individual* preference orderings can be represented graphically through an appropriate arrangement of the alternatives on the horizontal axis as a set of *single-peaked* curves only, then the *collective* preference ordering is *transitive* and there will be one alternative which, in a pairwise comparison with each of the other alternatives, always gets a majority. Therefore, on the left-hand side of figure 4.2, the collective preference ordering is transitive since all curves are single-peaked when alternative y is placed in the middle. There is also one alternative which will always be chosen by the majority: a and c choose x above y and x above z, and b does not succeed in forming a coalition that will undo this.

On the right-hand side of figure 4.2, the individual preferences of

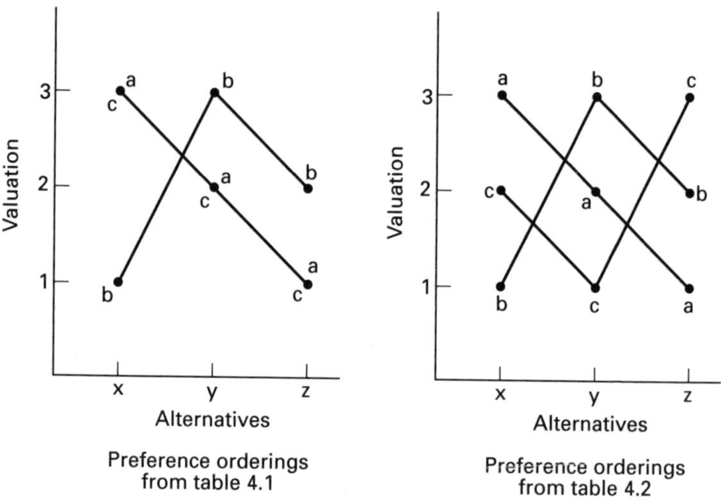

Figure 4.2 Single-peaked and multi-peaked preference orderings

table 4.2 are presented. The preference orderings of a (x > y > z) and b (y > z > x) are single-peaked. But the preference ordering of c (z > x > y) has two peaks. As the reader can check for himself, a different positioning of the alternatives on the horizontal axis resulting in all curves becoming single-peaked cannot be found. Therefore, the individual preferences of table 4.2 do not comply with the single-peakedness condition of Black; the collective preference ordering is not transitive.

One should not, however, conclude from this figure that c is the spoil-sport, who prefers both extreme alternatives to the moderate one. In this case, the fact that it is c's preference ordering which is multi-peaked, is a coincidence. We have simply drawn x at the left of the horizontal axis, y in the middle and z to the right. A different positioning, like y-z-x or z-x-y, would not only make c's curve single-peaked, but also result in a or b's curve being multi-peaked.

Later research has shown that Black has given a sufficient but not a necessary condition for collective transitivity. Sen (1970, pp. 168 and 174) attempted to formulate these necessary conditions using the concept of *value-restrictedness*. The 'value' of an alternative is the level of priority it enjoys, its ranking on the vertical axis. In our example, the value of an alternative is thus 1, 2 or 3. A set of individual preference orderings is value-restricted when there is one alternative that has in none of the preference orderings value 1, or in none of the preference orderings value 2, or in none the value 3. The set of preference orderings on the left-hand side of figure 4.2 is value-restricted in three ways – nowhere does alternative x have the value 1, nowhere does alternative y have the value 2, and nowhere does alternative z have the value 3. The set of individual preference orderings on the right-hand side of figure 4.2, on the other hand, is not value-restricted at all.

As Arrow (1951, p. 80) has already appreciated, conclusions such as those reached by Black and Sen (see also section 4.2.4) provide an insight into the significance of the *political culture* for a democracy. The political culture is the total of norms, values and goals in a society. According to Riker and Ordeshook (1973, pp. 104–6), political culture serves to realise a proper functioning of the majority rule. Single-peakedness of all preference orderings means that there is cultural agreement about the criteria on the basis of which decisions are made, although one can disagree about the decision itself. For example, all voters vote for the party closest to their own opinions; no one votes for the party the furthest away from their own point of view. Value-restrictedness means that some alternatives, although debated, will be ranked by no one as the best or the worst alternative. For instance, violence will only be accepted by everyone as a last resort. Both single-peakedness and value-restrictedness represent a cultural consensus without which a democracy cannot function.

4.2.7 *The median voter model*

Collective consistency of the majority rule is assured when the individual preferences are single-peaked. When this condition is met, we can formulate certain conclusions about a direct or referendum democracy with regard to the outcome of the political decision-making process.

When an individual preference ordering is single-peaked, this means two things. First, the individual appreciates one alternative as the highest; we could call that his ideal choice, his *policy optimum*. Second, according as an alternative is further away from such a policy optimum, either to the left or the right, the appreciation of the individual for the alternative involved decreases. Since each individual can have another view of what would be the optimal policy, the policy optima of the different group members can be found along the

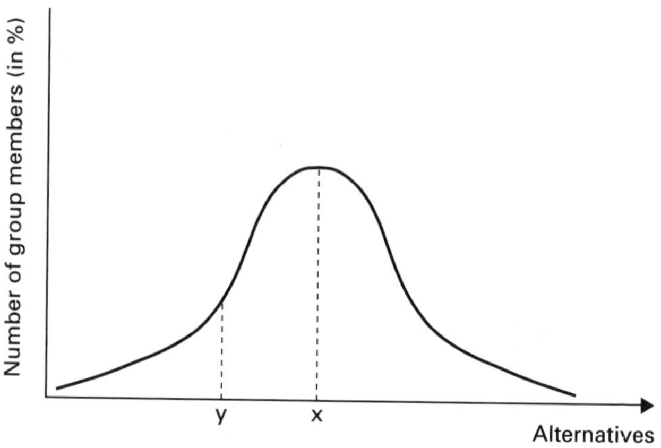

Figure 4.3 Distribution of policy optima

entire axis of alternatives. On the left-hand side of figure 4.2, for instance, alternative x is the policy optimum for two out of three group members and alternative y for one of the three group members.

The distribution of the policy optima of the group members along the axis of alternatives can be depicted graphically by drawing a function that represents the relative number of group members that considers a certain alternative to be optimal. The precise form of this function can vary from case to case. Figure 4.3 presents an example of such a function, based on a large number of group members and a continuum of alternatives; the distribution of policy optima is assumed to be symmetrical and unimodal. Depending on the specific situation, however, the distribution can as well be asymmetrical and/or multi-peaked.

Based on the distribution of individual policy optima, we can now predict which alternative will be chosen under the majority decision. That is the alternative that corresponds with the *median* of the distribution; see Black (1958, p. 18). The correctness of this statement can easily be seen. Compare alternative x in figure 4.3, the median of the distribution,[5] with any other alternative. Take, for instance, alternative y, left of x. On the right of the median, we find the group members who have a different alternative than x as their policy optimum, but for whom y is further from their own optimum than x. These group members, therefore, will value y lower than x and will, in a pairwise vote between x and y, vote for x. The reverse is the case for group members left of y; they will all vote for y. Finally, for those with a policy optimum between x and y, none of the alternatives is ideal and it depends on their individual preference ordering whether they will cast their vote for x or y. Taken together x will *at least* get all the votes on or to the right of the median, which is at least 50 per cent of the total, and also some of the votes of the group members between x and y. In other words, alternative y can never win from alternative x, the median. Under the majority decision, the alternative that corresponds with the median of the distribution will win. We can also say this in another way: the voter who has the median alternative as his policy optimum is decisive for the outcome of the collective decision-making process. This voter is often referred to as the *median voter*.

The median voter model acquires practical meaning when the median voter can be identified beforehand using particular characteristics (like income and tax level) and when an idea can be formed about his policy optimum from those characteristics. In literature, the median voter is for instance sought at the median position of the income distribution, and it is assumed that he carries the median tax burden.

A number of empirical studies has attempted to confront the median voter model with reality by analysing the level of local public expenditure in Switzerland and the United States (especially school expenditure). See, among others, Romer and Rosenthal (1979) for a survey, and Gramlich and Rubinfeld (1978). Most authors report that the median voter model is supported by their data. Pommerehne (1978) deserves to be mentioned specifically. He investigated the local public expenditures of the 110 largest Swiss municipalities, of which 48 could best be characterised as a referendum democracy and 62 as a representative democracy. The hypothesis that the median voter model would provide a satisfactory explanation for the first category and not or less so for the second category (see also chapter 5), could be confirmed. Romer and Rosenthal (1979), however, indicate that there are quite some methodological pitfalls in testing the median voter model, so that the empirical results thus far cannot be considered very reliable.

4.3 Majority decision and social welfare

4.3.1 Intensity of preferences

An important part of the welfare theoretical literature on the majority decision consists of discussions about which criteria a voting system must satisfy from the viewpoint of the pursuit of maximum social welfare. As we have seen, Arrow formulated a number of conditions that a fair voting system should meet. At the same time, however, he showed that when all these conditions are met, there is no certainty that group decisions will be consistent in their outcomes. He who strives for collective transitivity has to be ensured of adequate consensus among the individual preference orderings (single-peakedness, value-restrictedness). This means either that the first condition of Arrow cannot be met, or else that one of the other conditions has to be dropped. With regard to the other conditions, there is particularly doubt about the fairness of the third condition which holds that the outcome of a vote between two alternatives may only depend on the preferences the individuals have with regard to these two alternatives. This condition rests on the assumption that preferences are only ordinally ordered, i.e. that the individuals can indicate only whether they find the one alternative better than the other or vice versa.

For our line of reasoning, let us go back to the example in section 2.2.1 of a canteen where only one type of roll is served. The canteen is visited now by three, not two, visitors, of whom one person (a) prefers ham to cheese while the two others (b and c) prefer cheese to ham. The problem of whether ham or cheese rolls should be served, can easily be solved under the majority decision. A vote between ham and cheese will result in a victory for cheese. This is because each vote has equal value and all that is important is the number of votes for ham and cheese. There is no alternative, as long as the only meaning which can be attributed to the preference orderings of a, b and c is that two of them prefer cheese to ham and one ham to cheese; i.e. as long as their preferences are purely ordinal. With regard to social welfare, we must make ourselves content with the conclusion that there is a majority who wins, and a minority who loses.

As soon, however, as more information is available about the individual preference orderings, in the sense that a, b and c know how large their welfare difference is between ham and cheese, it can be worthwhile to take the *relative intensity* of the preferences into account. Dahl (1956), who systematically investigated the problem of preference intensity in *A preface to democratic theory*, states succinctly that the researcher who ignores this intensity wrongly equates 'most preferred' and 'preferred by the most' (p. 90). Information about the intensity of preferences can take various forms. One possibility is that the individual preferences can somehow be measured cardinally. Another possibility is that the preferences are ordered on an ordinal scale, but in such a manner that when individuals compare two alternatives, they can indicate which compensation (for instance, money) will undo the welfare difference.

The problem of preference intensity is especially important in those cases where a *relatively apathetic majority* is faced by a *passionate minority*. Dahl (1956, p. 99) characterised this situation as a *severe asymmetrical disagreement*. The difference of opinion is severe because one of the groups is passionate, and asymmetrical because the passion of the one group is in contrast to the disinterest of the other. In our example of the canteen, there would be a severe asymmetrical disagreement if person a would have a strong preference for ham because he does not like cheese at all, while b and c appreciate both types of rolls and only slightly prefer cheese. The question then arises whether social welfare is served by a simple majority decision in favour of cheese. The welfare theoretical problems that are related to (ignoring) the intensity of policy preferences will be the topic for the rest of this chapter.

4.3.2 Majority decision and the Pareto criterion

Political decision-making can lead to the realisation of collective provisions that are wanted by everyone. Unlike the unanimity rule, however, there is a chance under the majority decision that the coordination between individual (marginal) benefits and individual (marginal) costs (cf. section 2.3.6) is not optimal.

The majority decision allows for an unequal distribution of benefits, so that the difference between costs and benefits may become negative for a minority. That is, a redistribution of income may result. As a consequence other problems may arise. When the majority realises that the costs for collective provisions can be distributed unequally so that the costs for the decisive majority become accordingly lower, that same majority could decide on a level of collective provisions which is too high from a welfare theoretical point of view.

This can be illustrated with a simple example based on Buchanan and Tullock (1962, pp. 148ff.). A community of farmers has three members: a, b and c. A provincial road runs through the township where they live and work. Each of the farmers has access to that road by a road of his own. Maintenance costs of these access roads rest on the community and are being divided equally among its members. It is assumed that the intensity of individual policy preferences is known in the sense that the costs and benefits of road maintenance can be translated into money terms.

Suppose that for each access road the costs of maintenance are 600, while the benefits amount to 700. In the ideal situation, each road should be kept up since the benefits per road are higher than the costs: the net benefit is 100 per farmer. Under the majority rule it is possible that, for instance, a and b form a coalition, decide to maintain their roads only, and divide the costs of 1200 over the community through taxation. A simple calculation points out that the net benefit for a and b would then amount to $700-400=300$; farmer c is confronted with a net benefit of $0-400=-400$.

It will be immediately clear that with respect to the starting point *no Pareto improvement* has occurred, as farmer c has become worse off. Because farmer c pays taxes without receiving anything in return, there is an income redistribution in favour of a and b. The outcome is also *not Pareto-optimal.* If, indeed, farmer c could still decide to maintain his access road on his own account, his position would improve with a net benefit of $700-600=100$. The majority decision by a and b has led to an *improvement in the neo-Paretian sense* with respect to the starting point, since the majority is able to compensate the minority; if a and b would both pay c 200, c would be fully compensated and the net benefit of a and b would still be positive.

The conclusion that the majority decision may not lead to a Pareto improvement in the strict sense but can lead to an improvement in the neo-Paretian sense would be interesting and useful from a welfare theoretical point of view, if it were not for the fact that this conclusion depends on whether we are dealing with a positive-sum-game, a negative-sum-game or a zero-sum-game.

The above example concerns a positive-sum-game. Now assume that the benefits of road maintenance are 500 per road. Ideally, none of the access roads should be kept up, since the benefits lag behind the costs. However, a coalition could be formed here as well between two out of three farmers, say a and b, who decide by majority to maintain their access roads, and divide the costs over the community. The net benefit for a and b then amounts to $500-400=100$, and for c to $0-400=-400$. Since a and b are able to divide the costs over the community, two roads are kept up which by themselves are not worth it. From a social welfare point of view, the outcome is hardly satisfactory. In comparison with the starting point, the decision neither yields a strict Pareto improvement nor a neo-Paretian improvement. After all, it is evident that the majority is not able to compensate the minority. On the other hand, the minority is very well able to compensate the majority if the majority would abandon its plan. Through such a compensation, the minority would be better off than if the majority carried out its plan.

With the above we have demonstrated that, in general, one cannot expect that the majority decision will lead to maximum social welfare. The majority system is insufficient as a welfare indicator since it lacks a measurement of preference intensities.

4.3.3 Solutions

As it is important to take account of the relative intensity of preferences, the question arises whether in real practice there have not already been found solutions to this problem.

We argued above that under the majority decision it is possible that a minority is exploited. The problem is all the stronger when there is a stable majority that is able to exploit one and the same minority continuously over time. It is for this reason that guarantees against the infringement of certain fundamental rights are frequently inserted in the legislation, especially the constitution, and that rules exist pertaining to the fact that that constitution can only be changed by a qualified majority.

Furthermore, there are good reasons to assume that certain forces are at work in a majority system that will guard against a severe ill-treatment of a minority. First, when the minority loses more than the majority wins, it is to be expected that the political participation of the minority will be relatively larger than that of the majority. This somewhat increases the weight of the minority in political decision-making. When a minority suffers serious loss, it could change its attitude towards the voting procedure in the sense that it starts striving for a qualified majority rule. It is also possible that this minority no longer accepts the result of the vote, disregards the decision-making mechanisms and uses other means of power in order to change the situation to its advantage (from open conflict to civil war). Thus, it is in the own interest of the majority to guard against a too-severe exploitation of the minority. Although it could be defended on these grounds that within a formal majority system the preference intensities are taken into account, one needs to realise that the comparison of intensities is of a rather crude nature. It is dependent upon the judgment that the one voter has of the preference ordering of another voter, without the other voter being able to elaborate his differences in assessment more precisely.

The question of whether a method has been found to overcome the defects of the majority system can also be answered in the affirmative by pointing at the phenomenon of *vote trading*. The minority does not have to sit down in despair but can try to find ways within the voting procedure to achieve an improvement in its position; it can attempt to buy votes from the majority in order to have profitable plans implemented or to stop injurious plans from being carried through. This buying could take the form of a payment in cash. It is more usual that different issues are coupled to one another, so that an exchange of votes (*logrolling*) can take place. Logrolling means that the parties involved exchange their less urgent desires for their more urgent ones, which, under certain conditions, will lead to an optimal result for both parties. After all, an exchange will only take place if the welfare loss of the trading parties in one of the areas is compensated in another area. When all individuals would participate in the exchange, the result could even be optimal for the whole group.

We can illustrate the effects of vote trading with the example from section 4.3.2. Assuming that the benefits of the maintenance of each access road are 700 and the costs 600, we have seen that a and b could form a coalition. That result was not Pareto-optimal. But the process of decision-making does not need to stop there. For, although the road maintenance in principle is a community matter, farmer c could approach a and b with the request to allow him to maintain his own road at his own expense. If that is granted, then c's net position would improve with 700 − 600 = 100. Farmer c has a lot to win, and can be qualified as a passionate minority; a and b have nothing to lose and are a relatively apathetic majority. Given the potential profit, farmer c has some room to 'pay' a and b for their support. This payment could be in cash, but it could also be the promise of his support in future decisions. Assume that the payments to a and b could be valued at 20. The total financial picture would look thus:

for a and b each: 700 (benefit road maintenance) − 400 (taxes) + 20 (payment from c) equals 320;

for c: − 400 (taxes) + 700 (benefit road maintenance) − 600 (costs maintenance of own road) − 2 × 20 (payment to a and b) equals − 340.

From these figures it is clear that granting c the permission to maintain his own road through the vote-trading process just described yields a Pareto improvement in comparison with the majority decision by a and b to keep up only their own access roads (which resulted in a net benefit for a and b of 300 and for c of − 400). We can also observe that this final result is Pareto-optimal. All access roads that are worth it are being maintained. The total surplus is 320 + 320 − 340 = 300, which is the maximum to be achieved.

In the example thus far all members of the community were

involved in the trade, and in such a case the exchange can lead to a Pareto improvement and even to a Pareto-optimal outcome (cf. chapter 3). In general this does not need to be the case. It is conceivable that two passionate minorities will try to create a majority for both minority standpoints through vote trading. Then a third group may remain who in both issues belongs to the relatively apathetic majority who loses in both cases. Yet, from the point of view of social welfare, accounting for the intensity of policy preferences through vote trading can be considered an improvement on the grounds of the neo-Paretian criterion. When the scale is tipped towards a highly involved minority, that minority, provided it is not too small, will easily be able to compensate the majority. Even after such compensation, the net benefit of the minority would be positive. It is precisely the fact that the majority is apathetic that makes a relatively low compensation sufficient for them. If, on the other hand, a non-passionate majority forces its wishes upon a passionate minority, the majority would not be able to compensate the minority. Being passionate, the minority would require considerable compensation. The profit of the majority would not be sufficient to provide that. Both compensation tests lead to the same conclusion: on the grounds of a neo-Paretian criterion it is an improvement if the intensity of policy preferences is included in the decision-making process.

4.3.4 Logrolling: an empirical example

The welfare effects of logrolling can be illustrated with an empirical example regarding a *historic compromise* reached between Socialists and Christian-Democrats in the Netherlands in the beginning of this century. It is assumed in table 4.6 that there were three groups of voters at the time – Socialists, Liberals and Christian-Democrats – and that each represented about one-third of Dutch voters (the Liberal-Democrats who merged with the Socialists in 1946 have been included with the Socialists here). At the time, there were two important issues in Dutch politics – the introduction of universal suffrage and the 'schools struggle' which was concerned with whether private (mainly protestant and catholic) schools would be given the same financial support as public schools. In the table, $w > x$ indicates that w is preferred to x, while $w < x$ indicates that x is preferred to w. The sign $>$ means that the preference is weak, while the sign $\gg$ indicates that the preference is strongly felt.

Initially, the Liberals were strongly opposed to the financial

Table 4.6 *Dutch policy preferences in 1913*

groups of voters	relative size	suffrage			financing of private schools vis-a-vis public schools		
		universal (w)		limited (x)	equality (y)		discrimination (z)
Liberals	1/3	w	$<$	x	y	$<$	z
Socialists	1/3	w	$\gg$	x	y	$<$	z
Christian-Democrats	1/3	w	$<$	x	y	$\gg$	z

equation of private and public schools, but their opposition gradually weakened over the years. The same can be said about the suffrage issue. In 1907, the Liberal De Meester cabinet proposed some limited reforms of the voting system which were accepted by the Liberals. As yet, there was no movement in favour of universal suffrage.

The Socialists fought a passionate extra-parliamentary campaign for the introduction of universal suffrage. At the same time, they were not strongly against equal financial rights for private schools.

The Christian-Democrats passionately advocated equal financing of private and public schools, while their position on suffrage was not clear. The Protestants among them were initially in favour of a limited householders' suffrage, while the Catholics were divided. The principle of universal suffrage, however, was never an object of contention for the Christian-Democrats.

The alternatives chosen at the beginning of this century were 'limited suffrage' and 'financial discrimination against private schools'. This was also the case in the 1913 elections. Table 4.6 shows that limited suffrage won with the support of the Liberals and the Christian-Democrats, while the financial discrimination of private schools won with the support of the Liberals and the Socialists. In the matter of universal suffrage the Socialists were a passionate minority, whereas in the matter of education the Christian-Democrats were the passionate minority. The Socialists and Christian-Democrats then traded their votes in such a way that the Socialists agreed to support the financial equality of private and public schools, expecting the Christian-Democrats to advocate the introduction of universal suffrage. This logrolling was not realised explicitly but implicitly through party-congresses and 'extra-parliamentary' cabinets (meaning that the cabinet was not composed of representatives of both parties). As early as 1902, a Socialist party-congress passed a motion (on opportunistic grounds) that favoured the financial equality of private schools. In 1915 the extra-parliamentary Cort Van der Linden cabinet set up a 'Conciliation Commission' to advise on the suffrage and the schools struggle issue. In the same year the commission proposed to introduce a system of universal suffrage for men, based on proportional representation and compulsory voting. These proposals met with objections from the Christian-Democrats. This criticism died down, however, in 1916 when the commission also recommended that public and private schools should be given equal financial support. The Cort Van der Linden cabinet combined both issues in 1917 in a proposal to revise the constitution so that both universal suffrage and financial equality of private and public schools would become possible. The implicit logrolling then became manifest: the Socialists supported the financial equality of private schools and the Christian-Democrats voted in favour of universal suffrage to ensure that the revision of the constitution was accepted.

This logrolling meant that the Liberals lost in terms of welfare. The vote trading thus was no improvement in terms of the Pareto criterion. Whether it was an improvement in a neo-Paretian sense depends on the extent to which the Socialist and Christian-Democratic majority could compensate the Liberals. This would very probably have been the case. Since the Liberals did not have a strong preference for a certain policy alternative in the case of universal suffrage nor in the case of the schools struggle, the Socialists and Christian-Democrats would only have had to provide a limited compensation in order to satisfy the Liberals.

This example has been simplified somewhat but it illustrates that the general consequence of logrolling is that strongly preferred policy alternatives will more often be chosen by the majority than the weakly preferred alternatives. This occurs because the strongly preferred issues will form the contents of a negotiation offer and thus of a possible agreement. In the example, there were at first two passionate minorities, Socialists and Christian-Democrats, while after the logrolling none of the groups formed a passionate minority. Often those who are freed from a passionate minority position will profit to such an extent that they are able to provide adequate compensation. Logrolling meets the neo-Paretian requirement of optimum social welfare. In other words, logrolling is a positive-sum-game (cf. Mueller, 1989, pp. 82–94).

5 Representation

5.1 Elected representatives

In chapter 4 we explained why, under certain conditions, an iron law of oligarchy operates in a direct democracy; this is because, in order to avoid high decision-making costs, all individuals accept a decision rule by which decisions are made by a small group. This small group can consist of a minority which makes decisions completely independently of the other individuals. In a modern democracy, however, this small group consists of specialised 'agents' who have been chosen by all individuals. In such a case, there is no longer any question of a direct democracy, but of an *indirect* or *representative democracy*. Largely following Buchanan and Tullock (1962, pp. 211–17), we understand representative democracy to be a method which on the one hand avoids the high costs of decision-making associated with a large number of decision-makers and, on the other, precludes the external costs associated with dictatorship or oligarchy.

In this chapter, we shall assume that the individual voters will be represented by 'politicians' who combine the wishes of the voters and turn them into concrete proposals, weigh the interests of the various voters, and decide on the proposals by a majority of votes. In this definition, the category of politicians includes: committee members of societies and political parties; members of community councils, of town councils, of county councils; parliament; the prime minister and, except in a presidential system, also the members of the cabinet.

In the literature, the view predominates that representative democracy should be seen as an independent decision-making model. In this book, however, representation is taken to be an important part of the whole political process. This element is important because representation results in a clear division between demanders and suppliers. In a negotiations democracy, and in a referendum democracy, each person is both a demander and a supplier. In a representative democracy, individuals are specialised either as demanders or as suppliers.

In a representative democracy, the *demanders* are private citizens. They want a variety of government services (public goods, income transfers) and are prepared to pay a certain price for them. In the traditional literature on public finance, it is assumed that this price consists exclusively of the payment of collective costs (taxes, social insurance premiums). There are, however, a number of government services which are not financed from taxes or premiums (e.g. an expansive government policy in a period of economic depression), and there are many voters who contribute little or nothing to collective costs, yet continue to be demanders. The price which the demanders pay in all cases is to give political support to the politicians. This support consists, for example, of voting for a certain political party. Section 5.2 discusses the way in which the demanders exercise a demand in a representative democracy by providing political support.

Against the demanders, there are the *suppliers* who, in a representative democracy, are office-bearers; they have the office of elected representative or of civil servant. The role of civil servants will be discussed in chapter 6, while this chapter deals with the elected representatives, the politicians. The politicians supply the voters with a certain government policy in exchange for their support (i.e. their vote). The way in which this is achieved and what government policy results in an equilibrium between supply and demand is discussed in section 5.3.

Finally, the degree to which the equilibrium resulting from the decision-making model of the representative democracy yields a social welfare optimum, will be discussed in section 5.4.

5.2 The demand for government policy

5.2.1 Rationality of voters

In this chapter we shall confine ourselves to a specific form of political participation by citizens, namely, the exercise of a demand for government policy by voting or abstaining from voting. The decision on whether or not to vote depends in the model presented here and which is based on the work of Downs (1957) solely on the voters' policy preferences and the policy proposals of the various political parties.

The idea that voters evaluate the various policy alternatives and vote in accordance with their findings is disputed. Barry (1970, pp. 165–83) reminds us that political thinkers such as De Maistre, Hegel and Coleridge considered the citizen to be fairly irrational in his behaviour. They did not expect that the citizen would make a sensible choice from the various strategies even when he had complete information at his disposal. These ideas led to remarks such as 'Roman Catholics vote for Roman Catholics, no matter what policy is pursued.' Such a view links up with the sociological vision that political parties should be seen as 'natural' representatives of sharply distinct sections of the population. Voters' behaviour is largely explained by characteristics like religion, social class, education, age, sex, etc. In the US this approach has been curbed in a social-psychological direction by the work of Campbell, Converse, Miller and Stokes (1960). They argued that voters prefer candidates with whom they can identify even if it is not on the basis of all the policy proposals of the candidates, but on the basis of points of issue which happen to dominate the political scene at that moment. In the mid-1960s, however, the political sociologist Key concluded from empirical studies that what was until then considered an irrational identification with parties was in fact based on a weighing of policy alternatives in respect of the provision of public goods and the distribution of its costs: 'Vote switches occur in directions consistent with the assumption that voters are moved by a rational calculation of the instrumental impact of their vote' (Key, 1966, p. 47). Van der Eijk and Niemöller (1983) reach a similar conclusion starting from Dutch data: 'Electoral change . . . can be understood to emanate from the rational behaviour of voters who attempt to maximize with their vote the ideological congruity between themselves and the party they vote for' (p. 352).

5.2.2 *The political space*

For our purpose it is important now to take a closer look at the work of Downs (1957), who provided the theoretical foundation for the economic analysis of voter behaviour. Because of the central position of the political space concept, the economic theory of voter behaviour is also often designated as the *spatial theory of voting*.

We shall start the exposition with the assumption that elections are

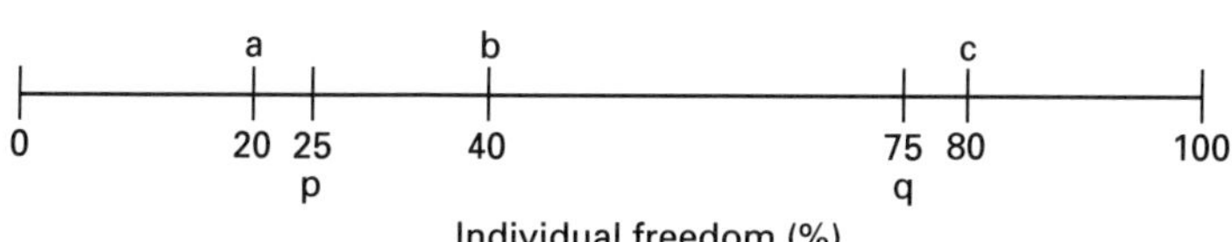

Figure 5.1 The political space

dominated by a single salient issue, e.g. by a complex of matters related to the question concerning the extent to which the government may limit the freedom of individuals. It is assumed that the *political space*, that is the set of all possible policy preferences with regard to the issue at hand, can be represented graphically in a *one-dimensional* continuum running from left to right. Such a continuum is shown in figure 5.1; the political space ranges from 0 per cent individual freedom at the far left to 100 per cent individual freedom at the far right. It is taken for granted that each citizen is able to indicate his own policy preference within this political space. In figure 5.1, for example, the preferences of the persons a, b and c are such that they are willing to limit the freedom of individuals to 20 per cent, 40 per cent and 80 per cent respectively.

In political parlance policy preferences are often described by the terms 'left' and 'right'. But it should be noted that such terms are vague in three respects. First, no one is ever absolutely left or right but at most left or right in relation to the average. Second, in these terms no indication is given of the degree to which someone is left or right. Third, it must not be forgotten that the degree to which a person is left or right can vary for each policy issue. On the score of figure 5.1 it cannot be decided whether b is left or right, but only that the position of b on this issue is more left than c and more right than a.

Within the framework of the political space voters decide on how they will vote. For that purpose they evaluate the position of the parties[1] in the political space. The two parties p and q in figure 5.1, for instance, which contend with each other for the favour of the electorate, advocate a policy characterised by, respectively, 25 and 75 per cent individual freedom. The voters compare their own policy preferences with those of the parties on hand and vote, in so far as they decide to vote, for that party which supports the policy position nearest to their own preference. In figure 5.1 this would mean that person a votes for party p and person c for party q. When it can further be assumed that the preferences of each voter are symmetrical around his policy optimum, so that person b dislikes 5 per cent less

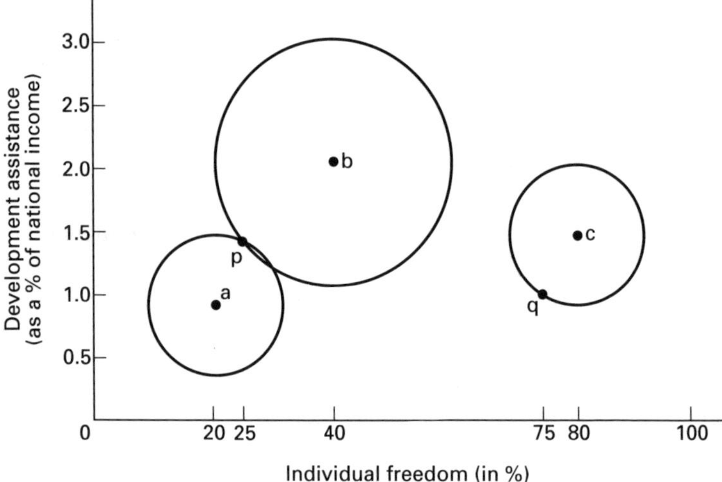

Figure 5.2 A two-dimensional political space

freedom with respect to his ideal of 40 per cent as much as he dislikes 5 per cent more freedom, it can be established that the distance between party p and the policy preference of b is smaller than for party q; so person b will vote for party p.

In a two-party system the voter will without doubt vote for that party which is nearest to his own position. In a multi-party system, it is claimed by Downs (1957, p. 49), a voter will also try to take account of the chance that his preferred party will actually come into power. When his favourite party has no chance whatsoever to win the election, the voter may consider the option to vote for another party, in order to withhold the party which he prefers least of all from governing.[2]

When there is more than one salient issue during the elections, then the political space can no longer be represented in one dimension by a single line. The political space becomes *multi-dimensional*, and must be represented conceptually by a set of straight lines, in which each separate line represents a continuum from left to right of possible opinions on a single salient issue. Although the content of the analysis becomes more complicated, the method remains the same.

Figure 5.2 portrays a two-dimensional political space; the horizontal axis represents, for example, the policy alternatives for the degree of individual freedom, the vertical axis the possible views on the financial aid to be given to developing countries as a percentage of national income. Taking for granted that voters have policy preferences with respect to both issues, their policy optima can be represented as points in the two-dimensional political space. When a voter has been able to ascertain the positions of the various parties, he can assess the distance between these positions and his own policy preferences. He will vote for the party with the closest position to his own policy optimum. To visualise the preferences of a voter we can draw indifference curves around his policy optimum. When the voter's preferences with respect to each issue are symmetrical around his policy optimum and when both issues are of equal weight to him, his indifference curves will have a circular form; to the degree that a circle is more remote from the policy optimum, the voter's appreciation for the policy alternatives involved is lower. From figure 5.2 it can then be read out that voters a and b prefer party p, while voter c opts for party q.

5.2.3 Information and ideology

Since voters in a representative democracy can only vote once in a certain period of time, there are always many issues at stake at an election. National elections nowadays deal with such divergent matters as environmental policy, tax-reform, defence budgets, unemployment and inflation, the trade deficit with Japan, the government budget deficit, problems of immigrants and fugitives, and abortion and AIDS. If a voter wants to assess the distance between his own policy preferences and those of the different political parties, he will have to know the position of the parties on all these issues.

First, the voter can find information in election programmes and promises of various parties. Since they do not have a binding nature, he will have to assess what the various parties might actually do once they are in power.[3] For the incumbent parties, he can look at the actual policies they pursued before the election. For the other parties, those in opposition, he will have to form a (hypothetical) judgement about their achievements had they been in power.

It will be clear that collecting and processing all of this *information* creates problems. Assuming that the human mind is able to grasp all the information regarding the standpoint of every political party with regard to all relevant issues, collecting and processing the information will at least take time and money. A rational voter will wonder whether these costs will weigh up to the benefits of a carefully considered choice. Those benefits will be very small, especially with national elections: the chance that the vote of one voter based on complete information and careful analysis will make a difference in the outcome of the election, is almost nil. Therefore, the average voter will act perfectly rational when he does not inform himself completely and thus limits his information costs.

According to Downs, this is why political ideologies are important to voters. A *political ideology* is 'a verbal image of the good society and of the chief means of constructing such a society'. 'Ideologies help him [a voter] focus attention on the differences between parties; therefore they can be used as samples of all the differentiating stands. With this short cut a voter can save himself the cost of being informed upon a wider range of issues.' 'Instead of comparing government behaviour with opposition proposals, he compares party ideologies and supports the one most like his own. Thus, he votes on ideological competency, not on specific issues' (1957, pp. 96, 98–9).

Given that political ideologies are of great importance to voter behaviour, it is interesting to know how many dimensions there are in the political space, as defined by these ideologies. Downs himself suggests that the political space can be reduced to a one-dimensional left–right scale that is socio-economic by nature: 'how much government intervention in the economy should there be? If we assume that the left end of the scale represents full government control, and the right end a completely free market, we can rank parties by their views on this issue in a way that might be universally recognized as accurate' (1957, p. 116). Other authors have stated that the ideological political space encompasses more than one dimension, and that – at the least – the religious-secular dimension should be added. How many dimensions the political space actually has in a concrete situation, seems in the end to be a matter of empirical research.

Ideological agreement between party and voter is the basis for party identification. Those voters who feel a sufficiently strong identification with a party are the core supporters of that party. Naturally, the ideological positions of both voters and parties can change in the course of time. This can lead to a change in party identification, and then to a change in voter behaviour.

More specifically, Kramer (1971) and Goodhart and Bhansali (1970) – see also Fiorina (1981) – have suggested that, at an aggregate level, the changes in voter behaviour can be explained by *macroeconomic developments*, like the development of real disposable income, unemployment and inflation.[4] Information about these developments is available to voters with hardly any costs, since they are given ample attention in the media. When the results of government policy are satisfactory in terms of income growth and decline of unemployment and inflation, then there is no reason for the supporters of the incumbent party (parties) to change their voting behaviour. When, on the other hand, the results are disappointing, the government will be held responsible; this can result in the incumbent party (parties) losing support, and the opposition being given the chance to take over.

The notion that the election results are strongly influenced by macroeconomic developments in the (recent) past, is not uncontested. Several authors have suggested that voters not only look backward at the actual course of things, but also try to assess the policies which have been pursued and whether these might offer certain opportunities for the future. It is pointed out that the government cannot always be held responsible for a disappointing economic development; for instance, developments abroad might play an important role. Furthermore, there is no clarity as to precisely which macroeconomic variables are of importance in determining voter behaviour. In this respect, Stigler (1973) has noticed that elections are predominantly about distribution issues that can hardly or not at all be captured in macroeconomic indicators. Finally, with regard to studies at the aggregate level, Hibbs (1977) has pointed out that it is wrong to consider the electorate as one whole; at the least, one needs to make a distinction between relevant socio-economic groups which meet with the advantages and disadvantages of macroeconomic developments in quite different ways.

5.2.4 Voter turnout and abstention

Until now we have assumed that everyone votes. This is, however, not at all self-evident within the economic theory of voter behaviour. The decision to vote or to abstain from voting is, in the vision of Downs (1957, pp. 260–74), likewise based on an individual cost-benefit analysis. In the formalisation of Riker and Ordeshook (1968; see also Davis, Hinich and Ordeshook, 1970) the citizens weigh the following factors one against the other:

P = the probability that the citizen will, by voting, materially affect the outcome of the election;

B = the differential benefit that he receives from the success of his preferred party over his less preferred one;

D = his personal satisfaction at having participated in the election;

C = the cost of voting;
and in such a way that the citizen only votes if:

$$P.B + D - C > 0.$$

The magnitude of P is negatively related to the size of the electorate. It will increase, on the other hand, when the election is expected to be close, such that every vote counts. The variable D is according to Downs (1957, p. 270) equal to the 'long-run participation value' of voting. 'Voting is a necessary prerequisite for democracy; hence democracy is in one sense a reward for voting.' Tullock (1967, p. 110) introduces for D the term 'civic duty'.

On the basis of the inequality introduced above we can conclude that there are two reasons why a voter could abstain, to wit indifference and alienation.

Indifference occurs when all parties propagate the same policy. For the voter's individual welfare it then becomes immaterial which party wins the election, so that the value of B approaches zero. However, there is still a chance that the indifferent voter will vote: he will vote if $D - C > 0$ and, in the opinion of the above-mentioned political scientists, D is relatively large. Indifference is related to the concept of positive apathy discussed in chapter 3: 'You don't participate – this time – because you feel you can rely on the fact that those who do participate will arrive at a reasonably acceptable decision and because you are able to use the time to do something else which is more enjoyable.'

Alienation exists when the distance between one's own preference and that of any party exceeds a certain critical limit. Because the voter does not recognise any of his own preferences in the proposed policies, he becomes demoralised, especially if his preferences are intense; he loses faith in the democratic system. Even if the programmes of the various parties differ, the voter still feels disheartened and useless, so that his feelings of personal satisfaction (D) approach zero. There is little likelihood that the alienated voter will vote: he will only vote if $P.B - C > 0$, and Olson has already shown that P will always be low in a large group. In his opinion, political alienation corresponds with negative apathy as discussed in chapter 3: 'When others have no sound policy, it is a waste of your time to try to change things.'

5.2.5 *Empirical findings*

Various studies set out to empirically test the theory of voter behaviour discussed above. In section 5.2.1, we already mentioned Key's study of the voter's policy orientation. Frohlich, Oppenheimer, Smith and Young (1978), following Shaffer (1972), attempted to empirically test the entire Downsian model against the US presidential elections of 1964 and to compare the results with those of an often applied social-psychological model. Since the empirical data for the indicators P, B, D and C figuring in the economic model, were lacking, they tried to operationalise these variables as well as possible using available indirect data. The voter's assessment of the probable influence his vote would have on the election result (P) was, according to Frohlich et al., dependent on the degree to which the outcome of the election would be close and was therefore measured as the margin with which, according to the voter, one of the rivals would win. The expected increase of individual welfare, should the preferred candidate be chosen (B), was based by Frohlich et al. on questions regarding the issues a voter considered to be important, the relative importance a voter attached to these issues, and from which candidate he expected the most on these issues. The expected influence of the election results on individual welfare was also taken into account. Furthermore, the less a voter was informed, the higher the importance which was attached by Frohlich et al. to party identification. The personal satisfaction from voting (D) was derived from answers to questions about the belief of the voters in the meaning of elections for the preservation of democracy. Data regarding the personal sacrifice of a voter (C) were lacking entirely. Frohlich et al. therefore tried a number of assumptions. The assumption that the costs of voting were lognormally distributed over the electorate, proved to be the most adequate.

Then, Frohlich et al. designed a computer simulation. The economic model appeared to predict no less than 86.6 per cent of the voter preferences for one of the candidates correctly. Also, the decision on whether or not to vote could be adequately predicted: the model explained 85 per cent of the variance in voter turnout. Furthermore, the simulation resulted in conclusions about the relative meaning of each individual variable. Only the variable 'information' as a component of variable B (the expected increase of individual welfare should the preferred candidate win) could be omitted without loss of model reliability.

The social-psychological model, based on questions about the voter attitude toward and his affective binding with candidates and their parties, also provided a good prediction of voter behaviour. Comparing the results of both models revealed that the results of the economic model regarding the preferences of voters for one of the candidates were a little less predictive, whereas the results with regard to the voter turnout were a little more predictive than in the social-psychological model. Since the *predictive value* of both models was roughly the same, and only the Downsian model was based on an elaborate theoretical *explanation* of voter behaviour, Frohlich et al. finally decided in favour of the Downsian model. They even went as far as suggesting that the attitudinal variables in the social-psychological model 'are actually surrogates for the components of the Downsian model' (p. 196).

More recently, Collier et al. (1989, p. 5) concluded from the results of experimental research that 'we should not be surprised to observe electorates which invest few resources in political information, especially if no great issues arise to upset the kind of equilibrium which is likely to prevail in stable democracies'.

The series of studies showing that the prevailing macroeconomic conditions have an important influence on the election results, is by now vast. Recent examples for the US are Marcus (1988) and Erikson (1989) and for Western Europe, Lewis-Beck (1986). It is generally found that voters are not so much interested in their strict personal financial situation, as in the role government policy plays with regard to that situation. These findings, which suggest that voters specifically rely on easily accessible information but pay heed in that to the policy which is being pursued, fit perfectly well in the Downsian model.

Other studies offering empirical support for (elements of) the economic model of voter behaviour are provided by Fiorina (1981) and Enelow and Hinich (1984, chapter 9).

It has also been investigated whether the Downsian model could provide an explanation for voter behaviour in *the Netherlands* which will serve as our prototype of a multi-party system. The study of Van der Eijk and Niemöller (1983) confirms that voters are led by motives related to forms of policy rationality. Policy rationality, however, is not directly related to political issues, but only indirectly through voter orientation to political ideologies in which the standpoints on political issues find their place. Van der Eijk and Niemöller are of the opinion that a one-dimensional left-right scale suffices to describe the spectrum of opinions among voters. The analysis indicates that the ideological identification of a voter is not specifically aimed at one party, but more generally to a particular segment of the political space. For the Netherlands, it is better to use the concept of *ideological identification* rather than party identification. Van der Eijk and Niemöller show that there is quite some stability in the ideological position of voters. This means that party-changers will usually shift between parties that look very much alike. Therefore, the general political power balance between the parties to the left and the right of the political spectrum is relatively stable, despite the large number of party-changers (see Van der Eijk and Niemöller, 1984).

The applicability of the Downsian model in the Netherlands and the one-dimensionality of the political space is not so readily accepted by all researchers. Irwin et al. (1987) analyse the voter behaviour at the national elections of 1986 by applying various explanatory models (the pillarisation perspective; standpoints about specific political issues; the assessment of pursued economic policy; the evaluation of leading politicians). None of them can be discarded as inapplicable, and none of them is clearly superior to the others; a combination of all perspectives provides the strongest explanation. It ultimately appears that the complete explanation can be brought together in two functions. The most important of these two strongly correlates with left-right, the appreciation of economic policy, opinions about a number of issues and sympathy towards politicians. The second correlates most strongly with religion and opinions about abortion.

Finally, let us look for a moment to the *turnout* at elections. Until 1970, voting was mandatory in the Netherlands with (a risk of) a fine in case of abstention; as a consequence, more then 90 per cent of the electorate turned out to vote. After 1970, this percentage dropped considerably. Voter turnout at elections for the national parliament varies between 80 and 90 per cent, for the municipal and provincial councils between 65 and 75 per cent, and for the European Parliament between 50 and 60 per cent. The differences between these figures appear to fit the economic theory of voter behaviour. The differences between political parties (think of factor B) are or seem to be considerably larger for the national parliamentary elections than for the other elections. On the one hand, this is because the media pay far more attention to these national elections, and, on the other, because the national parliament possesses more authority in collective decision-making than other bodies. With regard to the European Parliament, we can add that, due to the enormous size of the European electorate, the chance (P) that an individual vote will have influence, is even less than at national elections.

For other countries as well, it appears that the voter turnout reacts to differences in the probability of casting a decisive vote, even though that probability may be small. See, for instance, the studies of Cebula and Murphy (1980) for the US and of Darvish and Rosenberg (1988) for Israel. We must add to this that Foster (1984) has re-examined various studies on the basis of data for four US presidential elections. She reaches the conclusion that the effect of the closeness of the election on voter participation rates is present but also rather weak.

All in all, we can conclude that the findings above provide reasonable support for the economic theory of voter behaviour.

5.3 The supply of government policy

5.3.1 Aims of politicians

Citizens' demand for a certain government policy is met by a corresponding supply by politicians. During an election campaign the supply can be seen in the form of policy proposals which are presented to the voters alongside those of competing candidates. Of course, the decisions on these proposals are directed at achieving certain aims. In the previous section we assumed that the voters attempt to turn government policy, by their voting behaviour, in the direction of their policy optimum. Following Downs, we shall now assume that the parties, by their policy proposals, will try to turn the voters in the direction of an electoral optimum: 'parties formulate policies in order to win elections, rather than win elections in order to formulate policies' (1957, p. 28). In the opinion of a political party the election result is at an optimum when the party receives sufficient support to be able to participate as effectively as possible in government.

The idea that politicians strive for an electoral optimum needs further elucidation. Politicians can be divided into careerists and paternalists (or office-seekers and policy-pursuers). The pure *careerist* maximises the number of votes given to himself, to his party or to his regular coalition partners. The pure *paternalist* has 'merit wants' – he maximises the level of a set of values which are determined not so much by the voters as autonomously. The concept of careerists most closely corresponds to American politics. The concept of paternalists better fits in with European politics, even though just before actual elections a large number of careerists suddenly appear in European countries as well.

There is not necessarily always a clear distinction between the two ideal types. The careerist regards electoral support as an aim and the policy as a means. The paternalist, on the other hand, sees the policy as an aim and electoral support as a means. Under certain conditions the result is the same. As long as a politician does not have a monopoly position, obtaining electoral support is vital for him in order to realise the policy he prefers. Should a paternalist ignore this fact, he will be defeated by his opponent, and then be rudely awakened. When the politicians are able to obtain governing power solely by means of a competitive struggle for the people's vote, the paternalist will be obliged, on pain of the liquidation of his political power, to act as a careerist. The policy which he desires remains his *basic motivation*, but the support he must gain is his *immediate motivation* on the basis of which his behaviour can be described and predicted.

Hinich and Ordeshook (1970) have pointed out that the exact nature of the careerist's aims will depend on the party system. In a *multi-party system* parties can only take part in the government by forming a coalition; the more votes they collect, the stronger their position in a coalition becomes. It can therefore reasonably be assumed that, in the period preceding an election, parties in a multi-party system will try to *maximise the number of votes* given to them, while the number of votes cast in favour of their opponents does not matter. However, in a *two-party system* the situation is completely different. Here, a party is not so much concerned with getting more votes, irrespective of the electoral position of the opponent, as with defeating the opponent. The logical result, according to Hinich and Ordeshook, is that in a two-party system parties do not strive to obtain an absolute maximum of votes, but to achieve the greatest possible *majority* (plurality).

5.3.2 Dynamics of political parties in a two-party system

The models used by Downs and, following him, by authors like Riker, Davis, Hinich and Ordeshook to analyse the political strategies of parties are derived from the geometric model introduced by Hotelling (1929) to examine the location of grocers in a certain catchment area; see also Smithies (1941). In Hotelling's model the number of consumers served by a grocer varies with his geographical location. In the models of Downs et al. the numbers of voters represented by a party varies with the political location of that party, i.e. with its policy proposals in respect of a number of independent issues.

In order to simplify our analysis, we shall begin with the case that the elections are dominated by a *single issue*. Each voter will have his own view of what would be optimal with regard to this single issue. It is assumed that the policy optima of the voters can be represented as a left-right continuum of alternatives. The precise distribution of the voters over this continuum can be represented graphically by drawing a function which renders at each alternative the relative number of voters who consider that alternative to be the optimal policy (cf. figure 4.3). Various hypotheses can be formulated on the shape of that function. In the literature (Riker and Ordeshook, 1968 and 1973; Davis, Hinich and Ordeshook, 1970; Hinich and Ordeshook, 1970; Ordeshook, 1976) the shape of the distribution function is mostly taken to be *symmetrical*. This means that every voter who prefers a certain policy has an antipode in the voter who prefers a policy which is, with respect to the median, the diametrical opposite. A symmetrical distribution can be unimodal or multimodal. In this chapter we shall at first assume that the policy optima of the voters are *unimodally* distributed over the political space, as shown in figure 5.3. A unimodal distribution presupposes a certain degree of consensus among the voters. This need not imply, however, that most voters wish to maintain the status quo; it is quite possible that the consensus is concentrated on a policy which bends the existing situation in a progressive or a reactionary direction. A unimodal distribution only implies that there is one policy alternative (the so-called mode) which comes up to the preferences of more voters than any other alternative.

As regards the parties, the authors mentioned above assume that their political location is completely mobile, with the single restriction that the parties cannot pass each other. In a two-party system, a party does not strive simply to maximise its number of votes but to defeat its rival. Its success not only depends on the additional votes it receives itself, but also on the number of votes the opponent loses. It is quite attractive then to move towards the median. Every vote which a party gains from its rival near the median is doubly important: such a vote is not only added to its own total but is also deducted from the rival's total. The outcome of the model is that when one party takes a position at the median and the other does not, then the party at the median will in all cases receive the majority of votes. Thus, the party

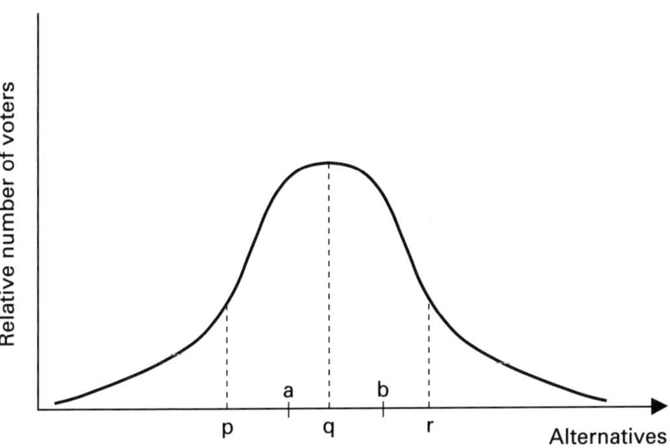

Figure 5.3 Distribution of the policy optima in a one-dimensional political space

which evolves most rapidly to the median has the greatest certainty that it will defeat its rival. Under these circumstances both rivals will want to be on the safe side and will occupy locations at the median. As a result, their policy will be subject to a process of *complete convergence*; there is no question of a supply of two fundamentally different policy alternatives. Hotelling illustrates this by the example of two shopkeepers who, in a main street which is equally busy throughout its length, both decide to locate their shops in the middle of the street.

When both parties indeed converge and end up by advocating the same policy, that policy will also be carried into effect, irrespective of which of the two parties exactly wins the election. Just as in section 4.2.7, we can conclude that it is the *median voter* who is decisive for the outcome of the process of collective decision-making.

Implicitly it has been taken for granted in the preceding argument that all voters always turn out to vote. *Abstention* can occur, however, as was argued in section 5.2.4, due to alienation and indifference, and hence should be taken into account. Now it is easy to see that, when the distribution of the policy optima of the voters is symmetrical and unimodal, both parties will be affected to the same degree by a loss of votes due to abstention when they move towards the median position. The conclusion that both parties converge to the median is thus not impeded by these kinds of vote abstention (Davis, Hinich and Ordeshook, 1970, p. 438).

When the elections are dominated not by one issue but by a *number of issues*, the argument remains essentially the same. In this case, the political space must not be seen as one straight line running from left to right, but by a set of left to right dimensions in which each dimension represents an independent salient political issue. When the relative importance of all issues is the same, i.e. when voters give all issues the same relative weight, then the policy outcome of a two-party system in each dimension separately corresponds with the median position.

5.3.3 Dynamics of political parties in a multi-party system

In a multi-party system parties aim at the maximisation of their number of votes. Taking account of political competition and of the possibility of abstention, the optimum location of a party in a multi-party system is determined by the tension between convergent and polarising forces.

Attention will first be paid to the *converging* forces. For that purpose we take figure 5.3 as our starting point, where the parties p, q and r form a three-party system and occupy the political locations as indicated. When party p, having a monopoly position at the left-hand side of the continuum, evolves in the direction of the median, it will lose the votes of the extreme left-wing voters who feel politically alienated. Initially it will win more right-wing votes than it loses in left-wing votes because there are, after all, more voters near the median than there are far away from it. The same argument applies to party r which occupies a monopoly position on the right-hand side of the continuum. On balance, evolution towards the median results in an advantage for extreme parties with a monopoly position. Hence, on the basis of this model, partial convergence can always be predicted in a multi-party system.

But no complete convergence occurs because there are also forces at work which favour a permanent *policy distance* between the parties. If all parties approach the median they must share the voters in the neighbourhood of the median with each other. They no longer win and lose votes only in a no-man's-land; they also do so at the expense of one another's monopolised votes. Thus they are no longer in a monopoly position, but they compete. Furthermore, voters will start abstaining due to indifference. As a result, when the evolution towards the median has reached a certain point, the gain in votes from voters near the median no longer compensates for the loss of votes from extreme voters. Once this point is reached, it is no longer worthwhile to evolve further: the extreme party in a monopoly position is now in equilibrium.

This situation changes as soon as the monopoly of the former extremist is broken by the entry of a new extremist party. The former extremist can now do one of two things: either it can try to restore its monopoly or it accepts its loss. In the former case it returns temporarily to its extremist base in order to defeat the newcomer or to join forces with it, and thereafter it will return to its natural point of equilibrium. In the latter case it will evolve completely to the median because, now that it has competition on both its left and right wing, its reason for preserving a policy distance to its opponents in the centre no longer applies, since there are more voters near the median than far away from it. As soon as it reaches the median it will either defeat its opponents there or it will join them. In the meantime the new extremist, who now occupies a monopoly among the extremist voters will move (for the reasons given at the beginning of this subsection) towards the equilibrium position of its predecessor, so that the whole story will repeat itself.

With this we have put the unambiguous result of Hinich and Ordeshook's mathematical calculations (1970, p. 787) somewhat crudely into words, namely that in a multi-party system in equilibrium three different political locations remain. It is not necessary that each location be occupied by a single party or candidate. It is equally possible that at one point more parties or candidates are located who agree to cooperate on a regular basis.

5.3.4 *Inconsistency and unreliability*

To form a stable cabinet a parliamentary majority is a minimum requirement. The problems which can follow from this requirement in a multi-party system can be illustrated with the help of figure 5.3. Assuming that the three parties p, q and r have occupied the political locations as indicated, there are many ways of arriving at a majority. However, in a study of coalition theories, De Swaan (1973, p. 288) has shown that not all possibilities will be used. A party will only form a coalition with the parties in the nearest locations and, in addition, it will not join any coalition which is larger than is absolutely necessary to obtain a majority.[5] In the example given by figure 5.3 this means that a coalition p + r is ruled out so that, to begin with, five possibilities remain to achieve a majority: p, q, r, p + q and q + r. In the last two cases, concerning the coalition between a centre party and one of the relatively extreme parties, either both parties can have equal influence or one party can dominate the other (e.g. p dominating q, or q dominating p). Each coalition thus has three variants, which means that there are nine possibilities: p, q, r, p + q, p + (q), q + (p), q + r, q + (r) and r + (q).

Uncertainty arises because the coalition which exists before an election is not necessarily the same as that which will be formed after the election. Assume that voter a in figure 5.3 votes for party q because q approaches his own policy optimum most closely. However, when party q forms a coalition q + r after the election, the policy pursued will approach position b. If a had known about this beforehand, he would not have voted for q but for p, because p approaches his optimum more closely than does b.

The continuing need to form a coalition means that, in the words of Downs (1957, pp. 105–7), the parties become inconsistent and unreliable. *Inconsistency* here means that at the beginning of a new parliamentary period of session the parties do not accept full responsibility for the policies pursued in the previous period. *Unreliability* here means that the political promises made during the election campaign give no definite answer as to what policies will be pursued by the new parliament.

The Netherlands offers us a neat example of the latter situation. Despite the considerable number of parties which took one or more seats in parliament, political life in the past decades has been dominated by three main parties: a relatively left, Social-Democratic party (PvdA); the Christian-Democrats at the centre (CDA); and a relatively right, Liberal-Conservative party (VVD). The parties which did not identify with one of these major political streams, have in general remained small. This picture is in perfect harmony with the prediction which flows from the theory of Hinich and Ordeshook, presented above in section 5.3.3.

The Christian-Democratic party, on the whole the largest of all, occupies a comfortable position in the centre of the political arena. Unless it is prevented by the election outcome, as in 1986, this party can choose to enter into a majority coalition with either the relatively right VVD or the relatively left PvdA. Both kinds of coalition have been tried in the past. Because the Christian-Democratic party almost never commits itself before the election to a continuation of the current government policy, while it does not speak out on the preferred coalition after the election either, the impact of the voter on coalition formation and future policy is very limited. A coalition party that wins the election can be expelled from government, as is shown by the fate of the Social-Democrats in 1977; and a coalition party that suffers a considerable loss at a national election can be maintained as government coalition partner, as happened to the Liberal-Conservatives in 1986.

In order to combat this evil political reformers in the Netherlands have, since the mid-sixties, often pleaded for the introduction of new procedural rules which should see to it that the election programmes of the coalition partners cannot be the subject of political negotiations after the elections. The proposals included the introduction of an elected prime-minister; the introduction of policy agreements between combinations of parties before the elections as to the intended composition and programme of the future cabinet; the transition from the system of proportional representation to a system of electoral districts with plurality rule; and a raise of the minimum fraction of the vote required to obtain a seat. These proposals should be seen as attempts to break the multi-party system open and to arrive at two parties or two permanent coalitions which would provide the voters with a clear choice between two essentially different policy alternatives (Van Thijn, 1967, pp. 59–61).

According to the political reformers, the polarisation of power is thus a way to achieve a polarisation of policy. As we concluded in section 5.3.2, however, a two-party system has a strong tendency to policy convergence. The expectations which these political reformers entertained with regard to a two-party system thus are not supported by the model discussed here.

By the way, all efforts in the past years to realise political reforms through amendments of the law and/or the constitution were wrecked in parliament.

5.3.5 *Implications of the assumptions of the model*

The conclusions which have been reached up till now (convergence to the median position in a two-party system; three political equilibrium locations in a multi-party system) depend on the assumptions on which the Downsian model is based. The most important assumptions (cf. Ordeshook, 1976) are:

1. The citizens evaluate the politicians solely on the basis of their policy preferences (section 5.2.2).
2. The set of political issues can be represented by a space of straight lines running from left to right (section 5.2.2).
3. Every citizen has a utility function, which consistently specifies

his relative utility at each point in this political space (section 2.1.1).

4. The utility function of each citizen has such a shape ('concave' or 'quasi-concave') that there is only one policy which is an optimum for the citizen (section 4.2.6).
5. The policy optima of the individual citizens are distributed symmetrically and unimodally over the political space (section 5.3.2).
6. Citizens can abstain from voting because they are indifferent or alienated (section 5.2.4).
7. The politicians aim to win the elections to enable them to (continue to) participate in government (section 5.3.1).
8. The positions taken by the politicians on each of the political issues are completely mobile, with the restriction that politicians cannot pass each other (section 5.3.2).
9. The citizens give the same relative weight to all issues (section 5.3.2).
10. There is perfect competition among the political parties (section 5.3.2/5.3.3).
11. Politicians have complete information on the voters' utility functions and the citizens have perfect information on the benefits and costs inherent in the policy positions taken by the politicians (section 5.2.2/5.3.2).

Several assumptions (especially 3, 4, 6 and 7) have already been discussed in earlier chapters and sections. The implications of some other assumptions will be examined somewhat more extensively below. The assumptions 9, 10 and 11 will (also) be addressed in section 5.4, which deals with representation and social welfare.

In the exposition in section 5.3 so far, we have assumed that the *voters* are *informed* about the different alternatives with regard to *every issue* and use this information to evaluate the politicians (assumptions 1 and 11). As we noted in section 5.2.3, it is because of the cost of collecting and processing information that most voters will not meet these assumptions. Voters will be led mostly by their political ideologies. When, however, these *ideologies* in turn form a political space that can be represented as a one-dimensional ideological left-right scale (cf. section 5.2.5), then the model can be considered to apply to that political space.

Of great importance for the outcome of the model are the assumptions 2 and 5 with regard to the number of dimensions of the political space and the symmetry and unimodality of the distribution of policy optima of the voters. Let us consider first the *unidimensional* political space. In section 5.3.2, we deduced that with a symmetrical and unimodal distribution of the policy optima of the voters, a two-party system converges to the median of the distribution whether or not voter abstention occurs. When the assumptions of symmetry and unimodality are abandoned, the conclusion of convergence to the median still holds, provided that there is no voter abstention. When, on the other hand, there is voter abstention, the convergence toward the median is no longer guaranteed. To be more precise, when the distribution of voters is unimodal but *asymmetrical*, the outcome is on or close to the mode (see Comanor, 1976). And when the distribution of the voters is symmetrical but *bimodal*, there is no general conclusion; either the parties find equilibrium locations in the vicinity of the two modes, or there is no equilibrium at all (see Davis, Hinich and Ordeshook, 1970, pp. 441–3).

Let us now examine the *multi-dimensional* political space. Several authors (Plott, 1967; Davis, DeGroot and Hinich, 1972; McKelvey, 1979) have proved that an equilibrium in a multi-dimensional political space can only exist when the condition of *strict symmetry* of the distribution of policy optima of the voters in all directions is met. With the slightest deviation in the preferences of whatever voter, this condition is no longer met, and there is no political equilibrium. When the symmetry condition is not met, then we have a major problem, due to the occurrence of the Arrow-paradox and cycling in the multi-dimensional space, which is indeed so serious that 'the usual situation will be that majority paths exist between *any* two points in the space' (McKelvey, 1979, p. 1106). In other words, from any starting point one can come out at every other alternative, with a proper choice of the agenda and sequence of voting. But then it will be impossible for the parties to choose for a more or less fixed political location. We can add to this that this problem is of a very general nature, because, as was argued in section 5.2.2, at elections in a representative democracy there are always more issues at stake than just one. The problem is especially relevant with distributional issues where as soon as more than two persons are involved, the options cannot be ordered one-dimensionally (cf. Aranson and Ordeshook, 1981; Coughlin, 1986).

Assumption 8 of *perfect mobility* of politicians and political parties has been criticised from various sides. In the opinion of Hirschman (1970, pp. 70–2), Downs et al. were too much influenced by Hotelling, who described a market system in which the consumer is unable to influence where shopkeepers locate their shops. After all, in the model consumers have nowhere else to go. But, according to Hirschman, voters are not powerless in a democracy. Did Dahl not say that nearly everyone has access to many still unused political resources? This applies in particular to *activists among the party officials*, who have an important influence on the designation of candidates and on the organisation of the election campaign. In Hirschman's view they will do everything to prevent their party from occupying a standpoint they detest. He therefore considers perfect mobility of political parties a naive assumption.

Incidentally, it must be noticed that Hirschman's argument seems to conflict with the picture which can be gained from participating observation. The argument most frequently used (even by parties dominated by a strong ideology) to convince a party cadre of the (in)correctness of a specific strategy, is a reference to the electoral effect of such a strategy. Of course, a party can, under the influence of activist cadres, take a decision which is undesirable from an electoral point of view. Among the examples most frequently given of such a wrong decision, are two from the US – Goldwater's Republican candidacy for the presidency in 1964, and McGovern's Democratic candidacy in 1972. However, such a mistake is immediately punished with an overwhelming defeat.

We can add to this that the chance that parties wield great influence will increase as the period between two elections becomes larger and the voters have fewer opportunities to voice their judgment about the standpoints of the parties.

A second consideration that limits the mobility of political parties is the necessity to remain sufficiently *credible* for incompletely informed voters who choose their party mainly on the basis of ideological identification. Changes made too suddenly in standpoints once taken can cause doubt about the ideological position of the party, so that the party could alienate and lose its core supporters. In this view, it is in the interest of parties to follow a more or less consistent policy, especially in a multi-party system with differentiated political locations, and to be influenced less by short-term considerations of maximisation of the number of votes or of the relative majority.

Finally, we have to take into consideration that political parties must *campaign* before election time in order to bring their own candidates, programme and ideological position to the attention of the voters, if, indeed, they are not completely informed. Hinich and

Ordeshook (1970) point out that campaigning becomes more important when political competition increases, and that it will cost more manpower and money. In relation to Olson's participation theory, important contributions to the election funds of political parties cannot so much be expected from the average voter, as from passionate minorities. A party set on acquiring funds will therefore have the inclination to hold onto certain standpoints which are favourable to specific minorities and deviate from the median position. See also Lindbeck and Weibull (1987).

There are also good reasons to put question marks at assumption 11. As we saw earlier, it is reasonable to assume that voters are not or not completely informed about the standpoints of politicians. It is, however, also unlikely that *politicians* are completely *informed* about the standpoints or the ideological position of the voters. And even if politicians would know the position of the voters on an ideological left-right scale, then it is still possible that the voters in their voting behaviour will, up to a certain extent, be led by personal opinions about the characteristics of the candidates and by the standpoints of the parties on specific issues regarded as personally important for every voter. About these latter aspects, which moreover will differ from one election to the other, the information of political parties will almost certainly be incomplete. This uncertainty about voting behaviour implies that political parties are not able to choose a position which is in perfect accordance with the Downsian theory.

Several authors (Hinich, 1977; Coughlin and Nitzan, 1981; Coughlin, 1986; Lindbeck and Weibull, 1987) have proved, by the way, that, as a consequence of this insecurity, the chance for the existence of a political equilibrium increases, although there has to be no need of convergence toward the median.

When we summarise the discussion above about the assumptions of the Downsian model, we can conclude: (1) that in many cases the existence of a political equilibrium cannot be proved, and (2) that in those cases where an equilibrium exists, there is not always a convergence toward the median.

5.3.6 *Empirical findings*

There have been relatively few attempts to test whether the assumptions of the Downsian model with regard to the interaction between voters and political parties are plausible. Several authors

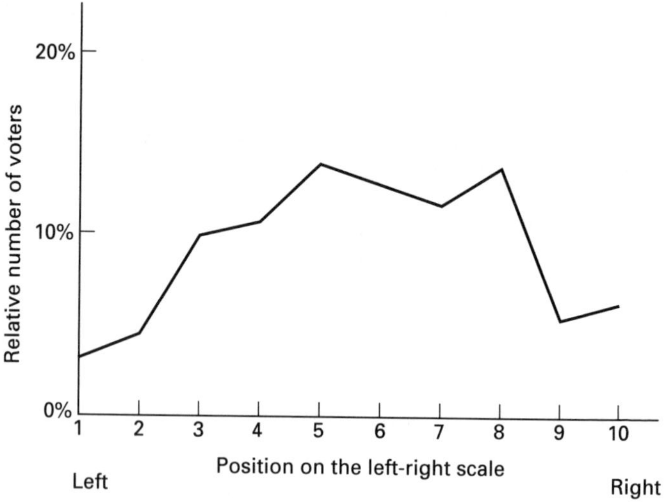

Figure 5.4 Distribution of the Dutch electorate in 1981 over a ten-point left–right scale
Source: Thomassen (1984), figure 3.1, p. 211.

have investigated the *distribution of voters* over the political space. Figure 5.4, derived from Thomassen (1984), presents the distribution of the Dutch voters on a *one-dimensional* ideological left-right scale in 1981. The figure suggests that this distribution meets the assumptions of symmetry and unimodality quite well.

Irwin and Thomassen (1975) analysed the distribution of the policy preferences of Dutch voters for seven *separate issues*. It appeared that the distribution of voters over the policy positions was asymmetrical but unimodal for half of the issues considered, while for the other half the distribution was symmetrical but bi- or trimodal. This ambiguous result may have partly been due to the fact that the policy positions were separated too much by the questions. When, for instance, with regard to income policy the left position is defined as 'the income distribution must become more equal' and the right position as 'the income distribution must remain as it is', it is not surprising that most voters appear as (extreme) left. When the left position, however, is defined as 'the income distribution has to be completely equal', then the advocates of a more equal income distribution would have been spread over different varieties of distribution policy, maybe in a bell-shaped form.

Irwin and Thomassen – see also Thomassen (1976) – then investigated the *degree of consensus* between the opinions of the voters and those of members of parliament with regard to the issues studied. For half of the issues there appeared to be a reasonable degree of consensus; such consensus was almost completely lacking for the issues public order, development aid and tax policy. According to the Downsian model, there is then reason to believe that the existing political parties should review their position, respectively that there is room for the entry of new parties.

A totally different line of empirical research analyses the *macroeconomic policy* of the government. Important contributions were furnished by Nordhaus (1975), Hibbs (1977), Frey and Schneider (1978) and Alesina and Sachs (1988); a summary of this literature can be found in Van Velthoven (1989). Without elaborating on the important differences between the studies mentioned, we can conclude from the available empirical results that the government is certainly not only led by short-term considerations of maximisation of the number of votes or by the chance for re-election, when deciding on macroeconomic policy; the ideological opinions and policy preferences of the government parties seem to carry weight as well.

The extent to which these empirical results do or do not indicate whether the Downsian model is correct is not entirely clear. On the one hand, political parties apparently do not immediately follow (changes in) the opinions of the electorate with regard to all kinds of specific issues. On the other, this does not have to be contradictory to the Downsian model as soon as it is acknowledged that collecting and processing information, decision-making, and entry all involve costs. Because of that, voters, for instance, will not be fully informed about all the separate political standpoints, but will be led by ideological identification. Indeed, in a multi-party system, with differentiated locations for political parties, parties can probably not adjust their standpoints with regard to all kinds of issues too rapidly without raising doubt about their ideological position and without jeopardising the ideological identification of their core supporters. Furthermore, the need to adjust the own position will also depend on the relative weight that voters attach to specific issues, and more data about this are lacking.

5.4 Representation and social welfare

5.4.1 Representation and the Pareto criterion

In chapter 2 we formulated the conditions under which social welfare, in so far as it depends on the provision of public goods and services, is at an optimum on the basis of the Pareto criterion. We shall now consider whether the institutions of representative democracy, discussed above, give a guarantee that these conditions will be met.

A multi-party system, in any case, does not give this guarantee. In such a system, three locations will be maintained in equilibrium, in which each location can be occupied by a group of parties which make a ballot-box agreement among themselves. Such ballot-box agreements are a useful means of preventing the number of independent parties from becoming larger than is necessary for a clear representation of the three policy alternatives, so that they make a substantial contribution to the rationality of the democratic process. But the need to form a cabinet after the elections generally remains in a three-party system. From the point of view of the rational voter, the parties, as they represent themselves before the elections, thus become inconsistent and unreliable. The policy outcome of a three-party system is indeterminate and the certainty that this result is at an optimum on the basis of the Pareto criterion cannot be guaranteed at all.

In a two-party system the policy outcome will be determinate, at least if certain conditions are satisfied (see section 5.3). Ordeshook (1971) has shown that this outcome is Pareto-optimal. After all, a Pareto improvement is an improvement in the position of some without a worsening in the position of others. Such an improvement always provides a gain in votes in the model discussed above. Should one of the two parties not choose a Pareto-optimal location, it could always be defeated by a rival who does.

However, that is not the final word to be said on the relation between representation and social welfare. In the first place, it should be observed that a political equilibrium does *not always exist*, certainly not in a multi-dimensional space. For those cases Kramer (1977) and Coughlin (1982) have pointed out that a two-party system converges in the course of a series of elections to the set of Pareto-optimal outcomes, provided the political parties strive for maximisation of the number of votes or the expected plurality.[6] In other words, the eventual outcome will satisfy the Pareto criterion. But it is generally unknown to which Pareto-optimal outcome – for there can be more – the two-party system will converge; there can also occur cycling among a number of Pareto-optimal outcomes.

Secondly, even if the eventual outcome is Pareto-optimal and thus no longer susceptible to any further Pareto improvement, that is not to say that that outcome is necessarily a Pareto improvement *with regard to the initial situation.* A policy which is supported by a majority of the electorate can very well be attended by a redistribution of income at the expense of a minority (see also section 4.3.2).

Finally, as we noted earlier in section 4.3, the above conclusion on Pareto optimality does not account for the *intensity of the preferences.* It is quite conceivable that the voters attach different relative weights to the various issues, and that, moreover, these weights vary from one voter or group of voters to the other. If so, assumption 9 from section 5.3.5 would no longer hold true.

5.4.2 Representation and the neo-Paretian criterion

When some voters are passionate in respect of certain problems, the chance of a party winning an election increases considerably when it combines issues and thus implicitly applies logrolling. Such *implicit logrolling* can take place between different parties but also within one party, which, after all, can be seen as a permanent coalition of various social groups. It is always possible for a party to bind a minority which is passionate in respect of a single issue, by meeting its wishes on this one point, provided that the majority which it goes against is relatively uninterested. Nevertheless, to prevent the loss of this majority to the opponent, it will have to accommodate this majority on other matters which it considers to be of especially great importance. Downs (1957, pp. 55–60), too, has already pointed at the possibility of forming a majority through a coalition of (passionate) minorities.

Van Thijn (1967, pp. 59–61) has shown that historically the two-party system derived its specific nature from such logrolling. He harks back to the origin of the parliamentary system in England. In the period 1721–42 Walpole held the reins of government and obtained an iron grip on the majority in parliament, partly through corruption. According to Van Thijn this had nothing to do with parliamentary democracy. Parliamentary democracy only came into being when the first leader of the opposition (Bolingbroke) succeeded in transforming the diversity of the groups of people, who were united solely by the fact that they had freed themselves from Walpole's powerful grip, into a more or less coherent opposition, which slowly developed into a majority which brought about Walpole's downfall in 1742.

Had a two-party system existed in the Netherlands at the beginning of this century, the elections would have been won by the politician (or the statesman) who combined the introduction of universal suffrage and the financial equation of public and private schools in a single platform (see section 4.3.4). In chapter 4 we showed that such logrolling could lead to an increase in social welfare in terms of the neo-Paretian criterion. In the example, the Liberals remained a minority but their loss in utility could be compensated by later statesmen, for instance by increasing the cultural freedom for which the Liberals strove passionately and against which the Christian-Democrats and the Socialists had no fundamental objections. Social welfare will be increased by each new case of logrolling until the optimum is reached. Of course, this conclusion applies on the condition that during this process of logrolling, which can take many years, no new issues are created.

From the above examples it becomes apparent that the abandonment of assumption 9 (stating that the voters give the same relative weight to all issues) has important consequences for the policy outcome in a representative democracy. After explicit or implicit logrolling has taken place, the policy outcome no longer always lies at the median of every left-right policy line but, depending on the issues involved, to the left or right of it.

Finally, we conclude that, in a democratic process, a two-party system stimulates most the attainment of a social welfare optimum. When we assess a two-party system using a (neo-) Paretian standard, the outcome of the decision-making process in a democracy is such that no voter can improve his position further without worsening that of another, and those voters who have improved their position at the expense of other voters would be able to compensate the losers completely. This conclusion applies not only to democracy in government, but also to democracy in clubs and in firms. In the case of a club, it would be worthwhile, in pursuit of a social welfare optimum, if the candidates for office were to merge into two competing groups.

5.4.3 The two-party system as ideal

The Downsian model of a two-party system is based on political competition. Frey (1970b) in particular made it clear that

Downs presented a model of *pure democracy*, which can be compared with the model of a market operating under perfect competition. At first this seems a strange conclusion. In a market, perfect competition is characterised by a large number of suppliers. In the political process pure democracy is characterised by the existence of only two political parties. The difference between these models is less important, however, than their similarity: in an optimum situation no one has any power. In the market model the absence of economic power results from economic indifference; the consumers are indifferent as to where they buy their goods at the current market prices, and the producers (since in the long run profits will be zero) are indifferent to whether they produce in the particular industry or not. In the political model the absence of political power manifests itself in political indifference. The voters are indifferent because, no matter which party is chosen, their utility will not be affected. The paternalists are indifferent because the policy is the same no matter whether they or their rivals govern. Only the careerists are interested in the outcome of the elections.

Another common characteristic of the models for a competitive market and for a pure democracy is that the optimum situation is achieved only when a number of ideal conditions have been met. For the political model, we summarised the most important of these conditions in section 5.3.5. To conclude this chapter we want to dwell a little longer on two of these conditions: that of perfect political competition and that of perfect political information.

Perfect competition here does not mean an active rivalry. Actually, the political equilibrium in which the two parties offer the same programme is very boring. All that is meant by 'perfect competition' is an institutional structure in which political power is in the hands of a large number of anonymous voters. This institutional structure is an ideal which is characterised by the continual occurrence of elections. Only when elections are held regularly do the political parties themselves have no power at all.

The competition between politicians is, of necessity, perfect during the election campaigns. After all, in a two-party system the election is a *zero-sum game* – what the one wins, is lost by the other. But as soon as the elections have been held, the stake is no longer in votes but in paternalistic policy satisfaction. The game then becomes a *positive-sum game*: more satisfaction for the one does not necessarily mean less satisfaction for the other. In such a case a restriction of competition can be beneficial to both parties (see also Wittman, 1973, p. 497). Just as oligopolies may reduce their price competition in the commodities market and maximise their revenue, it is conceivable that in a two-party system both parties will keep the costs of public goods out of the political arena and will stress the benefits of these goods. Lindblom (1968), among others, observed such conflict-minimising behaviour in respect of costs. In our opinion, this must be seen as a manifestation of political power resulting from the fact that all parties have little interest in gaining votes in the period between elections. The less attention politicians need to pay to the electoral effects of their policy, the greater the chance that public goods will be provided in non-optimal amounts at non-optimal prices.

The model of pure democracy is based not only on perfect competition but also on *perfect information*. Politicians are assumed to be informed about the voters' individual welfare functions, and voters to have insight in the benefits and costs of public goods. Neither assumption is valid.

Not only is it virtually impracticable to obtain information about the marginal benefits and disadvantages of a public good for each individual voter, but also it is theoretically not feasible. If a voter wants others to pay for a public good, he will hide his preference for that good. If he especially wants his individual wishes to be taken account of, he will exaggerate the urgency of his wishes.

The information voters have about the benefits and costs of public goods is also usually poor. According to Downs (1957) the benefits of some public provisions are far removed in time or space from the voters – these are 'hidden benefits' for the citizens. Examples of this include town and country planning, energy policy, development aid and foreign policy. To this we must add that there are also hidden costs – people are aware of indirect taxation, for example, only when the rates are raised or lowered. There is also the possibility that voters will see only the benefits of some provisions and only the costs of other provisions. In the former case they will support a utopian policy, i.e. a policy with detailed information about the aim, but with no information about the means of realising this aim. In the second case, they will vote for a technocratic policy in which the emphasis lies primarily on the means, but where the aims are kept vague.

In these cases there is no reason at all why the politician who wants to maximise the number of votes cast for him should strive for an optimum social welfare. Paternalist politicians run the risk of being defeated by their opponents unless they succeed in hiding their paternalism from the voters. In particular, it is impossible to conduct a long-term policy as long as the voters are geared to the short term. Statesmen who, in the words of a famous definition, do not plan for the next election but for the next generation, will, in the model, disappear very quickly indeed. The consequences of this can easily be imagined. Unless the voters either take a long view or can always remember which party in the past pursued policies directed at the future, each actual system of representative democracy has the built-in tendency for the government's policy horizon to be no longer than the period between two elections.

This conclusion shows the reverse side of the structure in which elections are continually taking place. If the period between two elections is long, this will reduce political competition. But if this period is short, then government policy in a real society will be dominated by the short-sightedness of the voters. As long as the voters do not take a long view or have a good memory, this dilemma is insoluble and the actual period of parliament will always be characterised by compromise.

6 Implementation

6.1 The power of bureaucracy

6.1.1 Bilateral monopoly

For a long time the literature on public administration suggested both that political decisions are made in parliament by elected politicians, including ministers, and that these decisions are implemented by bureaucrats appointed by the administration. This assumption goes back to Wilson ((1887)1970) and Weber ((1922) 1972) who regarded bureaucracy as the ideal type of a perfect hierarchy of trained professionals. According to this view the real bureaucrat is not engaged in politics but 'administers', i.e. he administers impartially. The bureaucrat will fulfil his duties 'sine ira et studio' (without passion and without partisanship). So he does not do what the politician always has to do, that is, fight. Taking sides, battle, passion – ira et studium – these are the essence of politics. The bureaucrat's professional honour lies in his ability at all times to carry out his superior's orders, conscientiously and scrupulously, irrespective of whether his objections to certain policies have been ignored (Weber, (1922)1972, pp. 551–79).

Yet, this classic view of bureaucracy must be discarded from an economic point of view. This became especially clear from an analysis of the bureaucracy in the Soviet Union. This bureaucracy had expanded to gigantic proportions so that phenomena which are inherent in every bureaucracy became caricatured and, because of this, became clearly visible. Nove (1961) and Ames (1965) broke new ground with the unmasking of the totalitarian myth, i.e. the myth that every Soviet bureaucrat actually did his duty. Williamson (1964), Galbraith (1967) and Niskanen (1971) reached a similar conclusion in respect of the administrations of the Western economies.

Not only do the voters and the politicians have the power to make economic decisions, so do the bureaucrats. In section 1.6 we defined an individual's power to make economic decisions as his influence in so far as it is used in accordance with his own aims and is backed by the possibility to apply economic sanctions. Pen (1971, pp. 110–12) illustrated the last part of this definition by an example. In this example the power to make economic decisions originates in a situation in which individual a has the more or less exclusive disposal over the means required by individual b to realise his aims. Two conditions must be met for person a to have economic power. First, that for the realisation of his aims b should in fact need the means controlled by the mighty a; second, that b can only obtain his requirements via a. It is only when a exercises more or less complete control over the means that he is able to apply a sanction by withholding these from b, thus hindering b in the realisation of his aims.

This example gives an insight into the balance of power between politicians and bureaucrats. Only politicians have the right to give orders to their departments and they alone can provide the funds necessary for executing these orders. The departments depend on their budgets which are allotted annually by the cabinet and parliament. On the other hand, the bureaucrats have the exclusive command over professional expertise and various types of information so that the cabinet and parliament are dependent on them for the production of the desired public goods. Niskanen (1971, p. 24) rightly concludes that because politicians and bureaucrats each have a certain degree of monopoly, the exchange relation between them can be termed *bilateral monopoly*.

This chapter will be devoted to a more detailed analysis of the (power) relations between politicians and bureaucrats and, in connection with that, of the influence of the bureaucracy on collective decision-making. In the sequel of this section we first of all take a look at the elements on which the decision power of the bureaucracy is based. We discuss: (1) the limited capability of the political leadership of a hierarchically structured bureaucratic organisation to control the implementation of orders at the foot of the pyramid; and (2) the own aims of the (leading) bureaucrats. In section 6.2 we present Niskanen's model of the interaction between politicians and bureaucrats, which starts from the premise that bureaucrats strive for the maximisation of the available budget. The presentation of this model is rounded off with a critical evaluation of its assumptions and a survey of the results of empirical research. In section 6.3, finally, we examine how the influence of the bureaucracy on political decision-making is related to the achievement of a social welfare optimum.

6.1.2 Limitation of the scope of control of politicians

The larger the public sector becomes, the less important is the right conferred on the politicians to give orders. After all, a minister's *scope of control*, i.e. his ability to let his political will penetrate all sections of his department, is limited. The same applies to the scope of control of his leading bureaucrats. The concept of scope of control can be divided into span of control and depth of control. *Span of control* refers to the number of individuals who can be controlled effectively by one departmental head, *depth of control* refers to the number of hierarchical levels that can be managed.

Graicunas stylised the span of control in a theorem which states that when the number of subordinates increases linearly there is an exponential growth in the number of relations between these subordinates so that it is efficient to have no more than four or five subordinates per civil servant. The validity of this theorem is no longer held absolute, but management consultants accept the conclusion that coordinating activities tend to increase more than in proportion to the increase in the number of subordinates. Ames (1965, p. 240) illustrates this by the example of a planning bureau. Consider a bureaucrat – with an arbitrary position in the hierarchy – who has the actual control over 15 subordinates. If he receives every month, say, 5 draft plans from above, he has to return 5 counter plans every month, he receives 5 definite plans back, and writes 5 reports about them; he also sends $5 \times 15 = 75$ draft plans downwards, receives 75 counterplans, returns 75 definite plans and later receives 75 reports. Both the 'input' and the 'output' of this bureaucrat is only documentary. His time is fully taken up by the multiplication of these documents for dispatch downward and their combination upward.

Attempts are made in bureaus to avoid the coordinating problems described above by increasing the number of hierarchical levels, but then a new problem looms up. At each intermediate level the chance that an order will be changed, either deliberately or accidentally, becomes greater, for it is possible that a subordinate will not understand the order, cannot execute it, or does not wish to execute it. The consequences of this are shown in table 6.1. A subordinate who,

Table 6.1 *Depth of control: an example*

orders executed at each level (in %)	ministerial orders eventually executed (in %) if the administration has: 2 levels	3 levels	4 levels	5 levels
95	90	86	81	77
90	81	73	65	59
80	64	51	41	32
70	49	34	24	17
60	36	21	13	8

Source: Ames (1965, p. 238)

for example, executes 90 per cent of his orders would reasonably comply with the Weberian model of altruism, but even in a chain of such good souls the result would be that at the fifth level only 59 per cent of the minister's order would be effective.

The combined results of a limited span and depth of control can be illustrated arithmetically by means of an exaggerated example. Let us assume that: (1) each bureaucrat supervises a maximum of six subordinates; (2) an average of 20 per cent of each bureaucrat's time is spent in being supervised, and the same amount of time is spent by each leading bureaucrat in supervisory activities; and (3) 90 per cent of the activities of a bureaucrat are in accordance with orders from above. Then it is easy to calculate that in a department numbering about 250 bureaucrats spread over three hierarchical levels, more than 100, i.e. a substantial minority, will be engaged in activities which can be regarded as either neutral towards or in opposition to ministerial policy. Should the activities of each bureaucrat accord for only 75 per cent with orders from above, then 170 bureaucrats, i.e. a significant majority, will make either a neutral or an obstructing contribution. This leads Tullock (1965, pp. 149–51) to conclude that a bureacracy, seen from the standpoint of a politician, is subject to the law of diminishing returns to scale: as the number of bureaucrats increases the effective productivity of the marginal bureaucrat drops and after a certain point this productivity even becomes negative. A few years earlier Parkinson (1957) reached a similar conclusion. There is a clear limit to a bureaucracy's ability to execute orders in conformity with ministerial intentions.

6.1.3 *Aims of bureaucrats*

Even if the ability of politicians to control the bureaucracy declines as the number of bureaucrats grows, our definition will only allow us to speak of decision-making power by bureaucrats if they can use the possibility to withhold cooperation and information in conformity with their aims. This brings us to the essence of the application of the new political economy to the bureaucracy: the *aims* of the bureaucrats, especially of the *leading bureaucrats*.

It is more difficult to formulate hypotheses on the aims of leading bureaucrats than on those of entrepreneurs or politicians. In conditions of perfect competition, entrepreneurs are forced to maximise their profits on pain of bankruptcy. As long as political competition is entirely open, politicians must try to gain votes or they will be cast out from the political scene. However, a bureaucracy is not characterised by perfect competition, so that it is not possible to get an unambiguous view of the aims of leading bureaucrats by just looking at the environment they are working in. As a result, any hypothesis on the aims of a bureaucrat will be somewhat speculative.

By analogy with the motives of politicians a distinction can be made to apply between the basic and immediate motives of politicians. Downs (1967) systematised the basic motives of bureaucrats. On the one hand he refers to the struggle for power, income, prestige or security, on the other to the need for loyalty, the desire to serve the public cause, and the involvement in a specific field of policy. It could be said that the first category of motives is that of the 'careerist', the second that of the 'paternalist'. It is not, however, the basic motivation that is important but the immediate motivation which can be used to explain and predict the behaviour of bureaucrats. Ames, Galbraith, Niskanen and Williamson have attempted to articulate these ideas theoretically by operationalising all the basic motives of both careerists and paternalists into one immediate motive.

Ames (1965, pp. 50–1) based his study of the Soviet bureaucracy completely on the assumption, which he himself considered simple, that all leading bureaucrats aim at the *maximum output* of goods and services by their factories and departments. Independently of Ames, Galbraith (1967, pp. 166–78) developed this idea further. Galbraith argued that in both the Soviet Union and the West a new élite, the technostructure, had become apparent, consisting of technical and managerial specialists of large firms and ministerial departments.

This technostructure gave high priority to the increase in the production of goods by firms, and its complement, the increase of services by government departments, because 'expansion of output means expansion of the technostructure itself'. Expansion means more security, greater prestige, a higher income, more power and greater satisfaction.

Niskanen (1971, pp. 36–41) who was the first economist to construct a mathematical model of bureaucratic behaviour, argues that bureaucrats do not aim at maximising their output of public goods but at *maximising their budget*. He considers the budget to be an adequate approximation for the utility of leading bureaucrats, including those bureaucrats who have relatively little interest in money and a great concern for public affairs. Even if there are a few bureaucrats prepared to accept a low budget, they will in his opinion not long survive in an environment of budget maximisation.

Under normal conditions, Galbraith's hypothesis (output maximisation) and Niskanen's (budget maximisation) will have identical results, as will be shown later. Williamson's hypothesis (1964, pp. 29–37) has entirely different results. He examined managerial behaviour within private firms on the assumption that appointed managers have an 'expense preference', especially for appointing new staff who will enable the manager to increase his own salary, security, status, power, or professional ability. At first sight, this hypothesis seems identical to Niskanen's. Yet, there is a real difference. Whereas the bureaucrat in Niskanen's model needs a budget to increase his output, the manager in Williamson's model needs a budget to *increase his input* (in the form of more staff) even when no extra output results from it.

Incidentally, the motives which were put forward by Niskanen and Williamson can be combined in one comprehensive objective function (see Migué and Bélanger, 1974; Niskanen, 1975). To that end it has to be recognised that the utility of the bureaucrats, at least in so far as it depends on their position in the governmental organisation, is being determined by their scale of salary and the non-monetary perquisites of their function. These, in their turn, are determined by the level of output and the discretionary budget of the department. This *discretionary budget*, also called 'slack', is the difference between the total available budget and the minimum costs which have to be made to realise the output; it can be employed by the bureaucrats within the department as they think fit, for instance for hiring extra staff, spacious reimbursements of all kinds of expenses, fancy trips abroad, etc. Utility maximisation by bureaucrats then corresponds to the maximisation of a combination – with proper weights – of the level of output and the discretionary budget.

In the sequel of our argument we shall at first follow Niskanen (1971) and assume that the head of a bureaucratic department strives for budget maximisation.

6.2 Bureaucratic behaviour

6.2.1 Niskanen's model

Niskanen's model (1971, pp. 45–8) is fairly simple. According to him the preference politicians have in respect of the level of output of public goods and services can be expressed by means of a 'budget-output-function'. Any point on this function represents the maximum budget (B) that the politicians, if necessary, would like to spend on a given level of output (Q). For the sake of convenience Niskanen writes the budget-output-function as follows:

$$(1)\ B = a.Q - b.Q^2 \quad (0 \leq Q \leq a/(2b)),$$

where a and b are positive coefficients.

In chapter 2 we did not speak of a budget-output-function but of a demand for public goods. It is not difficult to appreciate the connection between these two concepts. When (as in section 2.3.4) so-called income effects are ignored, the budget which politicians would, if necessary, be prepared to supply, coincides with their *total benefits*. However, demand depends on *marginal benefits*; at every level of output a demand function expresses which amount the individuals, in this case politicians, are prepared to pay for an additional unit of the good. Thus, the political demand function is the budget-output-function expressed in marginal terms:

$$(2)\ W = dB/dQ = a - 2b.Q \quad (0 \leq Q \leq a/(2b)).$$

The graphs in figure 6.1 show Niskanen's budget-output-curve and the political demand curve. The demand curve is downward sloping because politicians, in accordance with Gossen's first law, put the benefit of marginal public goods at less than that of intramarginal public goods, so that the amount budgeted for the last unit declines as the number of units increases. As a result the size of the total budget B which politicians are prepared to authorise for public goods will increase less than proportionally with the level of output. It reaches its

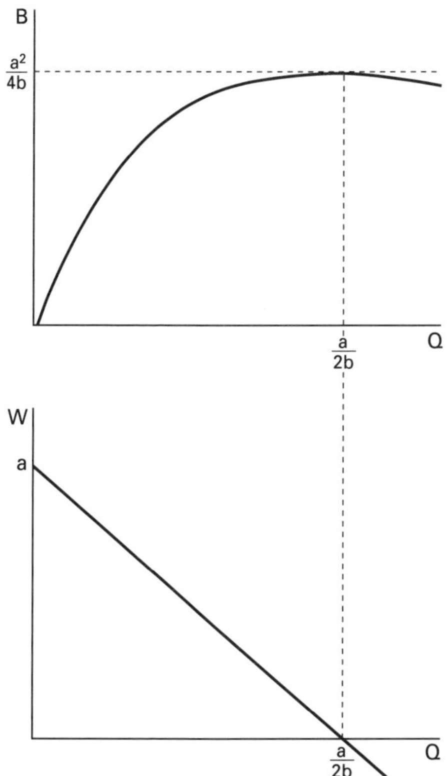

Figure 6.1 Total and marginal benefits from the viewpoint of politicians
B = size of the budget
W = marginal valuation of public goods
Q = level of output of public goods

maximum if the marginal valuation of an additional unit of output has dropped to zero.

Niskanen makes a clear distinction between the maximum amount of money which politicians would like to budget for a given level of output, and the minimum amount of money which must be paid to provide this output – the *costs*. According to him, these costs rise more rapidly in every phase than does the level of output of public goods and services. This assumption corresponds to Tullock's assumption of diminishing returns which we met in section 6.1.2. However, although it is quite plausible that the cost of producing public goods indeed rises more than proportionately with output, it is also conceivable that they rise equally or less than proportionately. In section 2.3.6 we ourselves assumed that the marginal costs of producing a social good are constant. We shall continue to adhere to this assumption in order to avoid less relevant complications in the presentation of Niskanen's argument. Our amendment to Niskanen's model thus means that total costs (C) do not increase quadraticly with the level of output:

$$C = c.Q + d.Q^2 \quad (Q \geq 0),$$

where c and d are positive coefficients, but linearly:

$$(3)\ C = c.Q \quad (Q \geq 0).$$

The positive coefficient c in equation (3) represents marginal costs:

$$(4)\ MC = dC/dQ = c.$$

If the coefficients a, b and c are given, the model has two equations (1 and 3) and three unknowns (B, C and Q). When an objective function is added to the model, the outcome is determined.

6.2.2 Political and bureaucratic optimum

The essence of Niskanen's model is that the objective functions of politicians and bureaucrats differ. This difference means that the politicians and department heads do not strive to achieve the same ratio between output and real costs.

From the point of view of the politicians a programme of public goods is most attractive when output is expanded to the point of maximum difference between total benefits and total costs; the surplus for the politicians is then at its maximum. In figure 6.2 it is shown that the *political optimum* is achieved at the point where the amount politicians are prepared to budget (B) maximally exceeds what they have to pay (C). Mathematically, the difference between total benefits and total costs reaches its maximum if marginal benefits equal marginal costs. For that reason, the political optimum can also be found in figure 6.2 at the intersection of the marginal benefit curve W and the marginal cost curve MC. At the political optimum the level of output is expanded to $(a-c)/(2b)$.[1]

In contrast to the politicians, the utility of the leading bureaucrats is relatively more affected by the benefits than by the costs. For the leading bureaucrats the benefits of public goods, as already noted, consist of a rise in salary, an increase in power and prestige, or

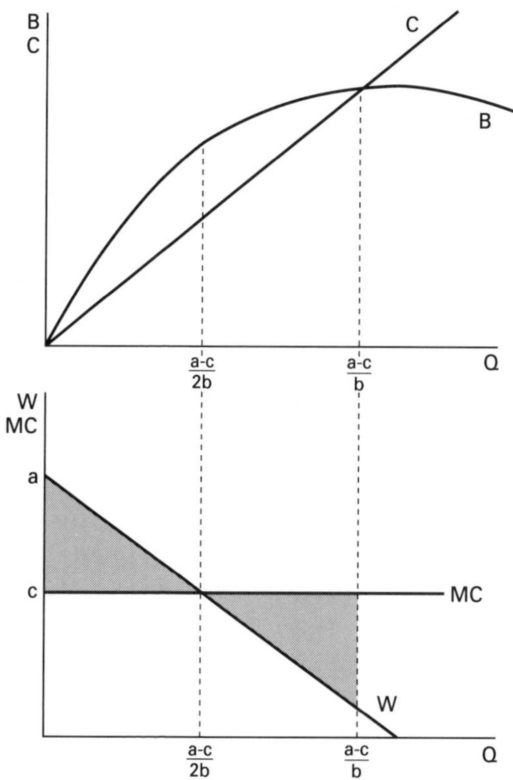

Figure 6.2 The political and bureaucratic optimum
C = total costs
MC = marginal costs
B = size of budget
W = marginal valuation of public goods
Q = level of output

satisfaction in their social usefulness. However, the cost of public goods is borne by the voters, in the form of taxation, and, as a result, by the politicians in the form of a loss of votes. To some extent the bureaucrats are indifferent to the sacrifices politicians have to make to provide funds. They only need bear in mind one factor, that is that the real costs must be covered by an authorised budget. The objective function of the leading bureaucrats thus reads: maximise the available budget finance (B), subject to the condition that the budget authorised by the politicians will at least equal the costs involved ($B \geq C$).

Figure 6.2 shows that the *bureaucratic optimum* in Niskanen's model is reached when the budget-output-curve cuts the total cost curve. At the bureaucratic optimum the level of output is equal to $(a-c)/b$.[2]

The political optimum is found where the budget the politicians are prepared to authorise is at a maximum distance from the costs they must pay. The bureaucratic optimum lies where the distance between the amount the politicians want to authorise and the amount they must pay is zero. At that point the bureaucrats have maximised their budget. In this simple model (which ignores the existence of (dis)economies of scale and income effects) the output desired by the bureaucrats, $(a-c)/b$, is twice as large as that desired by the politicians, $(a-c)/(2b)$.

In this model the consequence of such a doubling of output is that the political surplus vanishes completely, for the areas of the shaded triangles in figure 6.2 are equal. From the viewpoint of the politicians, marginal benefits exceed marginal costs before the point at which $Q=(a-c)/(2b)$; thereafter marginal costs exceed marginal benefits. The net political benefit of one part of the bureaucratic output is neutralised by the net loss of the other part. For the politicians it would have been ideal if all the public goods of which the marginal output resulted in a loss had never been provided. Leading bureaucrats, however, strive to increase their output far beyond the point of the political optimum.

Notice that it also follows from figure 6.2 that the bureaucratic objective of output maximisation (subject to the condition that the costs should be covered by the budget) leads to the same outcome as budget maximisation.

6.2.3 Compromise between politicians and bureaucracy

The political optimum gives the level of output the politicians would ideally demand; the bureaucratic optimum gives the level of output the leading bureaucracy would like to supply. As, according to Niskanen, the power relation between politicians and bureaucrats can be characterised as a bilateral monopoly, the outcome of negotiations between these two parties cannot be determined *theoretically*. The outcome will depend on the power balance and the strategies followed during the negotiations, and turn out somewhere between the political and the bureaucratic optimum.

In Niskanen's opinion, however, the bureaucrats *in practice* generally succeed in getting their own way. He explains this by pointing out that politicians are not aware of the real cost function; they know only one point of the cost function, the amount spent on costs at that moment. As a result the bureaucracy can set the agenda of political decision-making by leaving the politicians an *all-or-nothing choice*; either $Q=0$ or $Q=(a-c)/b$. In the absence of information on the specific form of the cost function the politicians cannot pass judgment on the cost-benefit-ratio of intermediate options, and are therefore almost forced to approve of the bureaucratic optimum for want of alternatives. Another possibility is that the bureaucracy provides the politicians with *inaccurate information* as to the form of the cost function; the ideal for the bureaucracy is to manipulate the information in such a manner that the politicians, if they maximise in good faith the difference between the total benefits and the total costs (as they know them), would exactly arrive at the bureaucratic optimum.

Niskanen thus predicts that the eventual level of output will coincide with the bureaucratic optimum. Note that at that point there is no *technical inefficiency*; the budget which is accorded is in perfect correspondence with the minimal costs which have to be made for the level of bureaucratic output.[3] At this point every managerial audit will show that the costs do not include any waste. After all, departments cannot reach the bureaucratic optimum by wasting money. Extravagance would force the cost function upwards and this would lead the politicians to propose cutting down on the output of a variety of public goods. From the bureaucratic point of view the ideal situation can only be attained by extending the production of public goods beyond the point the politicians find desirable. If there is inefficiency it must be sought not in the cost of any public good but in the level of output of these goods, i.e. the provision is characterised by *economic inefficiency*.

6.2.4 *The assumptions of the model*

The conclusions which have been reached hitherto (the level of bureaucratic output is given by the bureaucratic optimum and is twice the political optimum; possible inefficiencies are not of the technical but of the economic kind) are dependent on the assumptions on which the model is based. The most important assumptions are:

1. The cost curve C cuts the budget-output-function B at the left-hand side of its summit (figure 6.2).
2. Bureaucrats strive for budget maximisation, subject to the condition that the budget at least should cover the minimum costs (section 6.1.3).
3. The bureaucracy has a monopoly position with respect to

information on the costs of bureaucratic activities; in consequence it has a decisive influence on the process of political decision-making (section 6.2.3).

In this section we want to dwell a little longer on the meaning of these assumptions for the above-mentioned conclusions.

In figure 6.2 it is assumed that the marginal costs are so high that the total cost curve C cuts B at the *left-hand side* of its summit, i.e. at the left-hand side of $Q=a/(2b)$. This will be the case if $c>a/2$. The bureaucratic optimum which then results, to wit $Q=(a-c)/b$, is known in the literature as the 'cost-constrained solution'. At this level of output, the (maximum) budget the politicians are willing to supply is exactly equal to the minimum costs which have to be made for the realisation of that output level.

It is of course conceivable that marginal costs are lower, so that $c<a/2$. If so, the total cost curve C would cut B at the *right-hand side* of its summit. It is easily seen that the bureaucratic optimum then corresponds with the summit of the budget-output-function B, so that the level of output the bureaucrats are striving for is equal to $a/(2b)$. This is known as the 'demand-constrained solution'. In the latter case it is important to note that the maximum budget which the politicians would be prepared to authorise (and which they will indeed, according to the model, put at the disposal of the bureaucracy due to its decisive influence), exceeds the minimum cost of provision. Apart from possible economic inefficiency there surely will figure now technical inefficiency (Niskanen, 1971, p. 48). Stated differently, the bureaucracy now can dispose of a discretionary budget.

With respect to the second assumption it is known from section 6.1.3 that there are different views as to the *immediate motives* underlying bureaucratic behaviour. The hypothesis of budget maximisation (Niskanen) stands next to the hypotheses of output maximisation (Galbraith), the pursuit of an increase of inputs (Williamson), and the interest in the size of the discretionary budget (Migué and Bélanger). The differences, however, are not as large as it may seem at first sight. In section 6.2.2 it was already concluded that budget maximisation and output maximisation yield the same outcome. Furthermore, all hypotheses have in common that they predict that the government budget will be larger in a bureaucratic optimum than in the political optimum. The differences are especially related to the kind of inefficiency which results from this larger budget. According to the hypotheses of Galbraith and Niskanen the larger budget will primarily lead to a larger output, in other words to economic inefficiency; according to the hypotheses of Williamson and Migué/Bélanger (see also Wyckoff, 1990a,b) the larger budget will notably be used for employing extra inputs, hence lead to technical inefficiency.

Apart from that there are also authors who fundamentally question the alleged bureaucratic pursuit of budget increases. It is pointed out by Breton and Wintrobe (1975) and Dunleavy (1985) that the leading bureaucrats are not dependent upon just one department for the promotion of their individual welfare; they rather try to follow a career path along different departments in the governmental organisation. It is not at all self-evident that these career-oriented officials would be bent upon budget increases, on the contrary. It is quite plausible that they could enlarge their chances of a sweeping career by pleasing their political superiors and running their departments efficiently.

Also Niskanen's assumption that the bureaucracy has an *information monopoly* at its disposal and has in consequence a *decisive influence* on political decision-making, has made many authors take up their pens. From different sides it has been argued that the bureaucrats neither have the means nor the competence to put the politicians before an all-or-nothing choice. In the end the politicians have the final say as to the authorisation of the budget, not the bureaucrats (Thompson, 1973). When the politicians do not approve of certain budget proposals from the bureaucracy, it does not mean that the bureaucratic output is reduced to zero; the result rather is that the status quo level is being maintained, which will mostly be larger than zero (Romer and Rosenthal, 1978). Moreover, it is in the politicians' power to lay down the rules of the game for the negotiations between the bureaucracy and themselves, and to determine in which mould the exchange of information is cast (Miller and Moe, 1983). Experimental research by Eavey and Miller (1984) suggests that an information monopoly combined with control over the agenda indeed may give the bureaucracy a lead in the negotiations, but surely does not fully define the outcome.

It has further been contested from various sides that the bureaucracy takes up a monopoly position with respect to cost information, respectively that it can or will take an unfair advantage of this position. Thompson (1973) argues that when politicians are not informed about the real cost function, they are able to estimate it subjectively, by assuming, as we did in section 6.2.1, that marginal costs are constant. When they proceed in this manner, they will more likely end up in the neighbourhood of the political than of the bureaucratic optimum; see also Miller and Moe (1983). Information will furthermore, according to Thompson (1973), irrevocably ooze through to politicians as a result of the rivalry among bureaucrats as to the available top positions and the competition between departments to acquire certain parcels of the total bunch of public sector activities. Breton and Wintrobe (1975) have drawn attention to the fact that if politicians feel that they are insufficiently informed by the bureaucracy, they could unfold initiatives to get it elsewhere. Think of calling in external consultancy firms, asking offers from rival firms in the private sector, organising public hearings on the bureaucracy's performance by parliament or Congress, inspection of the bureaucracy's facilities, and the use of 'watchdog' organizations like the General Accounting Office in the US. Only in the extreme case of such information and monitoring devices being prohibitively expensive do Breton and Wintrobe agree with Niskanen's conclusion. In their view the outcome of the negotiations between bureaucrats and politicians will generally be a budget coinciding with the political equilibrium increased by the amount for which it is uneconomic to have audits. In this connection it has been noted by Niskanen (1975) that information on the costs of government provisions is for politicians a (pure) public good. Individual politicians will therefore not be inclined to spend much time and effort in collecting information outside the regular bureaucratic channels, and certainly not if it means that they should curtail the political and ombudsman services to the constituency on which they depend for their reelection; see also Fiorina and Noll (1978). At the same time it can be expected that that same constituency will interfere with its representative(s) at the time the inefficiencies in the bureaucratic government organisation become too ostentatious (McCubbins and Schwartz, 1984). Bendor, Taylor and Van Gaalen (1985), finally, point to the importance of the element of uncertainty. Bureaucrats do not have perfect insight into the budget-output-function; the composition of the representative bodies is, after all, regularly subject to changes due to recurring elections. And they cannot fully rely upon politicians being completely deprived of information on the real cost curve. As a result risk-averse bureaucrats might well be less inclined to deceive the politicians than Niskanen's model would make us believe.

6.2.5 *Results of empirical research*

In the previous sections several hypotheses regarding the influence of bureaucrats have been examined. First, the hypothesis of Niskanen and Galbraith according to which bureaucratic inefficiency is essentially economic and manifests itself in a too large volume of outputs. Second, Williamson's hypothesis which states that bureaucratic inefficiency is technical in nature and is shown by a waste of inputs, especially of staff. These two hypotheses contrast with a third one to which we could link the names of Thompson and Breton and Wintrobe, which contends that bureaucratic inefficiency either does not exist at all or is relatively unimportant. Empirical research must determine which of these hypotheses is right. However, so far such studies have been fragmentary.

The first question studies must answer is whether, independent of possible economic inefficiency, *technical inefficiency* occurs. Technical inefficiency can be proved by cost-effectiveness studies. Such studies regard policy aims as given; they are concerned solely with the costs of achieving these aims. On the basis of a comparative analysis of over 50 studies, for the larger part referring to the US, of the relationship between the costs and the effectiveness of autobus services, airlines, electric utilities, refuse collection, water supply, etc., Mueller (1989, pp. 261–6) observes that in over 40 studies public firms tend to be significantly less efficient than private firms supplying the same service. Previously, Orzechowski (1977, p. 248) concluded on account of a similar comparison: 'These studies show that public agencies operate at costs above private alternatives and exhibit slow or negative changes in productivity.' Technical inefficiency thus appears to be present in the governmental bureaucracy. The importance of the element of competition is underlined by Caves and Christensen (1980), who analysed the productivity of two Canadian railroad companies, of which one is in private and the other in public hands. Under the ruling competitive regime the public company appears to operate as efficiently as the private one: 'any tendency toward inefficiency resulting from public ownership has been overcome by the benefits of competition' (p. 958).

The second question investigation must answer is whether *economic inefficiency* can be found in addition to technical inefficiency. This question can never be answered by cost-effectiveness studies because such studies regard policy aims, i.e. the outputs, as given. In a cost-benefit analysis based on welfare economics, policy objectives are not given but are unknowns dependent on the joint welfare of the individuals. Such cost-benefit analysis will thus be able to provide a conclusion as to the degree of over-expansion of bureaucratic output. However, as far as we know, no cost-benefit studies have yet been made to demonstrate in particular the Niskanen-effect.

Research results which, more in general, indicate that it is likely that the bureaucracy has an influence on the size of the budget, can be found in Niskanen (1975) and Beck (1981). McGuire (1981), on the other hand, presents some empirical findings which do not fit Niskanen's model of section 6.2.3, at least not in a strict interpretation.

6.3 Bureaucracy and social welfare

6.3.1 Contraction or expansion?

The fact that the bureaucratic optimum differs from the political optimum does not necessarily mean that the former differs from the social welfare optimum. In section 5.4 we concluded that politicians in a two-party system who maximise their votes will achieve a Paretian optimum provided that political competition is perfect and that political information is complete. However, in point of fact, the political optimum will differ from the social welfare optimum because all conditions are rarely met. There are conflicting views on the nature of this difference.

On the strength of what was said in section 5.4.3 about it being difficult in a democracy to pursue a policy when the benefits will only become visible in the future, Downs concludes that the public sector of the economy in a democratic system will always be too small, i.e. smaller than the voter would choose if he were fully informed. Galbraith (1965) reached a similar conclusion; he claimed that the larger firms persuade the consumer, against his own interest, to concentrate on improving his present standard of living. The manipulation of information in advertising upsets the balance between the public and private sectors in Western economies and contrasts private wealth and public poverty ever more sharply.

The left-hand side of figure 6.3 illustrates the hypotheses of Downs and of Galbraith. The bureaucratic tendency to expand provides a valuable counter-weight to the short-sighted policies of politicians in respect of the size of the budget. If and when politicians and

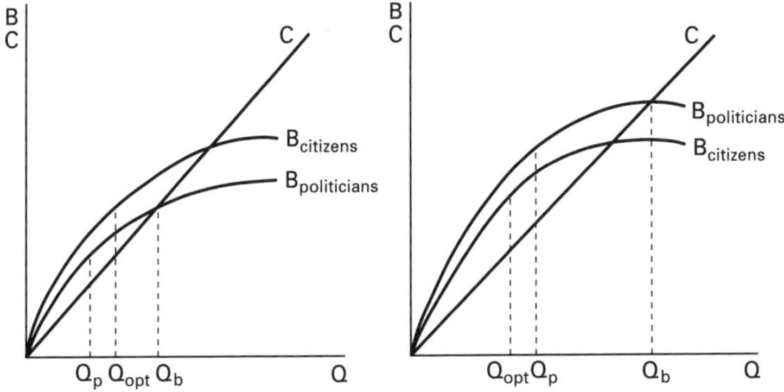

Figure 6.3 Budget, total costs and bureaucratic output
B = size of budget
C = total costs
Q = level of bureaucratic output
Q_{opt} = social welfare optimum
Q_p = political optimum
Q_b = bureaucratic optimum

bureaucrats are able to negotiate from positions of equal strength, these negotiations could result in a social welfare optimum.[4]

Drees' conclusions, however, are the exact opposite (Drees, 1955, pp. 61–71). In his opinion, the public sector in a democracy is too big, not too small. We have already pointed out in section 5.4.3 that political power which is the result of a reduction in political competition, causes the political parties to avoid conflicts about the costs of public goods. In our view this happens only when elections are unlikely to be held, but Drees maintains that it is a constant phenomenon. He claims that the way in which parliament behaves with respect to the budget depends largely on the dominating role of specialists who play down the costs of the public goods they advocate and concentrate on the benefits which would accrue to the voter.[5]

Drees' hypothesis is depicted on the right-hand side of figure 6.3. The mere paternalistic behaviour of politicians leads to a higher than optimum budget. The budget will become even higher if the bureaucrats have negotiation power. The positions desired by both politicians and bureaucrats lead away from optimum social welfare in the same direction. Put differently, the contra-optimal behaviour of politicians and of bureaucrats reinforce each other.

6.3.2 Private firms

One of the most common mistakes in the theory of economic systems is the rejection of a specific structure because it is not an optimum, without considering the extent to which the alternative structure is one. Those who make this mistake can be compared to judges in a beauty contest who, after having seen the first candidate, immediately crown the second. Thus, before discarding bureaucracy as an organisation, it must be compared with its alternatives.

Niskanen (1971, pp. 59–65 and 81–6) and Williamson (1975) compared the methods of coordination of bureaucracy and the market. Niskanen's conclusions especially are relevant to our argument. He says that the cabinet should get different and competing private firms to produce the public goods – in so far as the indivisibility of these goods allows this – and sell them to the cabinet at a price.[6]

We shall give Niskanen's analysis in our own words. A private firm is faced with a demand function similar to equation (2) given in section 6.2.1. A new element, however, is that the politicians now will demand so many units of the good until the marginal benefits (W) of the last unit are equal to the market price (P) so that the demand equation reads:

$$(2') \; P = a - 2b.Q.$$

The total revenue (R) of the firm, of course, equals the turnover in money terms:

$$(1') \; R = P.Q = a.Q - 2b.Q^2.$$

In respect of total costs (C) we shall, for the sake of presentation, continue with the previous simple assumption:

$$(3') \; C = c.Q,$$

such that marginal costs are constant:

$$(4') \; MC = c.$$

In respect of the objective function of private firms, Niskanen assumes that such firms maximise their profits. This is undoubtedly so in conditions of perfect competition. However, in the production of public goods there are often economies of scale which can only be obtained in a monopolistic market (see, e.g. Bohm, 1987, pp. 46–9 or Stiglitz, 1988, pp. 185–7). Perfect competition in the production of public goods seems a contradiction in terms and thus runs counter to reality where monopoly, oligopoly or monopolistic competition are

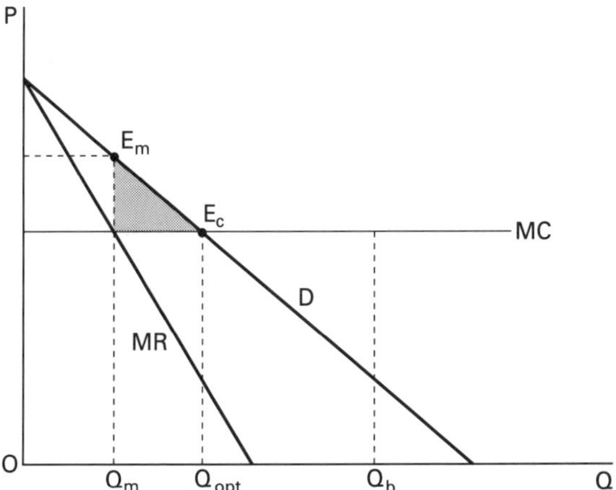

Figure 6.4 Private firms: industry equilibrium under perfect competition and monopoly
Q = level of output
P = price per unit
D = demand curve
MR = marginal revenue curve
MC = marginal cost curve
Q_m = optimum of a profit maximising monopoly
Q_{opt} = social welfare optimum
Q_b = bureaucratic optimum

more likely. This also means that the assumption that private firms seek to maximise their profits can no longer be maintained. In the first place, the type of market does not force this behaviour. In the second place, large monopolistic firms are bureaucratic, i.e. they are composed of a number of hierarchical departments which may maximise their output. Niskanen, to quote Nove (1961, p. 22), compares 'muddle with model': he makes the mistake of comparing the reality of a bureaucracy with an imaginary model of the market economy. To avoid making the same mistake as Niskanen, we shall assume that a number of aims is possible, not only maximum profits but also maximum output. The consequences of this model are shown in figure 6.4.

Irrespective of whether a firm is operating under perfect competition, it will, if it is trying to *maximise profits* (R − C), expand its output until its marginal costs equal its marginal revenue. The degree of competition, however, influences the marginal revenue.

In conditions of *perfect competition*, the firm will regard the market price as given. In this case the market price equals marginal revenue. Individual firms will increase sales until marginal costs equal the market price. Consequently, the point of equilibrium for the whole industry lies where the marginal cost curve cuts the demand curve. Figure 6.4 shows that in perfect competition the point of equilibrium lies at E_c, where $Q=(a-c)/2b$. In a perfect democracy this point is also the point of optimum welfare, because consumer surplus is at its maximum here.

The outcome is different when competition is restricted. In the extreme case of one supplier (*monopoly*), the demand curve for the firm will coincide with the demand curve for the industry. Market price and marginal revenue will no longer coincide so that there is a separate marginal revenue function (MR):

$$(5') \ MR=dR/dQ=a-4b.Q.$$

It follows from equation (5') that the MR curve must be drawn to the left of the demand curve; see figure 6.4. The firm will increase its output until its marginal cost curve cuts its marginal revenue curve. In this case equilibrium is at E_m where $Q=(a-c)/4b$. Whereas a government department in this simplified model wants to produce twice as many public goods as would be the social welfare optimum, a profit-maximising monopoly would like to produce only half that optimum. Production by a bureaucratic department means that the loss of social welfare (seen partially) would be so large that the whole surplus would vanish. The loss of social welfare when a private monopoly maximises profits would be less, namely it would equal the shaded area of the right-angled triangle with E_m and E_c on its hypotenuse.

The loss of social welfare will be neutralised as soon as the monopoly *maximises* not its profits but *the level of its output* (Q) provided that the revenues are sufficient to cover costs ($R \geq C$). Such a firm will try to find the point at which total costs equal revenue. In figure 6.4 this coincides with the social welfare optimum. A monopoly maximising its output therefore attempts to produce the same quantity as a firm maximising profits in perfect competition.[7]

The conclusion is that the output of private firms in this model equals or is less than the optimum. A private firm, however, achieves its optimum with a smaller social welfare loss than a government department. The cause of this difference lies in the price the politicians (and in fact the voters) must pay for the marginal unit of a public good. In the model, the firm sells a public good *per unit*. The price the politicians or the voters pay to a firm for the marginal unit in that case is never higher than the marginal benefits. As soon as the marginal costs exceed the marginal benefits, the politicians or the voters will no longer buy the marginal unit. But a government department does not sell a public good per unit but negotiates about the *total* supply of that good. The bureaucrats can give the politicians the choice between all or nothing and thus force them to buy the marginal units at a loss.

Yet in European countries the implementation of government decisions by private firms is an exception rather than the rule. For a shift from the private to the public sector can also mean a redistribution of income from profits to wages and salaries. In chapter 2 we noted that the economic norm contained in the Pareto criterion must always be weighed against an ethical norm, e.g. in respect of the income distribution. When production by a private firm satisfying the Paretian optimum is rejected on the grounds of an incomes objective, this is not necessarily irrational.

6.3.3 *Self-management by civil servants*

In our view the fact that bureaucracy does not work at an optimum can ultimately be explained by two factors – on the one hand the aims of leading bureaucrats, on the other, the possibility of realising these aims which results from the monopoly position of a department. If remedies are to be found, they must be sought in the removal of these causes. In order to start the discussion on this subject Van den Doel (1973) launched the idea of self-management by civil servants. At the same time Faludi (1973, p. 250), too, had concluded 'that departments formulating programmes, instead of being hierarchically structured, ought to be of a collegiate, self-directing type'. We define the characteristics of self-management by civil servants as follows: (1) all civil servants in a department are equal from an organisational point of view in so far as they choose representatives on a majority vote, who decide on the department's policy and on the appointment of departmental heads; (2) the department is financed exclusively by a budget authorised by the politicians; (3) the politicians negotiate with the departmental representatives about the tasks to be performed for the budget to be provided, and they secure the coordination between the departments; (4) no single department has the exclusive right to provide specific public goods.

If this idea has any value it lies in the fact that the basic characteristics of the model discussed are being extrapolated to the point of absurdity and thus made to reveal their consequences. The fact that the aims of departments are directed at expansion results from the hierarchical structure of a department. The prestige, the salary or the power of the head of the department are increased by raising the output or the budget. Irrespective of idealistic considerations, it is also in his own interests to maximise the output or the budget. The pattern of behaviour of the department in the model changes notably if the hierarchical structure is destroyed. In so far as the civil servants are motivated largely by selfish and not altruistic considerations, the decisions would be made to suit the interests of the lower-ranking rather than of the more senior civil servants. An increase in output (or in the budget) will, however, have different consequences for a lower-ranking civil servant than would have been the case for the person who was previously the head of his department.

An expansion of a department will inevitably mean that the work can no longer be overseen and that there will be a loss of social contacts for lower-ranking civil servants. On the other hand, he can benefit in three respects from expansion. First, the number of supervisors per civil servant will grow so that the freedom to pursue his own policy increases (cf. Tullock, 1965). Moreover, lower-ranking civil servants will have more chances of promotion. Finally, the existing amount of work can be divided among more civil servants.

However, in our opinion, many of the advantages of expansion for lower-ranking civil servants will be lost in a model of self-management by civil servants. For a lower-ranking civil servant the gain in policy freedom is wholly compensated by the loss of power because he must share his authority with his colleagues when his section is expanded. In a model of self-management by civil servants, 'promotion' occurs mainly when some civil servants are elected as representatives; it is probable that a civil servant who desires such a 'promotion' will hold up expansion because he fears competition from his new colleagues. When departmental expansion is not expressed in a greater output but in less effort per civil servant, this will be punished in the model of self-management not only by politicians but also by competing departments. 'It may well be that the best of all monopoly profits is a quiet life' (Hicks, 1935, p. 8), and that is precisely what is lost in this self-management model.

The managers appointed by the civil servants will also strive for expansion in a situation of self-management. But within their departments these managers do not possess the monopoly of information about the real cost function. Thus the stimulus to a large departmental expansion will be reduced if it does not disappear altogether.

Vanek (1970) examined the economic consequences of self-management within a firm. In a firm with a hierarchical structure the benefits (in this case the financial benefits) of the production process will primarily be of advantage to the managers and the shareholders. As soon as there is a workers' autonomy, however, the benefits will, in Vanek's model, be shared among all the participants in the firm. A number of hypotheses are possible in respect of a workers' collective in such a situation (Vanek, 1975 pp. 30–2). In a wide but vague conception the workers' collective has many aims as regards income, effort, collective consumption, the environment and community service. In a less wide but more operational conception the members of the workers' collective strive after their own interests, confining themselves largely to matters connected with their income. In this last conception, it is not profit (or output) as such which is maximised but the profit (or output) per worker. However, an increase in profit (or in output) is not possible without an increase in the number of workers. The extra profit must therefore be divided among more workers. This leads Vanek (1970, p. 119) to conclude that a self-managing firm does not tend towards overexpansion: 'Perhaps the most important conclusion is a far less danger of gigantism ... in labor-managed market structures than in just about any other economic regime.' By changing some mathematical equations in Vanek's model, Meade (1972, p. 417) has shown that a lessening of the tendency to expand is solely the result of the introduction of a cooperative element in the aims.

The simple mathematical model which was at the basis of the idea about self-management by civil servants (Van den Doel, 1974; Siccama, 1974) is put into a graph in figure 6.5. The horizontal axis does not give the output (Q) but the number of civil servants (L). The total costs (C) have been split into fixed capital costs (K) and variable wage costs (w.L, with w the remuneration per civil servant). The bureaucratic optimum and the social welfare optimum are found in the same way as in figures 6.2 and 6.3.

A new aspect is the optimum of a system of self-management by civil servants. If we adopt Vanek's less wide but more operational assumption and, moreover, assume that a civil servant is not interested in increasing fixed capital costs, then the civil servants no longer strive to maximise the total budget (or total output) but maximise the (for their remuneration) available *budget per civil servant*. That is,

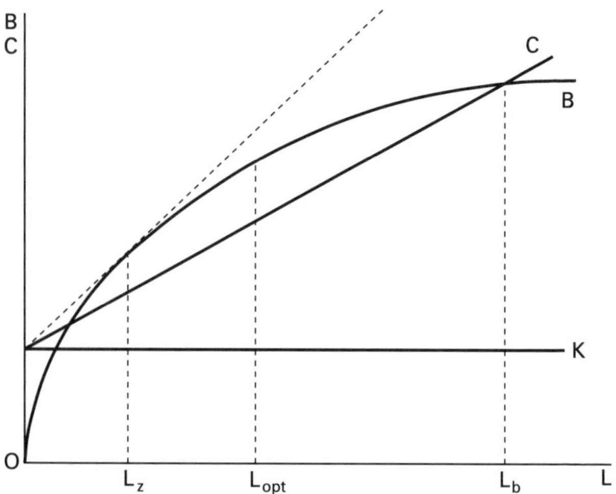

Figure 6.5 Self-management by civil servants without competition
C = total costs
K = fixed capital costs
L = number of civil servants
B = size of budget
L_z = optimum self-management without competition
L_{opt} = optimum social welfare
L_b = bureaucratic optimum

they strive for a maximum value of the quotient $(B-K)/L$ (subject to the condition $B \geq C$). The graph shows that after the establishment of self-management, the civil servants go from one extreme to another.[8] The excessive increase in the output of the hierarchical bureaucracy is succeeded by an excessive *contraction* in the output under self-management. A consequence of the implied aim is that in the short run the present service will, in a situation of self-management, exploit their monopoly to provide relevant services by preventing new colleagues from joining the civil service corps as is normal in professions, e.g. medicine.

This brings us to the second main problem of a bureaucracy, which is the monopoly position each department has. This monopoly position makes it possible for bureaucrats to make politicians choose between all or nothing, thus forcing them to buy their services at a loss.

Political reformers, faced with the power of a bureaucracy, are always trying to solve this problem by making proposals to sharpen the *external control* of the bureaucracy. The organisation of parliament must be improved, members of parliament should concern themselves more with their departments, ministers should give more guidance, an ombudsman should be appointed, a systematic policy analysis should be financed. In our opinion, these measures will have little effect. At the beginning of this chapter we explained why internal control is limited (cf. section 6.1.2). The same arguments apply to the limited effectiveness of external control. It is only by stimulating *competition* between bureaucrats that the foundations of bureaucratic power can be demolished.

It is also for this reason that our fourth characteristic of self-management by civil servants is that no single department should have the exclusive right to provide specific public goods. This means that other departments will have *free entry* or that existing departments can take over the tasks of other departments on condition that the government finances these initiatives. This condition allows a government to pursue a policy of entry which makes it possible to avoid waste from duplication.[9]

Under conditions of perfect competition in the administration, politicians are able to confine their executive task to comparing the various plans drawn up by a number of competing departments and choosing the best. In practice, competition will, however, never be perfect because it is difficult to set up a new bureaucratic department. Yet the possibility that a new department can be set up will work preventively. For fear of a potential competitor the existing departments will be more conducive to the wishes of the politicians. The market for administrative services will no longer be characterised by a bilateral monopoly between the politicians and the bureaucrats, but it will get an asymmetrical structure because the one group of politicians will be able to negotiate with competing departments. In the second characteristic of self-management it is laid down that in such a market structure the politicians will be the sole buyers (monopsony) which will give them a strong bargaining position.

Despite this optimistic conclusion, the significance of the model of self-management by civil servants is largely heuristic. We aimed to show that social welfare can be increased by replacing the traditional hierarchical structure in an administration wholly or in part by an 'entente' organisation such as is sometimes found in hospitals. The model of self-management by civil servants is more revolutionary than the conclusion already drawn by Weber ((1922)1972, pp. 158–9) and since forgotten, that stimulating collegiate management and administrative competition coincides with the pursuit by the public of optimum social welfare.

7 The political process

7.1 The political process as a number of production stages

Whereas chapters 3 to 6 dealt with separate stages of the political process, this chapter will consider the political process as a whole. In a political process the individual voter's demands on, and his support for, the government are converted into government policy, of which, in turn, certain effects are experienced by the individual voter. In our opinion, four methods of decision-making are applied in the course of this process of conversion: negotiation, majority decision, representation, and implementation. We have analysed these four methods of decision-making as independent decision-making models, i.e. as a negotiations democracy, a referendum democracy, a representative democracy and an implementation bureaucracy.

A *negotiations democracy* is the logical basis of every democracy. The basic pattern is split up into the other three decision-making models. In a negotiations democracy each individual is both supplier and demander. Using the method, described by Lindahl, of simultaneous negotiations the individuals reach an agreement. Then they implement this agreement.

A *referendum democracy* specialises in making binding decisions. Negotiations and decision-making are separated. Decision-making is not by way of a contract but by way of taking enforceable majority decisions.

In a *representative democracy* demanders and suppliers are separated. The demanders are private citizens, in their quality of voters or organised in pressure groups. The suppliers have an official function, e.g. elected representatives ('politicians') or bureaucrats.

In an *implementation bureaucracy* a function is once again split up.

A certain category of suppliers, the bureaucrats, now operates independently in respect of another category of suppliers, the politicians.

As is apparent from the description of the four decision-making models, their listing is not arbitrary. When the political process is compared to a branch of industry producing public goods, then this splitting up can be seen as a form of differentiation in which new stages have been added to the production process which links the primary producer to the final consumer.

The order of these decision-making models is not based on history or chronology but purely on logic. We are not concerned with the relative age of the decision-making models. We do not rule out the possibility that bureaucracy is the oldest method of decision-making, nor that historically there has been integration as well as differentiation. Nor are we concerned with the order in which decisions are actually made. We do not rule out the possibility that there is renewed negotiation after representation has been made and that once again a majority decision is made.

We are concerned here with a logical order, as the comparison with the stages of the production process shows. In a political system based on the political power of the voters, which, in principle, is equal, only the negotiations democracy can function as an independent model. All the other models we discussed necessarily contain elements of the preceding model. For example, a referendum democracy cannot exist unless negotiations have taken place on the voting system and the policy consequences of the outcome of the vote. A representative democracy, in turn, contains elements of a referendum democracy. The voters choose their parliament by a majority of votes; the politicians decide on policy by a majority of votes; all these decisions are binding. The examples of logrolling and of Arrow's paradox of voting, which we discussed in the chapter on referendum democracy, were deliberately taken from representative democracy. Last, an implementation bureaucracy cannot exist unless someone gives orders and checks whether these orders have been carried out. In a democratic political system these orders are given not by a dictator but by the masses. It is not possible to compress the multitude of conflicting interests into a single bunch of orders and also to ensure their implementation, unless the voters decide to elect representatives who are specialists in such work.

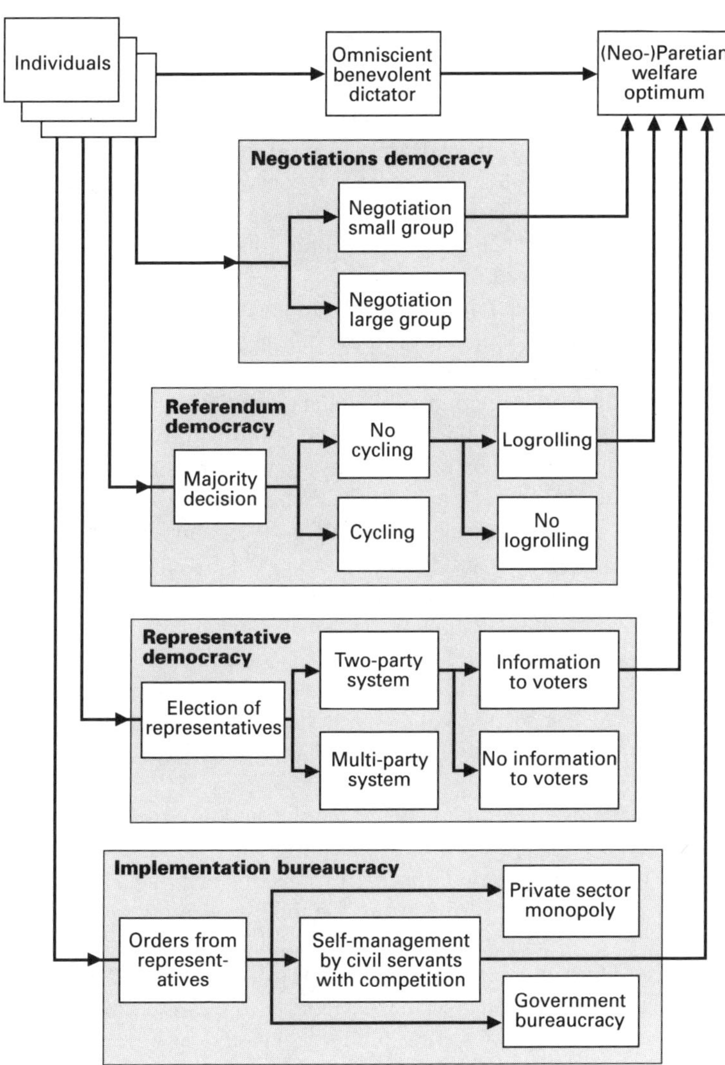

Figure 7.1 A greatly simplified scheme of this book

7.2 The welfare effects of the four decision-making models

In chapter 1 the problem of welfare economics examined in this book was described as the question of what organisation of the political system would provide a policy resulting in an optimum social welfare. Chapters 3 to 6 considered the answer to this question by examining each of the four decision-making models separately. In figure 7.1 the answer is summarised in a greatly simplified, though conveniently arranged form.

As has already been noted, *a negotiations democracy* is characterised by freedom of exit and non-commitment (section 3.1). If the individuals negotiate with each other in *small groups* it is not impossible that all individuals will reach an optimum (section 3.4.1). However, this does not guarantee that an optimum group welfare will always be reached. When negotiations are held on public and quasi-public goods the danger of parasitical behaviour is always present – people will profit from the benefits of public goods but will avoid contributing to their costs. The members of the group can sponge off each other; outsiders can also profit from the group's policy, and vice versa. Thus the small groups will achieve a social welfare optimum only if two conditions are met. The first condition is that selective stimuli are used to make parasitical behaviour within the group unattractive. The second condition is that the effects of the public goods remain limited to the group which negotiates about them (section 3.5.4).

When negotiations are held on public and quasi-public goods within *large groups*, it is practically impossible to achieve a social welfare optimum by way of the institutions of a negotiations democracy. As the members of the group are unable to apply sanctions to each other they will, in normal circumstances, be caught up in a Prisoners' Dilemma – each member of the group is tempted to sponge off the readiness of others to make sacrifices and at the same time he will fear that others will sponge off his generosity. As a result, hardly anyone is prepared to make a sacrifice and the public good will not be produced, not even when everyone very much wants to have it (section 3.5.2). However, an escape from the dilemma is possible when the group members decide democratically (e.g. by referendum or by electing representatives) to accept coercion, but then the institutions of a negotiations democracy will have served their term (sections 3.5.3 and 3.5.8).

In a *referendum democracy* group negotiations result in binding majority decisions without the intervention of representatives (section 4.1.1). The Prisoners' Dilemma of negotiations democracy can now be avoided, but the achievement of an optimum group welfare is threatened by the very high costs of decision-making, which can even mean that the group members leave decision-making to small oligarchies (section 4.1.4). But, also, if the problem of the costs of decision-making is ignored (as was done in figure 7.1), a majority decision can be afflicted by cycling, as a result of Arrow's paradox of voting (section 4.2.2). If cycling does occur, it is impossible to achieve an optimum group policy. Cycling can be avoided by reaching a consensus on the criteria upon which the decision will be based, although it continues to be possible to disagree about the decision itself (section 4.2.6). But, even if cycling is avoided, there is still no guarantee that a welfare optimum will be achieved. Another obstacle will have to be overcome – that of the tyranny of the majority. There are two ways to tackle this. The first is to use logrolling to influence political behaviour as is shown in figure 7.1, so that minorities can exchange their less urgent desires for the realisation of their more urgent desires (section 4.3.3). The second method is to change the political structure by introducing a voting system which takes more account of the urgent desires of minorities (section 4.2.2).

A *representative democracy* is characterised by the election of representatives, thus separating the demanders and suppliers of policy (section 5.1). The high costs of decision-making of a referendum democracy are avoided, but new problems arise in their stead. A social welfare optimum can be realised in the model only when a large number of conditions is met, the most important of which are summarised in section 5.3.5. But here, too, even if these conditions are satisfied, an optimum result cannot be assured. Political competition must be so strong that no one has any political power and the voters must have the requisite information about the costs and benefits of the aims of the political parties. A *multi-party system* cannot satisfy these two requirements. In such a system the parties on the relative left and on the relative right do not compete with each other at all and they compete only partly with the centre parties. They have already achieved an important share of their gains by mobilising their supporters (section 5.3.1). Also, in a multi-party system the political parties do not, before the elections, provide the voters with reliable information about their political views with respect to the coalition to be formed after the election (section 5.3.4). In a *two-party system* this objection does not apply. Both parties compete with each other and each vote captured from the opponent counts twice as much as each vote cast by a supporter. In addition, most voters have information about the strategies of the political parties after the election. However, a two-party system cannot rule out the possibility that, while voters are informed about the views of the parties, they know nothing about the related costs and benefits. If voters are so myopic (i.e. not directed at the future) a social welfare optimum will not be reached in a two-party system either.

An *implementation bureaucracy* is characterised by a hierarchy of bureaucrats, who, though they receive orders from elected representatives, have a certain range of choice in the extent to which they carry out these orders (section 6.1.2). They use this range of choice to exploit fully the preparedness of voters and politicians to accept a certain budget, if necessary, so that the output of the services provided by a bureaucracy in most cases exceeds that which would have been provided by the preferences of the voters and the politicians (section 6.2.2). There is, however, one exception to this conclusion – if the voters are myopic in respect of the future benefits of public goods but are fully informed about their future costs, the expansionist tendencies of bureaucracies can (from the viewpoint of an optimum) provide a valuable counterforce (section 6.3.1). As it is only possible to speculate on the relevance of this exception, we assumed in figure 7.1 that a government bureaucracy does not reach a social welfare optimum. In chapter 6 we examined two alternative methods of implementation on their welfare effects. First, we considered (following Niskanen) a private firm. If such a firm operates within a monopolistic market and also aims at maximising profits, we go from one extreme to another: the too great expansion of services by a government bureaucracy is now exchanged for a too great contraction by a private monopoly. However, figure 7.1 ignores the fact that if a monopolistic firm does not strive after maximum profits but after a maximum output instead, a social welfare optimum does become possible (section 6.3.2). The second alternative for an implementation bureaucracy is described in figure 7.1 as self-management by civil servants. The idea of this model is based on Weber's forgotten conclusion that the stimulation of collegiate management and administrative competition can have a favourable influence on government policy. In this model a social welfare optimum can be achieved if, at least, the four conditions listed in section 6.3.3 are met. Some of these conditions, especially the first one which, in principle, departs from the hierarchic decision-making method, will give many readers the impression of Utopia, so that, for the time being, this model can be given a heuristic value only.

7.3 The public sector: a huge Leviathan?

It was made clear in chapter 2 that if the production of public goods and of goods with public aspects (external effects, income redistribution) is to take place in optimum amounts and at optimum prices, then an institution is needed which is capable of adding the demand curves of individuals. In section 2.3.6 we demonstrated that this could be done by an omniscient and benevolent dictator. This conclusion is neither sensational nor relevant. The problem facing all Western economies is whether the methods of decision-making chosen by the voters themselves (a combination of negotiations, majority decisions, representation by politicians, and bureaucratic implementation) are also capable of realising the policy the same voters desire. In chapter 1, we argued that this problem has become more acute now that between one third and one-half of national income is in one way or another spent via the public sector.

In order to answer this question we conceived the public sector as that branch of industry producing public goods. However, the rate of expansion of this branch has put that of nearly all other industries in the shade. The problem is now whether the level of output and the nature of the products of this industry still comply with the wishes of the consumer.

At first sight it would not seem to matter whether expansion occurs in the production of a private firm or of the public sector. In fact there is, of course, one very important difference: the output of private firms is financed by the consumer and is evaluated in the market process, while the output of the public sector is both financed and evaluated by the political process. The study of the effects on social welfare of the growth of the public sector must therefore be concentrated on a comparison of the market and the political processes in all their aspects. This book cannot do more than just mention the most important points of such a comparison.

It is sometimes argued that the political process, of necessity, satisfies individual preferences to a lesser extent than does the market process because the latter is based on competition whereas the former is dominated by a single monopolist – the government. This idea fails to appreciate the fact that the political process, too, can be based on competition between political parties. According to Schumpeter

((1943)1976, p. 269) a political democracy is nothing else but an institutional arrangement of the decision-making process, in which the politicians acquire the power to decide by means of a competitive struggle for the people's vote. Economic theories of the political process build on this Schumpeterian thesis by regarding the political process, too, as a market process in which the voters are the demanders and the politicians and bureaucrats are the suppliers. One of the important conclusions reached with these theories is that under certain ideal conditions there is an invisible hand, which brings the self-interest of all individuals via the political process into harmony with one other, so that not only is an optimum (individual) utility achieved but also an optimum social (group) welfare. In this book these conditions have been discussed a number of times. In order to remove any misunderstanding we summarise the most important once again:

1. The citizens all have equal political power (section 1.7).
2. When public goods are of value to a large number of individuals, the decisions made democratically on their production and on the contribution to the costs are binding (section 3.5.3).
3. There is certain consensus among the voters about the criteria on the basis of which the decisions must be made, even though it is possible to disagree about the decisions themselves (section 4.2.6).
4. There is perfect competition between the political parties so that they are forced, on pain of liquidation, to strive after the maximisation of their political support by, among other things, implicit logrolling (section 5.4.3).
5. The voters have been informed about the benefits and costs associated with the politicians' plans for the present and the future (section 5.4.3).
6. The politicians have sufficient information about the costs of public goods to enable them to force the bureaucrats to carry out their orders scrupulously (section 6.2.3).

This book in no way wants to suggest that Western economies meet these ideal conditions. By the very formulation of these ideal conditions, insight can be obtained into the imperfect nature of the political process as it functions in the real world. Of course, it is possible to 'internalise' the external effects of public goods via the political process. But at the same time new external effects can be created. When decisions are not binding, many citizens refuse to contribute to the costs of public goods, even of those they strongly desire. When the decisions bind formally, but not materially, the individual contributions to the costs are evaded or shifted. If the decisions also bind materially, the majority will try to get the minority to pay for the public goods it (the majority) desires. When the politicians are not careerists but paternalists and make decisions within a multi-party system, and when they are not faced with elections for a relatively long period, they will add their preferences to those of the voters and will then pass these on to the heads of departments, who will, if the hierarchy is not perfectly arranged, distort preferences again. Without collective action the individuals' utility and social welfare cannot achieve an optimum, but even when there is collective action an optimum is rarely achieved under real conditions.

The important question now arises whether in a real situation the actual provision of public goods falls short of or exceeds the social welfare optimum when the provision is fixed by a political process. An answer to this question can only be given if all stages of the political process are considered in their relation to each other. After all, it is evident that the effect of each stage of the decision-making process on the size of the public sector will be different. We are concerned with the total result of all the stages. This book argues, for example, that two of the decision-making stages result in too small a public sector, and that two other stages lead to too large a public sector:

1. *Negotiations* lead to *too small* a public sector because the government does not decide on the size of wages and other incomes (hypothesis of Van den Doel, section 3.6.2).
2. *Majority decisions* stimulate the development of *too large* a public sector because the majority makes the minority contribute to the costs of those goods from which it (the majority) alone profits (hypothesis of Buchanan and Tullock, section 4.3.2).
3. *Representation*, on the other hand, produces *too small* a public sector because the citizens are informed only about the present costs of public goods and not about their future benefits (hypothesis of Downs and of Galbraith, section 6.3.1).
4. Finally, *implementation* leads to *too large* a public sector because leading bureaucrats strive after expansion (hypothesis of Niskanen, section 6.2.2).

Of course, other hypotheses can also be based on this book. In all cases, however, the size of the public sector is the result of forces which may conflict in the separate stages of the political process.

A large part of the literature has ignored this more differentiated approach. With the exception of Downs, most authors argue on a fairly elementary basis that at present the public sector in many democracies is considerably larger than the optimum. Some, following Hobbes, even conclude that the public sector is a 'Leviathan' which does not guarantee utility and social welfare, but threatens them (e.g. Buchanan, 1975 pp. 147ff.; Taylor, 1976, pp. 129ff.). We have two objections to this conclusion. First, the conclusion is insufficiently argued as we have already tried to show with our analysis of the effects of separate stages in decision-making. Second, such a conclusion could be seen by a scientific and political forum as a recommendation to reduce the size of the public sector in favour of the private sector. However, Buchanan has said clearly that such a recommendation may be made only when, in addition to the public sector, the private sector has been investigated on its social welfare aspects.

When comparing the 'public sector' industry and an arbitrary private sector industry as *ideals*, the public sector always has the advantage that, in contrast to the private sector, it is technically equipped to provide both public and private goods. When comparing the *reality* of the public and private sectors of industry the only possible conclusion is that the two sectors produce under circumstances of unequal power and imperfect competition, so that neither makes full use of the possibility of meeting the preferences of the consumers. Most market structures in the private sector are characterised by monopolistic conditions, incomplete information, shortsightedness and a slow adjustment to changing circumstances. In democratic decision-making in a large group all the forms of parasitical behaviour discussed above (exploitation by voters of each other, by the majority of minorities, by politicians of citizens, and by bureaucrats of politicians) are possible unless some changes in this democratic process are accepted democratically. Among other things, these changes can concern the acceptance of government coercion when fixing wages and other incomes; the strengthening of the two-party system; and the stimulation of collegiate management and administrative competition within the bureaucratic government organisation.

As the authors of this book, we do not draw the conclusion that these changes *must* be made. We do not regard welfare economics as a normative but as a positive science (section 2.2.3). Everyone is therefore fully within his rights not to accept the application of the welfare economist's conclusion for either ethical or distributional reasons. The conclusion of this book is only that, under favourable circumstances, the democratic decision-making procedure is able to realise the ideal of an optimum social welfare to a reasonable extent.

Notes

1 Economics and politics

1 Apart from this book the reader can find surveys of – important parts of – this literature in Riker and Ordeshook (1973), Frey (1978), Alt and Chrystal (1983), McLean (1986), Van Velthoven (1989) and Mueller (1989).

For completeness' sake it should be added that within political science a somewhat related approach has been developing in the past decade, the so-called political-institutional school, which is also interested in the interaction between economics and politics, tries to integrate economic and sociological elements in the analysis of the political system and the effects of government policy, and pays ample attention to the role of institutions. The methodology, however, is quite different, most notably because of the rejection of the postulate of methodological individualism. See, e.g., Keman and Lehner (1984), Scharpf (1987).

2 For an extensive discussion of this and other definitions of the concept of power, the reader is referred to the various contributions in Barry (1976).

2 Welfare and welfare optimum

1 Nevertheless it could be useful for a further elaboration of the theory to pay explicit attention to the learning and evolutionary processes in question. Cf. Thaler (1987), Mueller (1986), Opp (1985), who plead in favour of such an approach.

2 The question of whether the line ABC in figure 2.1 which resulted from the graphical representation of the consumer surplus can be equated to the demand curve, and conversely, whether an area under the demand curve which is shaded as in figure 2.1 can be equated to consumer surplus, has been much debated in the literature. The condition for this equality is that the so-called income effect is negligible. That is the case if the good takes up only a modest part of the total budget and/or if the income elasticity of the demand for the good is relatively small. Economists often tend to neglect

this income effect in practical applications anyhow because of problems with the quantification. For a thorough discussion of these matters the reader can be referred to Boadway and Bruce (1984, pp. 199–205, 216–19).

It should be observed that the said controversy is of no further importance for our purpose (we shall not set out empirically to measure the consumer surplus), so that we indeed shall equate the line ABC to the demand curve.

3 Notice that the area of this quadrilateral A′BCP exactly equals the sum of the areas of the triangles A″C″P and A′C′P, because D^{a+b} is the horizontal addition of D^a and D^b.

4 Notice that the area of this quadrilateral ABC'P is equal to the sum of the areas PC″q^bO and A′C′P, because D^{a+b} is the vertical addition of D^a and D^b.

3 Negotiation

1 Graphically seen S^b then is the vertical difference between MC and D^b.

2 Notice how by the construction of S^b, being the difference between MC and D^b, the line segment BC is as long as the line segment $Q_{opt}A$. The contribution of b in the purchase of canons, $P - p^a$, can on the one hand be read in the figure as the difference between the line segments $Q_{opt}C$ and $Q_{opt}A$, hence the line segment AC but, on the other, also as the difference between the line segments $Q_{opt}C$ and BC, hence the line segment $Q_{opt}B$. Clearly, the marginal benefits for b of extra canons between q^b and Q_{opt} are indeed higher than his contribution p^b, as indicated by the length of the line segment $Q_{opt}B$.

3 Through the construction of S^a, being the difference between MC and D^a, the length of the line segment $Q_{opt}B$ is equal to the length of line segment AC. The contribution of A in the costs, namely $P - p^b$, on the one hand is given by the difference between line segments $Q_{opt}C$ and $Q_{opt}B$, namely the line segment BC but, on the other, also by the difference between the line segments $Q_{opt}C$ and AC, namely the line segment $Q_{opt}A$. See also footnote 2.

4 That both negotiation processes will lead to the same outcome is a result of the fact that we again have not considered the so-called income effects (see section 2.3.4).

However, such income effects can occur depending on the route being taken during the negotiations. On the left-hand side of figure 3.1, for example, b fully pays for the *first* q^b units and contributes $p^b = P - p^a$ for the *extra* units between q^b and Q_{opt}; at the right side, on the other hand, b pays a contribution p^b for *all* units up to Q_{opt}. The rest of his income and his individual welfare level will be smaller in the first case than in the second. The reverse holds for person a. Such income effects could have consequences for the marginal valuation of the good, in other words, for the positioning of D^a and D^b. Shifts of D^a and D^b would make figure 3.1 very unclear, without – by the way – adding anything worthwhile to the analysis. Then, too, the negotiators would meet at the intersection of the relevant S and D curves. Furthermore, the conclusion (see the next paragraph in the text) that the outcome of the negotiation process is a Pareto optimum remains unchallenged. At the most, the amount belonging to the equilibrium would be a little higher or lower; see Buchanan (1968).

5 It should be noted that in game theory, a distinction is made between cooperative and non-cooperative games. In a cooperative game, an external mechanism exists through which agreements and obligations are made binding and can be enforced. Such does not exist in a non-cooperative game. Cooperative game theory concentrates on the group and the distribution problem: which coalition of players will be formed and how will the surplus be divided. Non-cooperative game theory emphasises the individual. Agreements between players only make sense if they are self-enforcing, that is to say when it is optimal for each player to keep to the agreement as long as the others will do so. Because freedom of exit and non-commitment are the starting point of the discussion in this chapter, the discussion will be limited to non-cooperative games.

6 For reasons of clarity, it should be remarked that the combinations (1;4) and (4;1) are also Pareto-optimal. Combination (2;2) clearly is not, because there is a combination (3;3) in which both players are better off.

7 Olson's analysis of the decision by individual members in a large group of whether or not to participate in collective action (see section 3.3.1) can also be formulated as a Prisoners' Dilemma Game. What holds for public goods in general, holds also for participation in particular. Up to a certain extent, participation too is a public good: the participant cannot exclude certain citizens from the effects of his participation, nor can those citizens exclude themselves from those effects. When one citizen participates, the effects are, therefore, open to other citizens.

8 In the example, other topics could be analysed. One example is a federal state in which two (or more) of the member states solve collective problems without coercion and based upon mutual agreement (including agreement about the distribution of the costs), like the construction of a national airport, a sea-wall, or the maintenance of national defence.

9 Other elements can also be important. Repeating Axelrod's computer experiments, Donninger (1986) shows that in a somewhat differently picked outcome matrix and a different set of possible strategies, Tit-for-Tat no longer has to be the most successful strategy in a Repeated Prisoners' Dilemma Game. More specifically, it might be profitable to take a not-so-nice, non-cooperative strategy.

4 Majority decision

1 This information is derived from *Relatie kiezers-beleidsvorming, referendum en volksinitiatief. Eindrapport van de staatscommissie inzake de relatie kiezers-beleidsvorming*, Staatsuitgeverij, 's-Gravenhage, 1985.

Some countries have an advisory referendum (Sweden for instance) or a people's initiative in which the final decision is made by parliament (like Italy and Austria). In these cases, one cannot speak of a referendum democracy because the final decision is not made by the electorate.

In addition to the national level Switzerland also has different kinds of referendum and people's initiatives on the local and the cantonal level.

2 As described in section 2.3.2, such jealousy effects and ideas about a just income distribution can be included in the individual welfare functions. In so far as that has happened and those effects and ideas have been taken into account when assessing whether or not a Pareto improvement occurred, the objections mentioned so far of course do not hold. See also Hennipman (1977, p. 239).

3 Cf. section 3.4.1, especially figure 3.1 and note 4. For the distribution of the (total) cost of canons purchased between the persons a and b, it made a difference who took the initiative.

4 The theoretical proof that under certain conditions all voting procedures can be manipulated has been given by Gibbard (1973) and Satterthwaite (1975). Hence, this proposition is known in the literature as the Gibbard-Satterthwaite theorem. However, this theorem 'not only precludes truth telling always being a dominant strategy, but also systematic lying in the sense of choosing some insincere ordering' (De Bruin, 1991, p. 187). See also Kelly (1988, pp. 101–18).

5 At a symmetrical and unimodal distribution mode and median coincide. At an asymmetrical and/or multi-peaked distribution, this does not need to be the case.

5 Representation

1 In so far as the election has no reference to parties but to persons, one should henceforth read candidates instead of political parties.

2 It has been observed in section 4.2.3 that, even if it is possible to vote strategically, it need not be profitable for an individual to state his own preferences falsely without sufficient information on the voting behaviour of others. That is why Barry (1970, p. 124) concludes that it is rational in a multi-party system to vote for the party of the own preference, 'for this *is* in general to increase the probability that the policies you prefer will be put into effect'.

3 This problem is the stronger in a multi-party system when none of the parties obtains a majority position and a coalition must be formed, with all its inevitable policy compromises.

4 For surveys of this – extensive – literature the reader can be referred to Kiewiet and Rivers (1984), Schneider (1984), Van Velthoven (1989, pp. 42–52), Schram (1991, pp. 9–21).

5 Such coalitions have been denoted as 'closed coalitions of minimal range' or 'minimal connected winning coalitions'. See, for the political theory of coalition formation, apart from De Swaan (1973), also Riker (1962), Van Winden (1984), Laver and Shepsle (1990).

6 When the parties are satisfied with achieving a single majority and do not strive for an optimal election outcome, McKelvey's (1979) result, mentioned in section 5.3.5, that cycling can occur through the whole political space, remains in force.

6 Implementation

1 This political optimum can be calculated by maximising the difference between B and C. From the equations (1) and (3) it follows: $B-C=-bQ^2+(a-c)Q$. Differentiating with respect to Q yields: $d(B-C)/dQ=-2bQ+(a-c)$. To determine the maximum this first derivative has to be set equal to zero, which implies $Q=(a-c)/(2b)$.

The political optimum can also be calculated – which, for that matter, comes to the same thing – by equating W and MC. From the equations (2) and (4) it follows: $W=MC$ if $a-2bQ=c$. The latter condition is satisfied if $Q=(a-c)/(2b)$.

2 The bureaucratic optimum can be calculated by equating B and C. From the equations (1) and (3) it follows that $B=C$ if $-bQ^2+(a-c)Q=0$. The latter equation has two solutions which correspond with the two intersections of B and C: either $Q=0$, or $Q=(a-c)/b$. From the figure it is obvious that only the second intersection yields a maximum budget. The bureaucratic optimum thus is reached at $Q=(a-c)/b$.

3 Economists discern two kinds of inefficiency, namely, technical and economic inefficiency. The first is also called productive or X-inefficiency, the second allocative inefficiency. As is apparent from the text, technical inefficiency is said to occur if a level of output is not produced at minimum costs. Economic inefficiency is said to occur if the size and/or the composition of the production does not correspond with the social welfare optimum.

4 The social welfare optimum, cf. section 2.3.6, is reached if the total marginal benefits of the citizens equal the marginal costs or, in other words, if the difference between the total benefits and the total costs (i.e. the consumer surplus) is at its maximum.

5 See also Niskanen (1971, pp. 138ff.), who analyses the situation that all budget proposals are extensively discussed and amended in committees, before they are put before the plenary assembly for a final vote. He assumes that, 'The committees for each service are dominated by representatives with the *highest* relative demand for the service' (p. 139). See further Miller and Moe (1983).

6 Observe that even if public goods are characterised by indivisibilities in the sphere of *consumption* (for instance, in the case of defence, lighthouses, a sea-wall; see section 2.3.3), it is not necessarily excluded that the *production* is put out to contract to private industry, say the firm asking the lowest price. Combat airplanes and tanks, lighthouses and dikes are mostly built by private firms.

7 The conclusion that the optimum for the output maximising monopoly is

exactly equal to the social welfare optimum, is due to our simplifying assumption with regard to the cost function; see equation (3′). When the cost function has the more general form $C = c.Q + d.Q^2$, the two optima will no longer coincide. The optimal level of output of the output maximising monopoly will then in general be larger than the social welfare optimum, but always *smaller* than the bureaucratic optimum. The latter result is what really counts for our argument.

8 That L_z represents the optimum position under self-management by civil servants can be seen as follows. For each L one can draw an auxiliary line from the corresponding point on the budget line B to the point K on the vertical axis. Then look at the angle between this (auxiliary) line and the horizontal fixed capital costs line K. The tangent of this angle or, differently said, the slope of the auxiliary line, is equal to $(B - K)/L$. To maximise the quotient $(B - K)/L$ one should thus find the auxiliary line with the largest angle towards the fixed capital costs line. If we try so, we come out at L_z.

9 Bendor (1985) has shown with a number of examples that duplication, apart from the disadvantage of potential waste, can also have advantages, such as a lower chance of total failure and more competition.

References

Alesina, Alberto, and Jeffrey Sachs, 'Political parties and the business cycle in the United States, 1948–1984', *Journal of Money, Credit, and Banking*, vol. 20, 1988, pp. 63–82.

Alt, James E., and K. Alec Chrystal, *Political economics*, Wheatsheaf Books, Brighton, 1983.

Ames, E., *Soviet economic processes*, Irwin, Homewood Ill., 1965.

Aranson, Peter H., and Peter C. Ordeshook, 'Regulation, redistribution and, public choice', *Public Choice*, vol. 37, 1981, pp. 69–100.

Arrow, Kenneth J., *Social choice and individual values*, Wiley, New York, 1951; 2nd edition, Yale University Press, New Haven/London, 1963.

Axelrod, Robert, *The evolution of cooperation*, Basic Books, New York, 1984.

Barry, Brian, *Sociologists, economists and democracy*, Collier-Macmillan, London, 1970.

Barry, Brian (ed.), *Power and political theory. Some European perspectives*, Wiley, London/New York, 1976.

Beck, John H., 'Budget-maximizing bureaucracy and the effects of state aid on school expenditures', *Public Finance Quarterly*, vol. 9, 1981, pp. 159–82.

Bendor, Jonathan, *Parallel systems. Redundancy in government*, University of California Press, Berkeley and Los Angeles, 1985.

Bendor, Jonathan, Serge Taylor and Roland van Gaalen, 'Bureaucratic expertise versus legislative authority: a model of deception and monitoring in budgeting', *American Political Science Review*, vol. 79, 1985, pp. 1041–60.

Berg, Sven, 'Paradox of voting under an urn model: the effect of homogeneity', *Public Choice*, vol. 47, 1985, pp. 377–87.

Berg, Sven, and Bo Bjurulf, 'A note on the paradox of voting: anonymous preference profiles and May's formula', *Public Choice*, vol. 40, 1983, pp. 307–16.

Bergson, Abram, 'A reformulation of certain aspects of welfare economics', *Quarterly Journal of Economics*, vol. 52, 1938, pp. 310–34. Reprinted in Kenneth J. Arrow and Tibor Scitovsky, *Readings in welfare economics*, Irwin, Homewood Ill., 1969, pp. 7–25.

Black, Duncan, *The theory of committees and elections*, Cambridge University Press, Cambridge, 1958.

Blydenburgh, John C., 'The closed rule and the paradox of voting', *Journal of Politics*, vol. 33, 1971, pp. 57–71.

Boadway, Robin W., and Neil Bruce, *Welfare economics*, Basil Blackwell, Oxford, 1984.

Bohm, Peter, *Social efficiency. A concise introduction to welfare economics*, Macmillan, Basingstoke/London, 2nd edition, 1987.

Brams, Steven J., and Peter C. Fishburn, *Approval voting*, Birkhäuser, Boston, 1983.

Brennan, Geoffrey, and James M. Buchanan, *The reason of rules. Constitutional political economy*, Cambridge University Press, Cambridge, 1985.

Breton, Albert, and Ronald Wintrobe, 'The equilibrium size of a budget-maximizing bureau: a note on Niskanen's theory of bureaucracy', *Journal of Political Economy*, vol. 83, 1975, pp. 195–207.

Buchanan, James M., *The demand and supply of public goods*, Rand McNally, Chicago, 1968.

The limits of liberty. Between anarchy and Leviathan, University of Chicago Press, Chicago/London, 1975.

'Towards the simple economics of natural liberty: an exploratory analysis', *Kyklos*, vol. 40, 1987, pp. 3–20.

Buchanan, James M., and Wm. Craig Stubblebine, 'Externality', *Economica*, N.S. vol. 29, 1962, pp. 371–84. Reprinted in Kenneth J. Arrow and Tibor Scitovsky (eds.), *Readings in welfare economics*, Irwin, Homewood Ill., 1969, pp. 199–212.

Buchanan, James M., and Gordon Tullock, *The calculus of consent. Logical foundations of constitutional democracy*, The University of Michigan Press, 1962.

Campbell, Angus, Philip E. Converse, Warren E. Miller and Donald E. Stokes, *The American voter*, Wiley, New York, 1960.

Caves, Douglas W., and Laurits R. Christensen, 'The relative efficiency of public and private firms in a competitive environment: the case of Canadian railroads', *Journal of Political Economy*, vol. 88, 1980, pp. 958–76.

Cebula, Richard J., and Dennis R. Murphy, 'The Electoral College and voter participation rates: an exploratory note', *Public Choice*, vol. 35, 1980, pp. 185–90.

Coase, Ronald H., 'The problem of social cost', *Journal of Law and Economics*, vol. 3, 1960, pp. 1–44.

Collier, Kenneth, Peter C. Ordeshook and Kenneth Williams, 'The rationally uninformed electorate: some experimental evidence', *Public Choice*, vol. 60, 1989, pp. 3–29.

Comanor, William S., 'The median voter rule and the theory of political choice', *Journal of Public Economics*, vol. 5, 1976, pp. 169–77.

Cooter, Robert, and Thomas Ulen, *Law and economics*, Scott, Foresman and Company, Glenview Ill./London, 1988.

Cornes, Richard, and Todd Sandler, *The theory of externalities, public goods, and club goods*, Cambridge University Press, Cambridge, 1986.

Coughlin, Peter, 'Pareto optimality of policy proposals with probabilistic voting', *Public Choice*, vol. 39, 1982, pp. 427–33.

'Elections and income redistribution', *Public Choice*, vol. 50, 1986, pp. 27–91.

Coughlin, Peter, and Shmuel Nitzan, 'Electoral outcomes with probabilistic voting and Nash social welfare maxima', *Journal of Public Economics*, vol. 15, 1981, pp. 113–21.

Cyert, Richard M., and James G. March, *A behavioral theory of the firm*, Prentice-Hall, Englewood Cliffs NJ., 1963.

Dahl, Robert A., *A preface to democratic theory*, University of Chicago Press, Chicago/London, 1956.

Darvish, Tikva, and Jacob Rosenberg, 'The economic model of voter participation: a further test', *Public Choice*, vol. 56, 1988, pp. 185–92.

Davis, Otto A., Morris H. DeGroot and Melvin J. Hinich, 'Social preference orderings and majority rule', *Econometrica*, vol. 40, 1972, pp. 147–57.

Davis, Otto A., Melvin J. Hinich and Peter C. Ordeshook, 'An expository development of a mathematical model of the electoral process', *American Political Science Review*, vol. 64, 1970, pp. 426–48.

De Bruin, Gert P., *Decision-making on public goods. An exploration into the borderland of politics and economics*, Het Spinhuis, Amsterdam, 1991.

DeMeyer, Frank, and Charles R. Plott, 'The probability of a cyclical majority', *Econometrica*, vol. 38, 1970, pp. 345–54.

De Swaan, Abram, *Coalition theories and cabinet formations*, Elsevier, Amsterdam, 1973.

Donninger, Christian, 'Is it always efficient to be nice? A computer simulation of Axelrod's computer tournament', in Andreas Diekmann and Peter Mitter (eds.), *Paradoxical effects of social behavior. Essays in honor of Anatol Rapoport*, Physica-Verlag, Heidelberg/Wien, 1986, pp. 123–34.

Downs, Anthony, *An economic theory of democracy*, Harper and Row, New York, 1957.

Inside bureaucracy, Little, Brown and Co, Boston, 1967.

Drees, W. Jr., *On the level of government expenditure in the Netherlands after the war*, Stenfert Kroese, Leiden, 1955.

Dror, Yehezkel, *Public policymaking reexamined*, Chandler, San Francisco, 1968.

Dudley, Leonard, 'Foreign aid and the theory of alliances', *Review of Economics and Statistics*, vol. 61, 1979, pp. 564–71.

Dunleavy, Patrick, 'Bureaucrats, budgets and the growth of the state: reconstructing an instrumental model', *British Journal of Political Science*, vol. 15, 1985, pp. 299–328.

Easton, David, *The political system. An inquiry into the state of political science*, Alfred A. Knopf, New York, 1953.

A framework for political analysis, Prentice-Hall, Englewood Cliffs NJ., 1965a.

A systems analysis of political life, Wiley, New York, 1965b.

Eavey, Cheryl L., and Gary J. Miller, 'Bureaucratic agenda control: imposition or bargaining?', *American Political Science Review*, vol. 78, 1984, pp. 719–33.

Elster, Jon, *The cement of society. A study of social order*, Cambridge University Press, Cambridge, 1989.

Enelow, James M., and Melvin J. Hinich, *The spatial theory of voting. An introduction*, Cambridge University Press, Cambridge, 1984.

Erikson, Robert S., 'Economic conditions and the presidential vote', *American Political Science Review*, vol. 83, 1989, pp. 567–73.

Etzioni, Amitai, 'On thoughtless rationality (rules of thumb)', *Kyklos*, vol. 40, 1987, pp. 496–514.

Eucken, Walter, *Die Grundlagen der Nationalökonomie*, Fischer, Jena, 1940.

Faludi, Andreas, *Planning theory*, Pergamon Press, Oxford, 1973.

Farquharson, Robin, *Theory of voting*, Yale University Press, New Haven, 1969.

Fiorina, Morris, 'Short- and long-term effects of economic conditions on individual voting decisions', in D.A. Hibbs Jr. and H. Fassbender (eds.), *Contemporary political economy*, North-Holland, Amsterdam, 1981, pp. 73–100.

Fiorina, Morris P., and Roger G. Noll, 'Voters, bureaucrats and legislators. A rational choice perspective on the growth of bureaucracy', *Journal of Public Economics*, vol. 9, 1978, pp. 239–54.

Foster, Carroll B., 'The performance of rational voter models in recent presidential elections', *American Political Science Review*, vol. 78, 1984, pp. 678–90.

Frey, Bruno S., 'Die ökonomische Theorie der Politik oder die neue politische Okonomie: eine Ubersicht', *Zeitschrift für die gesamte Staatswissenschaft*, vol. 126, 1970a, pp. 1–23.

'Models of perfect competition and pure democracy', *Kyklos*, vol. 23, 1970b, pp. 736–55.

Modern political economy, Martin Robertson, London, 1978.

International Political Economics, Basil Blackwell, Oxford/New York, 1984.

Frey, Bruno S., and Friedrich Schneider, 'An empirical study of politico-economic interaction in the United States', *Review of Economics and Statistics*, vol. 60, 1978, pp. 174–83.

Frohlich, Norman, Joe A. Oppenheimer, Jeffrey Smith and Oran R. Young, 'A test of Downsian voter rationality: 1964 presidential voting', *American Political Science Review*, vol. 72, 1978, pp. 178–97.

Galbraith, John Kenneth, 'The dependence effect and social balance', in

Edmund S. Phelps, *Private wants and public needs*, New York, 2nd edition, 1965, pp. 13–36.

The new industrial state, Hamish Hamilton, London, 1967.

Garman, Mark B., and Morton I. Kamien, 'The paradox of voting: probability calculations', *Behavioral Science*, vol. 13, 1968, pp. 306–16.

Gehrlein, William V., and Peter C. Fishburn, 'The probability of the paradox of voting: a computable solution', *Journal of Economic Theory*, vol. 13, 1976, pp. 14–25.

Gibbard, Allan, 'Manipulation of voting schemes: a general result', *Econometrica*, vol. 41, 1973, pp. 587–601.

Goodhart, C.A.E., and R.J. Bhansali, 'Political economy', *Political Studies*, vol. 18, 1970, pp. 43–106.

Gramlich, Edward M., and Daniel L. Rubinfeld, 'Micro estimates of public spending demand functions and tests of the Tiebout and median-voter hypotheses', *Journal of Political Economy*, vol. 90, 1982, pp. 536–60.

Hardin, Russell, *Collective action*, John Hopkins University Press, Baltimore/London, 1982.

Hayek, F.A., *The road to serfdom*, London, 1944.

Heckathorn, Douglas D., and Steven M. Maser, 'Bargaining and constitutional contracts', *American Journal of Political Science*, vol. 31, 1987, pp. 142–68.

Hennipman, P., *Welvaartstheorie en economische politiek*, Samsom, Alphen aan den Rijn/Brussel, 1977.

Hibbs, Douglas A. Jr., 'Political parties and macroeconomic policy', *American Political Science Review*, vol. 71, 1977, pp. 1467–87.

Hicks, John R., 'Annual survey of economic theory: the theory of monopoly', *Econometrica*, vol. 3, 1935, pp. 1–20.

'The foundations of welfare economics', *Economic Journal*, vol. 49, 1939, pp. 696–712.

Hinich, Melvin J., 'Equilibrium in spatial voting: the median voter is an artifact', *Journal of Economic Theory*, vol. 16, 1977, pp. 208–219.

Hinich, Melvin J., and Peter C. Ordeshook, 'Plurality maximization vs vote maximization: a spatial analysis with variable participation', *American Political Science Review*, vol. 64, 1970, pp. 772–91.

Hirsch, Fred, *Social limits to growth*, Harvard University Press, Cambridge Mass., 1976.

Hirschman, Albert O., *Exit, voice and loyalty: responses to decline in firms, organizations and states*, Harvard University Press, Cambridge Mass., 1970.

Hochman, Harold M., and James D. Rodgers, 'Pareto optimal redistribution', *American Economic Review*, vol. 59, 1969, pp. 542–57.

Hotelling, Harold, 'Stability in competition', *Economic Journal*, vol.39, 1929, pp. 41–57.

Irwin, Galen A., and Jacques Thomassen, 'Issue-consensus in a multi-party system: voters and leaders in the Netherlands', *Acta Politica*, vol. 10, 1975, pp. 389–420.

Irwin, G.A., C. van der Eijk, J.M. van Holsteyn and B. Niemöller, 'Verzuiling, issues, kandidaten en ideologie in de verkiezingen van 1986', *Acta Politica*, vol. 22, 1987, pp. 129–79.

Jamison, Dean T., 'The probability of intransitive majority rule: an empirical study', *Public Choice*, vol. 23, 1975, pp. 87–94.

Johansen, Leif, *Public economics*, North-Holland, Amsterdam, 1965.

Kafoglis, M.Z., *Welfare economics and subsidy programs*, Gainesville Fl., 1962.

Kaldor, Nicholas, 'Welfare propositions and interpersonal comparisons of utility', *Economic Journal*, vol. 49, 1939, pp. 549–52. Reprinted in Kenneth J. Arrow and Tibor Scitovsky, *Readings in welfare economics*, Irwin, Homewood Ill., 1969, pp. 387–9.

Kapteyn, Arie, 'Utility and economics', *De Economist*, vol. 133, 1985, pp. 1–20.

Kelly, Jerry S., *Social choice theory. An introduction*, Springer, Heidelberg/Berlin, 1988.

Keman, Hans, and Franz Lehner, 'Economic crisis and political management: an introduction to the problem of political-economic interdependence', *European Journal of Political Research*, vol. 12, 1984, pp. 121–9.

Kennedy, Gavin, *Burden sharing in NATO*, Duckworth, London, 1979.

Defense economics, Duckworth, London, 1983.

Key, V.O. Jr., *The responsible electorate. Rationality in presidential voting 1936–1960*, The Belknap Press of Harvard University Press, Cambridge Mass., 1966.

Kiewiet, Roderick D., and Douglas Rivers, 'A retrospective on retrospective voting', *Political Behavior*, vol. 6, 1984, pp. 369–93.

Kornai, Janos, *Anti-equilibrium. On economic systems theory and the tasks of research*, North-Holland, Amsterdam, 1971.

Kramer, Gerald H., 'Short-term fluctuations in U.S. voting behavior, 1896–1964', *American Political Science Review*, vol. 65, 1971, pp. 131–43.

'A dynamical model of political equilibrium', *Journal of Economic Theory*, vol. 16, 1977, pp. 310–34.

Krech, David, Richard S. Crutchfield and Egerton L. Ballachey, *Individual in society: a textbook of social psychology*, McGraw-Hill, New York, 1962.

Kreps, David M., Paul Milgrom, John Roberts and Robert Wilson, 'Rational cooperation in the finitely repeated Prisoners' Dilemma', *Journal of Economic Theory*, vol. 27, 1982, pp. 245–52.

Laver, Michael A., and Kenneth A. Shepsle, 'Coalitions and cabinet government', *American Political Science Review*, vol. 84, 1990, pp. 873–90.

Lewis-Beck, Michael S., 'Comparative economic voting: Britain, France, Germany, Italy', *American Journal of Political Science*, vol. 30, 1986, pp. 315–46.

Lindahl, Erik, *Die Gerechtigkeit der Besteuerung*, Lund, 1919. Partly reprinted as 'Just taxation – a positive solution', in Musgrave and Peacock, 1958, pp. 168–76.

Lindbeck, Assar, and Jörgen W. Weibull, 'Balanced-budget redistribution as the outcome of political competition', *Public Choice*, vol. 52, 1987, pp. 273–97.

Lindblom, Charles E., *The policy-making process*, Prentice-Hall, Englewood Cliffs NJ., 1968.

Loasby, Brian J., *Choice, complexity and ignorance: an enquiry into economic theory and the practice of decision-making*, Cambridge University Press, Cambridge, 1976.

Luce, R. Duncan, and Howard Raiffa, *Games and decisions*, Wiley, New York, 1957.

Maizels, A., and M.K. Nissanke, 'Motivations for aid to developing countries', *World Development*, vol. 12, 1984.

Marcus, Gregory B., 'The impact of personal and national economic conditions on the presidential vote: a pooled cross-sectional analysis', *American Journal of Political Science*, vol. 32, 1988, pp. 137–54.

Marx, Karl, and Friedrich Engels, *Manifest der Kommunistischen Partei*, 1848, London. English translation: *The manifesto of the communist league*, 1888, reprinted in Dan N. Jacobs, *The new communist manifesto and related documents*, Harper, New York, 1962.

May, Kenneth O., 'Intransitivity, utility, and the aggregation of preference patterns', *Econometrica*, vol. 22, 1954, pp. 1–13.

McCubbins, Matthew, and Thomas Schwartz, 'Congressional oversight overlooked: police patrols versus fire alarms', *American Journal of Political Science*, vol. 28, 1984, pp. 165–79.

McGuire, Thomas G., 'Budget-maximizing governmental agencies: an empirical test', *Public Choice*, vol. 36, 1981, pp. 313–22.

McKelvey, Richard D., 'General conditions for global intransitivities in formal voting models', *Econometrica*, vol. 47, 1979, pp. 1085–112.

McKinlay, R.D., 'The German aid relationship: a test of the recipient need and the donor interest models of the distribution of German bilateral aid 1961–1970', *European Journal of Political Research*, vol. 6, 1978, pp. 235–57.

McLean, Iain, 'Review article: some recent work in public choice', *British Journal of Political Science*, vol. 16, 1986, pp. 377–94.

Meade, J.E., 'The theory of labour-managed firms and of profit sharing', *Economic Journal*, vol. 82, 1972, pp. 402–28.

Merkies, A.H.Q.M., and A.J. Vermaat, 'De onmacht van een kabinet. Een empirisch onderzoek naar sociaal-economische preferentiefuncties en hun gebruik als welvaartsindicator', *Maandschrift Economie*, vol. 45, 1981, pp. 101–18.

Michels, Robert, *Zur Soziologie des Parteiwesens in der modernen Demokratie*, Alfred Kröner Verlag, Stuttgart, 1911.

Migué, Jean-Luc, and Gérard Bélanger, 'Toward a general theory of managerial discretion', *Public Choice*, vol. 17, 1974, pp. 27–43.

Miller, Gary J., and Terry M. Moe, 'Bureaucrats, legislators, and the size of government', *American Political Science Review*, vol. 77, 1983, pp. 297–322.

Mills, C. Wright, *White collar: the American middle classes*, Oxford University Press, New York, 1951.

Mosley, Paul, *The making of economic policy. Theory and evidence from Britain and the US since 1945*, Wheatsheaf Books, Brighton, 1984.

'The political economy of foreign aid: a model of the market for a public good', *Economic Development and Cultural Change*, vol. 33, 1985, pp. 373–93.

Mueller, Dennis C., 'Rational egoism versus adaptive egoism as fundamental postulate for a descriptive theory of human behavior', *Public Choice*, vol. 51, 1986, pp. 3–23.

Public choice II, Cambridge University Press, Cambridge, 1989.

Mueller, Dennis C., and Peter Murrell, 'Interest groups and the size of government', *Public Choice*, vol. 48, 1986, pp. 125–45.

Murdoch, James C., and Todd Sandler, 'Complementarity, free riding, and the military expenditures of NATO allies', *Journal of Public Economics*, vol. 25, 1984, pp. 83–101.

Murrell, Peter, 'An examination of the factors affecting the formation of interest groups in OECD countries', *Public Choice*, vol. 43, 1984, pp. 151–71.

Musgrave, R.A., and A.T. Peacock, *Classics in the theory of public finance*, Macmillan, London/New York, 1958.

Naylor, Robin, 'A social custom model of collective action', *European Journal of Political Economy*, vol. 6, 1990, pp. 201–16.

Niemi, Richard G., and Herbert F. Weisberg, 'A mathematical solution for the probability of the paradox of voting', *Behavioral Science*, vol. 13, 1968, pp. 317–23.

Niskanen, William A., *Bureaucracy and representative government*, Aldine, Chicago, 1971.

'Bureaucrats and politicians', *Journal of Law and Economics*, vol. 18, 1975, pp. 617–43.

Nordhaus, William D., 'The political business cycle', *Review of Economic Studies*, vol. 42, 1975, pp. 169–90.

Nove, Alec, *The soviet economy. An introduction*, Allen and Unwin, London, 1961.

Nozick, R., *Anarchy, state, and utopia*, Basic Books, New York, 1974.

Olson, Mancur, *The logic of collective action. Public goods and the theory of groups*, Harvard University Press, Cambridge Mass./London, 1965.

The rise and decline of nations. Economic growth, stagflation, and social rigidities, Yale University Press, New Haven/London, 1982.

Olson, Mancur, and Richard Zeckhauser, 'An economic theory of alliances', *Review of Economics and Statistics*, vol. 48, 1966, pp. 266–79. Reprinted in Bruce M. Russett (ed.), *Economic theories of international politics*, Markham, Chicago, 1968, pp. 25–49.

Oneal, John R., 'Testing the theory of collective action. NATO defense burdens 1950–1984', *Journal of Conflict Resolution*, vol. 34, 1990, pp. 426–48.

Oneal, John R., and Mark A. Elrod, 'NATO burden sharing and the forces of change', *International Studies Quarterly*, vol. 33, 1989, pp. 435–56.

Opp, Karl-Dieter, 'Sociology and economic man', *Zeitschrift für die gesamte Staatswissenschaft*, vol. 141, 1985, pp. 213–43.

'Soft incentives and collective action: participation in the anti-nuclear movement', *British Journal of Political Science*, vol. 16, 1986, pp. 87–112.

Ordeshook, Peter C., 'Pareto optimality in electoral competition', *American Political Science Review*, vol. 65, 1971, pp. 1141–5.

'The spatial theory of elections: a review and a critique', in Ian Budge, Ivor Crewe and Dennis Farlie (eds.), *Party identification and beyond: representations of voting and party competition*, Wiley, London, 1976, pp. 285–314.

Ordeshook, Peter C., and Thomas Schwartz, 'Agendas and the control of political outcomes', *American Political Science Review*, vol. 81, 1987, pp. 179–99.

Orzechowski, William, 'Economic models of bureaucracy: survey, extensions, and evidence', in Thomas E. Borcherding (ed.), *Budgets and bureaucrats. The sources of government growth*, Duke University Press, Durham, 1977, pp. 229–59.

Ostrom, Elinor, *Governing the commons. The evolution of institutions for collective action*, Cambridge University Press, Cambridge, 1990.

Pareto, Vilfredo, *Manuale di economia politica*, 1906. French edition: *Manuel d'economie politique*, Paris, 1909. English edition: *Manual of political economy*, New York, 1971.

Parkinson, C. Northcote, *Parkinson's law and other studies in administration*, Ballantine Books, New York, 1957.

Parry, Geraint, George Moyser and Neil Day, *Political participation and democracy in Britain*, Cambridge University Press, Cambridge, 1992.

Pen, J., 'Bilateral monopoly, bargaining and the concept of economic power', in K.W. Rothschild (ed.), *Power in economics*, Penguin, Harmondsworth, 1971, pp. 97–115.

Pigou, A.C., *The economics of welfare*, 1920; 4th edition, London, 1946.

Plott, Charles R., 'A notion of equilibrium and its possibility under majority rule', *American Economic Review*, vol. 57, 1967, pp. 787–806.

Pommerehne, Werner W., 'Institutional approaches to public expenditure. Empirical evidence from Swiss municipalities', *Journal of Public Economics*, vol. 9, 1978, pp. 255–80.

Rawls, J., *A theory of justice*, Harvard University Press, Cambridge Mass., 1971.

Riker, William H., 'The paradox of voting and congressional rules for voting on amendments', *American Political Science Review*, vol. 52, 1958, pp. 349–66.

The theory of political coalitions, Yale University Press, New Haven, 1962.

'Arrow's theorem and some examples of the paradox of voting', in J.M. Claunch (ed.), *Mathematical applications in political science*, vol. 1, 1965, Southern Methodist University Press, Dallas, pp. 41–60.

Riker, William H., and Peter C. Ordeshook, 'A theory of the calculus of voting', *American Political Science Review*, vol. 62, 1968, pp. 25–42.

An introduction to positive political theory, Prentice Hall, Englewood Cliffs NJ., 1973.

Robbins, Lionel, *An essay on the nature and significance of economic science*, Macmillan, London, 2nd edition revised and extended, 1935.

Roberts, Donald John, 'The Lindahl solution for economies with public goods', *Journal of Public Economics*, vol. 3, 1974, pp. 23–42.

Romer, Thomas, and Howard Rosenthal, 'Political resource allocation, controlled agendas, and the status quo', *Public Choice*, vol. 33, 1978, pp. 27–43.

'The elusive median voter', *Journal of Public Economics*, vol. 12, 1979, pp. 143–70.

Röpke, Wilhelm, *Die Lehre von der Wirtschaft*, Zürich, 1954.

Rowley, Charles K., and Alan T. Peacock, *Welfare economics. A liberal restatement*, Wiley, New York, 1975.

Saari, Donald G., and Jill Van Newenhizen, 'The problem of indeterminacy in approval, multiple, and truncated voting systems', *Public Choice*, vol. 59, 1988, pp. 101–20.

Samuelson, Paul A., *Foundations of economic analysis*, Harvard University Press, Cambridge Mass., 1947.

'The pure theory of public expenditure', *Review of Economics and Statistics*, vol. 36, 1954, pp. 387–9. Reprinted in Kenneth J. Arrow and Tibor Scitovsky, *Readings in welfare economics*, Irwin, Homewood Ill., 1969, pp. 179–82.

'A diagrammatic exposition of a theory of public expenditure', *Review of Economics and Statistics*, vol. 37, 1955, pp. 350–6.

Satterthwaite, Mark A., 'Strategy proofness and Arrow's conditions: existence and correspondence theorems for voting procedures and social welfare functions', *Journal of Economic Theory*, vol. 10, 1975, pp. 187–217.

Scharpf, F.W., 'A game-theoretical interpretation of inflation and unemployment in Western Europe', *Journal of Public Policy*, vol. 7, 1987, pp. 227–58.

Schneider, Friedrich, 'Public attitudes toward economic conditions and their impact on government behavior', *Political Behavior*, vol. 6, 1984, pp. 211–27.

Schram, Arthur J.H.C. *Voter behaviour in economic perspective*, Springer-Verlag, Berlin/Heidelberg, 1991.

Schumacher, E.F., *Small is beautiful: a study of economics as if people mattered*, Blond + Briggs, London, 1973.

Schumpeter, Joseph A., *Capitalism, socialism and democracy*, Harper, New York, 1943; 5th edition, Allen and Unwin, London, 1976.

Scitovsky, Tibor, 'A note on welfare propositions in economics', *Review of Economic Studies*, vol. 9, 1941, pp. 77–88. Reprinted in Kenneth J. Arrow and Tibor Scitovsky, *Readings in welfare economics*, Irwin, Homewood Ill., 1969, pp. 390–401.

Sen, Amarty K., *Collective choice and social welfare*, North-Holland, Amsterdam, 1970.

Sen, Amartya, 'Choice, orderings and morality', in Stephan Körner (ed.), *Practical reason*, Basil Blackwell, Oxford, 1974.

Shaffer, William R., *Computer simulations of voting behavior*, Oxford University Press, New York/London/Toronto, 1972.

Shepsle, Kenneth A., and Barry Weingast, 'Structure-induced equilibrium and legislative choice', *Public Choice*, vol. 37, 1981, pp. 503–19.

Siccama, J.G., 'Ekonomie en demokratie in het staatsbestuur: Een kritische reaktie', *Acta Politica*, vol. 9, 1974, pp. 413–32.

Simon, Herbert A., *Models of man: social and rational. Mathematical essays on rational human behavior in a social setting*, Wiley, New York, 1957.

'Rationality as process and as product of thought', *American Economic Review*, vol. 68, 1978, Papers and proceedings, pp. 1–16.

Smithies, Arthur, 'Optimum location in spatial competition', *Journal of Political Economy*, vol. 49, 1941, pp. 423–39.

Stigler, George J., 'General economic conditions and national elections', *American Economic Review*, vol. 63, 1973, Papers and Proceedings, pp. 160–7.

Stiglitz, Joseph E., *Economics of the public sector*, Norton, New York/London, 2nd edition, 1988.

Taylor, Michael, *Anarchy and cooperation*, Wiley, London, 1976.

Taylor, Michael, and Hugh Ward, 'Chickens, whales and lumpy goods: alternative models of public-goods provision', *Political Studies*, vol. 30, 1982, pp. 350–70.

Thaler, Richard, 'The psychology of choice and the assumptions of economics', in Alvin E. Roth (ed.), *Laboratory experimentation in economics. Six points of view*, Cambridge University Press, Cambridge, 1987, pp. 99–130.

Thomassen, J.J.A., *Kiezers en gekozenen in een representatieve demokratie*, Samsom, Alphen aan den Rijn, 1976.

'Beleidsopvattingen van burgers en politieke stabiliteit', *Beleid en Maatschappij*, vol. 11, 1984, pp. 205–13.

Thompson, Earl A., 'Review of: Bureaucracy and representative government by William A. Niskanen', *Journal of Economic Literature*, vol. 11, 1973, pp. 950–3.

Tiebout, Charles M., 'A pure theory of local expenditures', *Journal of Political Economy*, vol. 64, 1956, pp. 416–24.

Tinbergen, J., 'The theory of the optimum regime', in L.H. Klaassen et al. (eds.), *Jan Tinbergen selected papers*, North-Holland, Amsterdam, 1959, pp. 264–304.

'Gegenwartige Probleme der Theorie des volkswirtschaftlichen Wohlstands', *Statistische Hefte*, Heft 3, 1967.

Todaro, Michael P., *Economic development in the Third World*, Longman, New York/London, 4th edition, 1989.

Tullock, Gordon, *The politics of bureaucracy*, Public Affairs Press, Washington, 1965.

Toward a mathematics of politics, University of Michigan Press, Ann Arbor, 1967.

Tversky, Amos, and Daniel Kahneman, 'The framing of decisions and the psychology of choice', *Science*, 1981, pp. 453–8.

Van den Doel, J., *Ekonomie en demokratie in het staatsbestuur*, Inaugural lecture Katholieke Universiteit Nijmegen, Kluwer, Deventer, 1973.

'Baten en offers in het bestuurlijk systeem', *Acta Politica*, vol. 9, 1974, pp. 423–31.

'De macro-politieke paradox van Arrow's nachts in het parlement', *Acta Politica*, vol. 10, 1975, pp. 199–205.

'Carry out the revolution and increase production! The evolution of the Chinese economic order to an optimum', *De Economist*, vol. 125, 1977, pp. 211–37.

Van den Doel, J., C. de Galan and J. Tinbergen, 'Pleidooi voor een geleide loonpolitiek', *Economisch Statistische Berichten*, vol. 61, 1976, pp. 264–8 (I) and 828–31 (II).

Van der Eijk, C., and B. Niemöller, *Electoral change in the Netherlands. Empirical results and methods of measurement*, CT-press, Amsterdam, 1983.

'Het potentiële electoraat van de Nederlandse politieke partijen', *Beleid en Maatschappij*, vol. 11, 1984, pp. 192–204.

Van Doorn, J.A.A., 'Inleiding tot Robert Michels en zijn thematiek', pp. 13–38 in Robert Michels, *Democratie en organisatie. Een klassieke theorie*, Universitaire Pers Rotterdam, 1969.

Van Eijk, C.J., and J. Sandee, 'Quantitative determination of an optimum economic policy', *Econometrica*, vol. 27, 1959, pp. 1–13.

Vanek, Jaroslav, *The general theory of labor-managed market economies*, Cornell University Press, Ithaca/London, 1970.

Self-management: economic liberation of man, Penguin, Harmondsworth, 1975.

Van Praag, B.M.S., *Individual welfare functions and consumer behavior*, North-Holland, Amsterdam, 1968.

Van Praag, Bernard M.S., and Arie Kapteyn, 'Further evidence on the individual welfare function of income: an empirical investigation in the Netherlands', *European Economic Review*, vol. 4, 1973, pp. 33–62.

Van Thijn, E., 'Van partijen naar stembusaccoorden', in: E. Jurgens et al., *Partijvernieuwing?*, Arbeiderspers, Amsterdam, 1967.

Van Velthoven, Ben C.J., *The endogenization of government behaviour in macroeconomic models*, Springer-Verlag, Berlin/Heidelberg, 1989.

Van Winden, F.A.A.M., 'Towards a dynamic theory of cabinet formation', in Manfred J. Holler (ed.), *Coalitions and collective action*, Physica-Verlag, Würzburg, 1984, pp. 145–59.

Von Neumann, John, and Oskar Morgenstern, *Theory of games and economic behavior*, Princeton University Press, Princeton NJ., 1944.

Wansbeek, Tom, and Arie Kapteyn, 'Tackling hard questions by means of soft methods: the use of individual welfare functions in socio-economic policy', *Kyklos*, vol. 36, 1983, pp. 249–69.

Weber, Max, *Wirtschaft und Gesellschaft*, Berlin, 1922; 5th edition, J.C.B. Mohr, Tübingen, 1972.

Wicksell, Knut, *Finanztheoretische Untersuchungen*, Jena, 1896. Partly reprinted as 'A new principle of just taxation', in Musgrave and Peacock, 1958, pp. 72–118.

Williamson, Oliver E., *Economics of discretionary behavior: managerial incentives in a theory of the firm*, Prentice-Hall, Englewood Cliffs NJ., 1964.

Markets and hierarchies: analysis and antitrust implications, Free Press, New York, 1975.

Wilson, Woodrow, 'The study of administration', *Political Science Quarterly*, vol. 2, 1887, pp. 197–222. Reprinted in Louis C. Gawthrop (ed.), *The administrative process and democratic theory*, Houghton Mifflin, Boston, 1970, pp. 77–85.

Wittman, Donald A., 'Parties as utility maximizers', *American Political Science Review*, vol. 67, 1973, pp. 490–8.

Wyckoff, Paul Gary, 'The simple analytics of slack-maximizing bureaucracy', *Public Choice*, vol. 67, 1990a, pp. 35–47.

'Bureaucracy, inefficiency, and time', *Public Choice*, vol. 67, 1990b, pp. 167–79.

Index